Publicity on the Internet

STANDARD

Publicity on the Internet

Creating Successful Publicity Campaigns on the Internet and the Commercial Online Services

Steve O'Keefe

Wiley Computer Publishing

John Wiley & Sons, Inc.

New York • Chichester • Brisbane • Toronto • Singapore • Weinheim

Executive Publisher: Katherine Schowalter
Editor: Tim Ryan
Managing Editor: Mark Hayden
Text Design & Composition: SunCliff Graphic Productions

Designations used by companies to distinguish their products are often claimed as trademarks. In all instances where John Wiley & Sons, Inc. is aware of a claim, the product names appear in initial capital or all capital letters. Readers, however, should contact the appropriate companies for more complete information regarding trademarks and registration.

This text is printed on acid-free paper.

Library of Congress Cataloging-in-Publication Data

O'Keefe, Steve, 1959–
    Publicity on the Internet : creating successful publicity campaigns on the Internet and the commercial online services / Steve O'Keefe.
        p.   cm.
    Includes index.
    ISBN 0-471-16175-6 (pbk. : alk. paper)
    1. Internet (Computer network) in publicity.   2. Internet advertising.   I. Title.
HM263.05925   1997
659'.0285'467- -dc20   96-32539
                                                                          CIP

Printed in the United States of America

10 9 8 7 6 5 4 3 2 1

Contents

Acknowledgments

Special thanks to Jill Ellsworth, for her support, suggestions, gentle nudging, matchmaking, and enthusiasm; and to Jesse Vohs, for his graphics work and overall technical wizardry.

CHAPTER 1

The Power of Internet Publicity

The Internet is at once a publicist's dream and nightmare. Floating out there in the ether are about 20 million people from every country on the planet. Conveniently, they are segmented by their special interests, whether that be vegetarian cooking or cyberpunk fiction. With a few keystrokes, you can send a message to thousands or millions of them, and the cost of delivery is *absolutely zero*. This is an irresistible scenario. But before you fire up your personal computer and deliver your first salvo, you should be aware of the Net's darker side. The Internet has its own code of behavior, called *netiquette*, which includes a loose prohibition on commercial activity. If you transgress this unwritten code, you risk the wrath of a cabal of hackers and self-appointed "judges" who are capable of wreaking havoc with your computer system.

You *can* conduct commercial activity on the Internet, but it requires finesse. I know; I've been engaged in marketing on the Net for many years. I've been *flamed* for violating netiquette, but it has taught me how to contribute to the Net in a manner that is appreciated, not excoriated. I can help you reach this lucrative market without going through the painful learning curve of the Net novice. Let me show you.

The Benefits of Internet Publicity

Imagine having the ability to send a direct mail piece about your product or service to a sharply targeted mailing list of thousands of known

1

enthusiasts spanning the globe. Now imagine that your cost for printing the piece is *zero*, your cost for postage is *zero*, the likelihood of your piece being thrown away unopened is nearly *zero*, and the cost to the consumer to respond to your message is *zero*. Now you understand the awesome power of Internet publicity.

The Internet is the most amazing communications tool ever invented. It provides a low-cost vehicle for sending, receiving, and storing massive quantities of information. It can deliver words, pictures, audio, video, animation, software, money. It is nearly instantaneous, allowing people to have telephone-style conversations through the speakers built into their computers. It is international, facilitating unprecedented access to foreign cultures and markets without any intermediaries. Thanks to the Internet, we no longer have to pay to deliver information—only to create it.

All the costs of marketing on the Internet are in the makeready. You must carefully craft your copy to avoid the Net's prejudice against advertising. You must provide information, not a sales pitch. You must meticulously research the potential audience, selecting the appropriate individuals and discussion groups to send your messages to. You must gain facility with the array of tools available on the Net and the arcane commands that activate them. And you must make a commitment to maintaining a presence on the Net; hit-and-run operations are frowned upon. If you want the Net's respect, you must provide follow-up.

To indiscriminately place ads all over the Internet results in flaming, but product information sent to an appropriately targeted audience is welcome. It's a fine line, but I know how to walk it like a Wallenda and I can teach you the same skills. The key to successful marketing on the Internet is *publicity*, not advertising.

The Dangers of Internet Publicity

In the summer of 1994, Laurence Canter and Martha Siegel flooded the Internet with ads for their legal services. The results? The "Green Card Lawyers" were bombarded with hate mail and death threats; they were hunted across cyberspace by digital vigilantes; their messages were destroyed by "cancelbots"; their ability to communicate online was blocked by hackers. Their personal lives were subjected to intense scrutiny, and unflattering information, whether true or not, was spread all over the Net. This, too, is the power of Internet publicity.

There are many dangers awaiting those who would market their goods in cyberspace. Intel found out the hard way when someone posted a message to a Usenet newsgroup about a tiny defect in the popular Pentium chip. Intel acknowledged the bug and explained how insignificant it was and that it had been fixed. But that wasn't good enough for the online community. People demanded a recall, and when Intel refused, the company became the butt of many unflattering jokes. The bad publicity escalated, taking the wind out of Intel's Pentium promotion, cutting into sales, and even hurting the company's stock price. Intel eventually modified its stance and mollified the protesters, but not before significant damage had been done.

But much of the bad PR companies get online is self-inflicted. Apple Computer rolled out one of the biggest Internet promotions ever with its companion Web site for the film *Mission Impossible*. The campaign included television spots touting the Web site, but when users clicked, there was nothing there. The site wasn't ready on time and thus Apple got baked online. Other sites have been so poorly designed they had to be pulled to reduce the embarrassment to the parent company.

The point is, the Internet audience is a tough crowd. If you want to reach the millions of people working and playing online, you have to be very careful. That's what this book is all about. I will show you how to promote your products and services online without being flamed or kicked out. These techniques were forged in the school of hard knocks, and I not only graduated with honors, I now teach there.

About the Author

The Internet used to be a graveyard where my working day went to die. I spent years mastering the cryptic commands needed to exchange information there: sending and receiving mail; downloading and uploading files; reading newsgroups and posting to them; manipulating mailing lists. I realized few benefits for all the effort I put in—until that magic day when I first discovered the power of Internet publicity. I was promoting a book called *Secrets of a Super Hacker*, by The Knightmare (Loompanics Unlimited, 1994). A friend posted a review of the book to a handful of Usenet newsgroups. Within minutes, the fax machine began humming with orders from Sweden, Japan, South Africa, the United Kingdom, and the United States. The response was dramatic, instantaneous, gratifying.

I asked permission to reprint the review on other newsgroups and forums. Inquiries and sales continued to pour in. The publisher made a bulk sale to a U.S. spy agency. Within weeks, Spanish-language rights were sold to a company in South America. I negotiated the entire deal via e-mail. The book became a best-seller for the publisher, and I became an Internet junkie.

Secrets of a Super Hacker was uniquely suited to Internet promotion. It appealed to many of the Net's strongest demographic groups: computer fanatics, businesspeople, young males. But almost any product or service will benefit from a well-built Internet publicity campaign. In the years since that first fateful fax, I honed the art of conducting publicity on the Internet. I constructed one of the first book catalogs on the Internet. I obsessively developed what may be the world's best list of media e-mail addresses. I ran contests that were complete disasters. I promoted the first Web site to be spun off into a television series. I booked online author tours and created snappy little promotions. I learned how to tap the power of the Internet publicity. So can you.

From my early days coaxing a beat-up Ford down the Infobahn, I now drive a Mercedes-Benz soundtruck. It is a well-oiled, finely tuned machine. This book is the owner's manual.

About This Book

"This is all about throwing money at a wall and seeing what sticks."

Dan Rosenbaum, editor of *Netguide* magazine, used these words to describe Microsoft's $200 million agreement with NBC to build an online news service. "It's exactly Microsoft's job to be putting speculative money like this into unproven ventures," Rosenbaum was quoted as saying, appropriately enough in the *Seattle Post-Intelligencer*.

This book is for people who can't afford that strategy. It is also for people who demand results from their online efforts. It takes work and it takes time, but the benefits are not imaginary. You will learn exactly how to find your target audience online, how to create a message that will appeal to them, how to distribute that message through a number of different channels, and what to do when people respond. This book is for people who can't afford to wait for the market to find them.

Publicity on the Internet will help you build traffic at your Web site. I'll show you how to seed the Net with links to your site. I'll help you make your directory listings more enticing, and teach you how to get the media to review your web site. I'll help you craft promotions that bring the target audience to your virtual door.

What makes the difference between a great Internet promotion and a dud? Money seldom has anything to do with it. It takes creativity. I can't give you that, but I can provide you with a sourcebook of ideas that might spark your creative engine. A good promotion requires planning; this book has checklists, worksheets, time lines, and everything else you need to execute successful campaigns. Without a follow-up plan, you have only half a promotion. This book will show you how to measure response, modify your campaigns on the fly, and magnify your results with timely follow-up. In short, this book will help you develop promotions that sizzle, not fizzle.

What this book is *not* about is throwing money or messages at a wall; it's about methodically researching your target market, painstakingly crafting promotions that will appeal to that market, and delivering those promotions with near-surgical precision. This book will show you how to reach an online audience that *wants* to hear from you without disturbing those who don't. This book will teach you to tap the power of Internet publicity. Let me show you.

CHAPTER 2

Who's Online?

About three minutes after the Internet opened for commercial traffic, people started trying to size up the online audience, asking how many people are online, how old are they, how much money do they have; where do they hang out; and what services do they use? Advertisers aren't satisfied with vague answers for very long. It's hard to tailor a pitch without knowing who's in the audience. But there's a problem measuring Internet demographics, because it was designed to be a decentralized system that would be difficult to knock out in a terrorist attack. Thus, there's no good way of collecting information about who's online. Like television, there's no way of determining exactly who is watching what. The best you can do is take a statistical sample and generalize from that. But surveys of the Net have, for the most part, been poorly conducted, so that the results are almost useless.

I could follow a typical path and give you the numbers from all the surveys and then explain why none of them means anything, and you would come away from this chapter with a feeling for the difficulty of measuring online activity, but little else. Instead, I'm going to try to give you some insight, from years of experience, of what exactly is going on out there.

I still cover the basic numbers, and tell you where to find reams of misleading statistics about Internet demographics. But I hope you'll finish this chapter *without* that glazed-over look that comes from trying to understand the Internet audience by the numbers. Here are some of the topics we'll cover:

- **The Main Studies:** The biggest names in audience measurement have taken their tape measures to the Net, but their math comes up short. Nevertheless, we'll look at the best stats available: MIDS, GVU, Nielsen, O'Reilly, and FIND/SVP.

- **Demographics of the Net:** There seems to be a consensus emerging about the size and basic demographics of the Internet, including gender, income, and education. I'll tell you what that consensus has determined so far.

- **What People Do Online:** Are most people swapping e-mail or playing DOOM? The statistics are shakier than the demographic data, but they tell us something about how people play and work online. We'll also hear some personal opinions about what people like and what they hate to do on the Net. We'll go where the in-crowd goes.

- **Commercial Online Services:** Half the people on the Net are coming through America Online, CompuServe, Prodigy, and the other online services. We'll look at what makes them click.

- **Online Publics:** For a slightly different approach, we'll look at the audience we're trying to reach and see what they're doing online, including consumers, businesses, the media, government, education, investors, and employees.

- **Custom-Tailored Promotions:** For most marketers, it's not important to know who's online as long as you know where to find your target market. We'll talk about some of the amazing possibilities for personalizing your pitches.

The Main Studies

On a recent swing through cyberspace, I counted a dozen different organizations researching Internet demographics. Some are affiliated with universities, others with Internet content providers, still others are market research firms moving into the new territory of cyberspace. Many of the studies are proprietary, charging up to $25,000 to view the complete results, although they often make general conclusions available to the public.

Chapter 12 has a good set of bookmarks for finding demographic information on the Web. As of this writing, there were five major surveys available: GVU, FIND/SVP, MIDS, Nielsen, and O'Reilly. Let's take a look at them now.

GVU's Web User Survey

http://www.cc.gatech.edu/gvu/user_surveys/User_Survey_Home.html

Every six months, the Graphics, Visualization & Usability (GVU) Center at Georgia Tech University conducts a survey of World Wide Web users (Figure 2.1). The first survey took place in January 1994. Later that year, GVU was joined by the Hermes Project from the University of Michigan Business School. Hermes, headed by Sunil Gupta, is charged with researching the commercial uses of the Web. GVU is headed by Jim Pitkow and Colleen Kehoe. The latest survey results are from May 1996.

The GVU survey makes no effort to be representative of the Internet population as a whole; it is neither random, nor impartial. Questionnaires are distributed on the Net, the results are tallied, and the averages are made public. While the GVU survey asks some demographic questions, the other surveys are much more accurate. What makes the GVU survey interesting are questions such as "Why do you save Web pages?" or "How did you learn to use HTML?" You'll gain insights

Figure 2.1 The GVU Web User Survey provides keen insight into surfer behavior.

from looking at GVU's survey results, but it would be a mistake to try and generalize them to the Internet population.

MIDS Survey

http://www.mids.org/index.html

MIDS stands for Matrix Information and Directory Services, a research organization headed by John Quarterman. If the GVU survey is loosely constructed, John Quarterman's work is positively rigorous. He is fussy about his methodology and the meaning of the numbers that result. His main focus is quantifying the size and spread of the Internet.

MIDS sends questionnaires to Internet service providers and other domain administrators, asking them to quantify their customers. Quarterman tallies the results and performs standard statistical analyses. MIDS makes the conclusions of their survey freely available and charges a nominal fee for the full details. They also sell a variety of maps and reports showing the size and distribution of the Internet audience. The latest survey results are from October 1995.

Nielsen/CommerceNet Survey

http://www.nielsenmedia.com/demo.htm

Released in October 1995, the Nielsen survey attempted to apply rigorous polling methods to determine the number and makeup of online users. They used a telephone poll with a random-digit dialing structure, conducting a total of 4,200 telephone interviews. The Nielsen survey included not only Web users, but also Internet users, commercial online service users, and nonusers. Even though this may be the most accurate survey available to the public, some people claim that the methods used do not result in the statistical validity that Nielsen claims.

FIND/SVP Survey

http://etrg.findsvp.com/features/internet_demo.html

In December 1995, FIND/SVP conducted a random-digit dialing telephone survey finding 1,000 Internet users who were polled about their use of the Net. The result is *The American Internet User Survey*, containing a cross of factual measurements and more conceptual questions.

The survey contains some interesting numbers dealing with commercial online services.

O'Reilly Survey

http://www.ora.com/www/info/research/users/index.html

O'Reilly & Associates, book publishers and founders of the popular Global Network Navigator (GNN) Web site, joined with Trish Information Services for this telephone survey of 30,000 randomly chosen households (Figure 2.2). The survey was released in October 1995, but most of the results are available only to the study's sponsors. The survey focused on people with a direct Internet connection. Separate interviews were done with users of commercial online services.

Other Studies

Jupiter Communications (http://www.jup.com/) offers a dozen research reports at prices ranging from $345 to $1,895 that cover advertising, banking, shopping, and other online activities. Jupiter is a good source of information for the demographics of commercial online services such as America Online, CompuServe, and Prodigy.

InterNIC, the organization that manages domain names, provides a lot of statistical information about the growth of the Net. You can find an analysis of these numbers at the InterNet Info Web page, http://www.webcom.com/~walsh/stats.html.

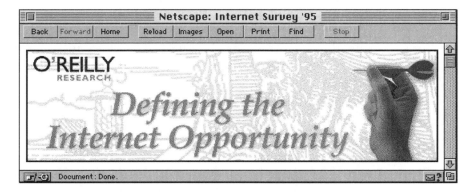

Figure 2.2 O'Reilly's 1995 Internet survey used some of the best methodology to date for measuring the online audience.

Figure 2.3 Hoffman and Novak's Project 2000 is known for deflating Internet hype and subjecting Internet surveys to intelligent, articulate analysis.

Two sites that provide intelligent analysis of Internet demographics are Project 2000 and CyberAtlas. Project 2000 (Figure 2.3) is a research study into the marketing implications of Internet-style communications. It is headed by professors Donna L. Hoffman and Thomas P. Novak. Hoffman and Novak have a reputation for debunking bogus surveys, and are two of the smartest people providing commentary on Internet demographics. You'll find their Web site at http://www2000.ogsm.vanderbilt.edu/.

CyberAtlas is sort of a clearinghouse of information about Internet demographics. It tracks the work of others, compiling and comparing the final results. I think you'll find their Web site is the best starting place for exploring the subject of Internet demographics. It's located at: http://www.cyberatlas.com/ (Figure 2.4).

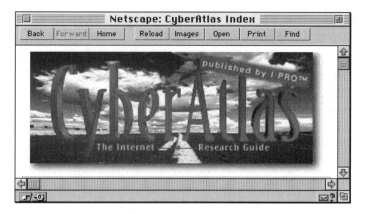

Figure 2.4 CyberAtlas is the best place to go for a summary of Internet studies in easy-to-understand language and charts.

Demographics of the Net

Those are the major studies and Web sites. Now let's look at what they tell us about who's using the Net.

How Big Is the Net?

This is one of the more difficult numbers to ascertain. Table 2.1 shows the most-often-cited estimates of Internet size, but each survey is measuring something slightly different. A consensus appears to be emerging based on the data collected for the Nielsen survey as reviewed by Hoffman and Novak. They concluded that 16.4 million people used the

Table 2.1 Number of Internet and Web Users (millions).

Survey	Internet	Web
MIDS February 96	26.4	16.0
Nielsen October 95	24.0	18.0
O'Reilly July 95	5.8	—
FIND/SVP January 96	9.5	7.5
Hoffman & Novak April 96	16.4	11.5
Wall St. Journal March 96	17.6	—

Internet in the United States in 1995. A recent survey by Computer Intelligence Corporation put the number of U.S. Internet users at about 15 million.

The MIDS numbers measure people who can exchange e-mail, which is the broadest measure used; it is referred to as The Matrix. The FIND/SVP numbers don't include e-mail-only accounts. Some surveys measure the number of people who have used the Internet, while others measure the number with Internet accounts. Until better measurements are developed, a safe guess would be about 15 million U.S. Internet users at the end of 1995.

How Fast Is It Growing?

Through the beginning of 1996, MIDS showed Internet growth at 100 percent per year for the last six years. This rate is confirmed in the FIND/SVP survey, where half the people polled began using the Net in 1995. Network hosts increased 95 percent from January 1995 to January 1996. The numbers seem to indicate a steady doubling of users every year. While this trend must eventually slow, there is still a lot of room for growth; less than 10 percent of U.S. households were connected to the Net at the end of 1995.

Geography

Not many surveys have tackled the question of geographical spread. The "nonscientific" GVU survey shows 73 percent of respondents from the United States, 11 percent from Europe. California is the dominant state, accounting for 11 percent of all Web browsers, followed by Texas (4.8 percent) and New York (4.4 percent). An analysis of area codes shows that 21 percent of commercial domains registered with InterNIC are in California, 5 percent are in New York, and 1.5 percent are in the United Kingdom.

Gender

The gender balance is slowly leveling on the Internet. As you can see from Table 2.2 on Internet demographics, most surveys peg the split at two-to-one male. A survey by San Francisco State University in early 1996 showed almost half of Bay Area Internet users were female. Males

Table 2.2 Internet Demographics Summary.

Survey	Gender	Average Age	Median Income	College Degree
MIDS February 96	66% male	—	—	—
Nielsen October 95	66% male	34	$60,000	64%
O'Reilly July 95	66% male	32	$50,000	—
FIND/SVP January 96	65% male	—	$62,000	—
GVU/Hermes May 96	69% male	33	$59,000	57%

spend more time online than females, according to the Nielsen survey, which shows males accounting for 75 percent of all time spent online.

Income

Yeah, they're rich. Nielsen found that one-quarter of Internet users had an annual income in excess of $80,000 compared to only 10 percent of the general population. FIND/SVP showed an average household income of $62,000. O'Reilly pegged median income at $50,000. Nielsen put median income at $60,000. That's double the median household income in the 1990 U.S. census ($30,000).

Education

Internet users have a higher-than-average education. Given that many people first access the Internet from a college or university, this isn't surprising. The Nielsen survey shows 64 percent of Internet users have college degrees. The latest GVU survey has 57 percent of Web browsers with college degrees. Compare these numbers with the 1995 U.S. census which estimates that 20 percent of the population has a college degree.

What People Do Online

When we begin to examine what people do online, some of the more interesting results come from the less scientific surveys, especially the latest GVU study, which is more focused on user activities than on raw demographic data.

Work or Home?

It appears that more people access the Internet from work than from home, although many people access it from both work *and* home. The Nielsen survey shows 66 percent accessing the Net from work, 44 percent from home, and 8 percent from school. However, the latest GVU survey gives home users the edge, at 55 percent of all Web browsers. The FIND/SVP survey shows most users logging in from both work and home, with only 20 percent using the Net exclusively from work, and only 37 percent exclusively from home.

But just because they login from work doesn't mean their activities are work-related. The FIND/SVP survey shows 60 percent of Internet users are engaging in both business and personal use of the Net. With the rising number of home office workers, it's fair to say that the lines between personal and business use of the Net are blurred. People play on the Net at the office and work on the Net at home.

Shopping

They like to browse, but do they buy? The answer to this question is more important to marketers than to publicists. A publicist is using the Net as one more component of a campaign to raise awareness about a client, and there are many positive results derived from this awareness that have little to do with sales (for example, making a company more attractive to investors). Marketers, on the other hand, are measured by the bottom line: what are the sales?

Most of the surveys show that Internet users are a hard sell. Nielsen shows 13 percent of Web users bought something over the Net. GVU's fourth survey shows shopping is virtually the last thing people want to do on the Web, with only 11 percent of respondents using it that way. On the fifth GVU survey, 47 percent of respondents have never made an online purchase. I feel almost certain that Internet response is much lower than the 1 to 3 percent required for a successful direct mail promotion, but the cost of message delivery is also far less.

People don't buy online for a variety of reasons. One reason is insecurity about putting credit card numbers on the Net. It doesn't matter to Web users that transmitting credit card information online is far safer than, say, giving a credit card to a waiter in a restaurant. What counts is their *perception* of insecurity. The media helps foster this perception by playing up online rip-offs, but that's to be expected. After all, plane crashes get more press coverage than automobile fatalities, even though airplane travel is safer.

A more valuable statistic for marketers is how many people use the Internet to get product information or comparison shop. More than half of the people online use the Web to gather information on products and services. The fifth GVU survey has 42 percent of respondents using the Web at least once a week to get product information. One survey I saw showed that for every sale online, three more sales took place offline as a result of information gathered on the Internet.

Research

The Internet is used more for gathering information than any other activity. You can call this research if you like. FIND/SVP shows that a quarter of Internet users search for information on a daily basis. Nielsen shows 73 percent of Internet users are after information. People look to the Internet more for information than they do for entertainment (see below), and this is natural, since the Net is good at providing information and can't compete with motion picture or television production standards for entertainment. Nielsen shows less than 20 percent of Internet users accessing audio or video.

Entertainment

People like to browse the Web, with roughly 80 percent of users just "surfing." Browsing is a way to become familiar with what's available online and since half of all users have been online for less than a year, it's to be expected that they spend most of their time getting acclimated to the environment.

According to the fourth GVU survey, 64 percent of the people on the Web use it for entertainment. The Web is much more entertaining than, say, e-mail, so people spend a higher percentage of their Web time enjoying sites such as ESPNet. The FIND/SVP survey shows that time spent on the Internet is cutting into television watching time more than any other activity among home users. Accessing electronic news and magazines is another of the more popular reasons for being online, but because many of these publications are work-related, it's hard to say whether people are reading them more for work or pleasure.

Getting a Feel for the Net

To better understand how to conduct publicity on the Internet, you need more than just numbers. Numbers lead to thoughts such as "If I can post this message to 20,000 newsgroups, and only 1 percent of the people respond, I'll be rich!" Beyond the numbers, there's a feeling for the Internet that you get when you've been around awhile. As a professional publicist and veteran surfer, here are some biased opinions.

The Web

As far as a direct connection to the Net goes, the Web is where the action's at. The Web is colorful and easy to use. Point-and-click hyperlinks make navigation simple and fun. Senior citizens and little kids take to the Web just as quickly as experienced computer users. Many Web users will never go near Usenet or Internet mailing lists. They will use Gopher, FTP, audio, and video if those features are seamlessly integrated with their Web browsers.

The Web is exciting because new content comes online every day. There's a thrill waiting to see who is going to come up with "the next big thing." Web surfers have a "herd" mentality; we hear about a new movie site, or contest, or stupid Web trick, and we just gotta check it out. Novelty—not size—is the crucial factor in getting noticed.

Fame on the Net is fleeting, though. You could get a million hits one week, a hundred hits the next. Maybe you were named "Cool Site of the Day" by Glenn Davis and your server got a good workout? But people won't come back unless they have a compelling reason to do so. So far, the most compelling reasons are that you either have a great search engine or you display pictures of naked people.

Very few Web sites have what it takes to be a continuous draw. HotWired is probably the most successful new media site, and it has constantly struggled to maintain attendance. The site has been redesigned several times (Figure 2.5). It has gone from requiring registration to a hybrid to no registration. It has been interesting, watching the designers learn the lessons and adapt to the Internet audience.

I think I can speak for my fellow surfers when I say most Web sites are a disappointment. We're so accustomed to the high production levels on television that the Web experience is simply not competitive en-

Figure 2.5 HotWired's home page has been redesigned several times based on user feedback.

tertainment to us. And, as an avid reader of magazines, newsletters, and journals, I haven't seen a single transformation to the small screen that I enjoyed reading as much as its print counterpart. The best *webzines* I've seen are not transplants, but were born in the new media, such as Word and Suck and HotWired, or chronicle the new media, such as Netsurfer Digest and Seidman's Online Insider.

Usenet

Usenet is all but dead for me. What was once fertile territory for people exchanging information of a personal or valuable nature has degenerated into a war of words between spammers and flamers. Both sides are equally guilty for ruining Usenet. The spammers don't seem to understand that not everyone wants to see their ads, and the flamers make even the most innocent contributors feel unwelcome.

Usenet used to be like a daily newspaper with a short dispatch from everyone in the neighborhood. Although most posts were repetitive and a lot were poorly written, there was always something authentic and interesting about it all. Then the neighborhood grew so big it became harder to find anything of value, more fights erupted between incompatible neighbors, and the whole thing got out of hand.

Today, intelligent discussion has moved away from Usenet into moderated discussion forums. Moderators keep out the blatant spam and put out flame wars before they spread, but, consequently, some of the spontaneity is lost. Occasionally, I come across something in Usenet that touches me. But the experience is so rare it's barely worth looking for.

Mailing Lists

Mailing lists are great. They're like Usenet discussions without all the debris. Messages tend to be longer, more thoughtful, less heated, with a higher proportion of useful content. But it takes a good moderator to keep a mailing list rolling. Someone has to keep the list free from technical problems, spam, and flames. A good moderator provokes discussion and sometimes curtails it when the subject has been beaten to death.

You'll find the audiences on mailing lists are quite knowledgeable and very responsive. The subscription mechanism will be intimidating to many beginners, so you won't reach a broad market. Promotional postings to mailing lists require more care than Usenet, too, because the audience is dedicated and discriminating. But they're worth the effort. I posted a message for Jim Sterne's book, *World Wide Web Marketing* on Market-L, a healthy mailing list for marketing discussions, and I received more than 100 requests for a sample chapter from the book. Nothing I've done on Usenet compares.

Chat

Chat is cool, but chatting on the Internet has been disappointing until recently. Internet Relay Chat, or IRC, used to be too complicated to appeal to a broad audience. If you wanted to chat with hacker wannabes, great; otherwise, it was pretty disappointing. New IRC software is changing chat, but it hasn't reached high enough saturation to attract the kind of guests that appear on America Online or Prodigy.

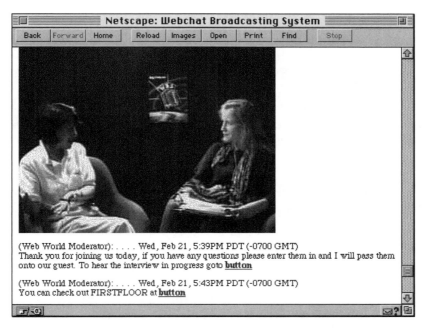

Figure 2.6 Graphical chat combines the best features of television talk shows and talk radio. It has the potential to attract a huge, consistent following.

WebChat has potential, but it's not there yet (Figure 2.6). Telnet chat is a drag. HotWired may be one of the most popular sites on the Net, but check out some of its chat transcripts. You'll find a couple of hosts, the guest, and maybe a couple of regulars in the audience, and that's it. A lot of the chats get virtually no attendance, and if you've ever been to one, you'll know why. Most are completely chaotic. You can't tell what question the guest is responding to. There's all sorts of "chat noise" from people logging on and logging off. It's a mess. But the crazy, chaotic energy of chat is part of its appeal, especially for a younger audience that takes it all in stride.

Chat is one of the best prospects on the Internet, even though the current software is not very sophisticated. When the software improves, look out. People are attracted to celebrities large and small. Someday, chat will be bigger than TV talk shows and talk radio combined. And it will become a major vehicle for the publicist and the marketer.

E-Mail

E-mail is the most commonly distributed and used Internet application. It is so plain and ordinary that it's taken for granted, buried beneath the hype over the Web. Everybody checks their e-mail. If there's any time left, they go surf the Web. E-mail is the low-cost, direct way to reach a large, diverse audience, one person at a time. Ask any marketer if he or she would rather have an ad on a Web site seen by a million people or the e-mail of addresses of 10,000 people whose demographics match the target audience.

Commercial Online Services

Commercial online services have a separate but overlapping audience with direct Internet users. The four largest services are America Online (AOL), CompuServe (CIS), Prodigy (PDY), and The Microsoft Network (MSN). Other services include GEnie, Delphi, WOW (a CompuServe brand), GNN (an America Online Brand), among others. Most commercial online services have thoroughly integrated the Internet into their offerings, so that users can browse the Web, participate in newsgroups and mailing lists, use FTP and Gopher, and exchange e-mail with people throughout the Internet.

How Big Are They?

America Online is the largest service with almost 6 million U.S. members in mid-1996. AOL is roughly three times the size of rival CompuServe, which had about 2 million U.S. members in 1996. Prodigy was holding steady at about 1.5 million members, and the Microsoft Network had about 1 million.

According to these numbers, about half of all Internet users come from commercial online services. That's exactly what the FIND/SVP survey showed, with AOL accounting for 30 percent, CIS 11 percent, and PDY 9 percent of Internet users. Many people have more than one Internet account, with about one-quarter having both a direct connection and a commercial service account. People with multiple accounts tend to play havoc with demographics surveys.

The structure of Internet connectivity is in serious flux right now. The Microsoft Network abandoned plans to be a full-fledged competitor to AOL and CIS and is instead gravitating to a glorified Web site. America Online has attempted to straddle both markets, retaining AOL as a low-cost commercial service and using GNN as a direct connection brand. Several of GNN's best content features have been cut recently, including Web Review and The Story Cafe. eWorld bit the dust, Delphi and GEnie don't figure to last much longer, and Prodigy and CompuServe are both up for sale as of this writing.

If people vote with their fingers, it appears that America Online and a direct connection are going to be the dominant ways of connecting to the Net through the end of the century. After that, it's anyone's guess as Microsoft and Netscape battle over the Internet software market, and cable companies, phone companies, and Internet service providers battle over the pipeline.

America Online

America Online has a vibrant, youthful feel (Figure 2.7). It has better artwork and an easier interface than its competitors, even though the artwork causes the system to be very slow. When I do promotions on AOL, I find it easier to get people to open a sample chapter from a forum library than to get them to visit a Web site. Experienced Web

Figure 2.7 America Online has a young and restless membership.

surfers are likely to move to a direct Internet connection to avoid AOL's hourly charges.

The forums on America Online are open and responsive. Forum hosts are compensated according to the time people spend in their forums. Consequently, they act less like cops and more like facilitators. Members are given broad latitude in the messages they post. I've had good luck on AOL with promotions that appeal to entrepreneurs, small-business people, families, women, children, and seniors.

America Online's chat is a combination of good facilities for celebrity chat and weak facilities for forum chat. The People Connection chat rooms are notorious for their raunchy, sophomoric, party-line atmosphere. They really aren't a good place to hold a serious discussion. Conversely, the auditorium chats are well-promoted and well-attended, but it can be impossible to book one. AOL's largest "auditorium" holds 50,000 visitors—far surpassing chat capabilities anywhere else on the Net. AOL needs to start building private chat rooms for its popular forums so that there are more opportunities to book meaningful chats with noncelebrity guests.

CompuServe

CompuServe (Figure 2.8) has an older, more professional feel to it than America Online. CIS has been slower to add graphics, making its inter-

Figure 2.8 CompuServe attracts professional, intelligent users.

face less appealing on the surface, but much faster for the experienced user. I've had good luck with promotions aimed at businesses, the media, executives, professionals, women, writers, programmers, and teachers.

CompuServe's forums all have a similar look, making it harder for their personalities to come through. Each has its own chat room for serious chat of an educational nature. Unless you're a headliner on CIS, your chat won't get much promotion beyond the forum sponsoring it. You need to publicize the chat yourself.

The forum hosts on CIS run a tighter ship than on AOL. They seem more like administrators than facilitators; they seldom encourage contributions and are quick to remove messages that appear commercial. I'm not sure whether the hosts on CIS are compensated according to the traffic they draw, but they don't act like it. Attitudes are starting to change, though, and I have more forum hosts working with me now to bring good content to their forums.

CompuServe has good connections to the Internet and a membership that seems a little more computer-savvy than AOL's. While I can get people to visit Web pages from CompuServe, they still prefer to grab sample chapters from forum libraries. CompuServe has excellent research tools and resources that attract a more educated crowd. Members aren't intimidated by promotions that involve downloading and installing software.

Prodigy

Prodigy's audience is an interesting mix of young and old (Figure 2.9). The service is well-suited to small children, with its graphics and parental controls. I've been very successful with promotions that appeal to kids and parents. Prodigy also attracts older, professional users who aren't Web-surfing cybernauts—they just want to have an e-mail address and keep an eye on what all the hype is about.

Prodigy has relatively few special-interest forums, and its interface is so cumbersome that the forums don't get much traffic. Those who do stop by seem like a community of lurkers, preferring to read rather than actively participate. You *can* get Prodigy users to visit Web sites because they've gotten used to going outside the service in search of good content, but it's hard to get them to sign up for a newsletter, use an autoresponder, or download files.

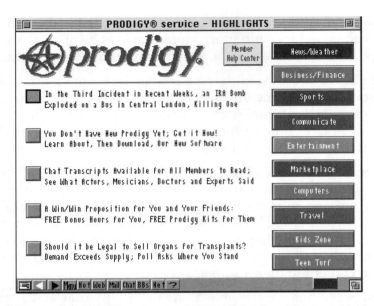

Figure 2.9 Prodigy does a better job of putting on chats than anyone else.

For all its flaws, Prodigy does an excellent job with celebrity chats. The Spotlight auditoriums are large (5,000 capacity) and they get headline talent every night. Unlike America Online, where e-mail to chat hosts seldom gets answered, Prodigy will go to great lengths to put chat guests on the service. Even if Prodigy can't survive as a full-featured online service, it should consider running a chat service on the Web—they know how to do it right.

Online Publics

Most publicity efforts are aimed at familiar target audiences: consumers, businesses, the media, government, educational institutions, investors, and employees. In this section, we'll examine each group to see how strongly they are represented online and how to reach them.

Consumers

Every person online is a consumer, but do they act like consumers when they're online? Not really. Studies show that people don't jump on the Net to buy something. They're attracted by the Net's communication features and the availability of a wide range of information. They enjoy being entertained when they're online; browsing around, playing games, participating in chat, reading electronic publications. But they don't purchase much.

That said, there are several retailers who have prospered online. Most are experienced direct-mail marketers who are used to competing on a national scale. They have low prices combined with superb facilities for processing orders and shipping merchandise. My experience with online retailers shows that people will purchase unusual items, things they can't readily find in their hometowns or are taboo to purchase in person. Nothing succeeds online like a provocative, hard-to-find product line.

People online are able to price products and services very easily. For example, you can find lower prices for computer equipment on America Online's classified ads boards than anywhere else. The ads are free, and with millions of users, asking prices quickly plummet to the lowest motivational level. So, if there is a clear price advantage to buying online, people *will* buy. Several online retailers have told me that customers will start small, gradually increasing the size of their orders as their confidence in the merchant grows.

Whether or not people purchase products online, they are susceptible to advertising that promotes brand awareness. For advertisers, the biggest problem has been getting people to browse the Web with graphics turned on, so they can see the ads. A great deal of money has been spent building Web sites that consumers don't want to visit instead of placing ads on sites they *do* visit. By and large, consumers don't come to merchant Web sites for entertainment but for information.

Businesses

Businesses are online in big numbers now. Almost every business possesses the equipment needed to access the Net, so the additional cost of going online has been minimal. There is a huge business-to-business market online that was ignored by most companies in the early going. Unfortunately, most commercial Web sites have been designed to appeal to a consumer who is *not* online rather than a business client who is.

Most manufacturers will find a wholesale audience online ready and willing to buy if only they could. More Web sites need to court the trade by making it easy for wholesale customers to check stock and prices and place orders over the Net. More promotions should be geared toward the trade instead of the general public. The trade has a stronger incentive to use your Web site, substituting low-cost online communications for long-distance phone calls and faxes.

You can use your Web site to educate wholesalers about your product line, to introduce new products, to demonstrate products, to provide sales literature, and to teach merchants how to sell your products to their customers. Wholesale customers are also probably more interested in your news releases and newsletters than the general public. If most of your customers are wholesalers, distributors, jobbers, sales representatives, or stores, then build your Web site to serve them, and let *them* serve the retail customer.

The Net is a fantastic tool for promoting international trade. On the Net, the buyer in Singapore is just as close as the customer down the block. E-mail significantly reduces telephone charges for companies doing business overseas. More documents are being transmitted over the Net, saving time and delivery charges. If you publicize your Web site properly, international buyers will hear about your products and be able to find your Web site. You might not find a responsive consumer market online, but you might find people who can open up global markets for your products and services.

The Media

Certainly, the media is online in a huge way. Walk into any television, radio, or newspaper newsroom and what do you see? Computers. Lots of them. Journalists live by the word. They were early users of word processing equipment and they have adapted to the Internet faster than almost anyone else. For them, the Net is a way to find leads, research stories, prepare articles for publication, and even deliver those articles.

Consequently, it's very easy to reach the media online. The novelty of the Internet has not yet worn off. News releases that would be ignored through other channels get noticed in e-mail. Stories that would not be worth covering are suddenly interesting because they happened online.

Almost every journalist who is on the Internet has his or her own e-mail address. As you will see in Chapter 6 on news releases, it's possible to find almost anyone's e-mail address if you're willing to look hard enough. The press is swarming the Internet looking for good stories. Giving them what they're after is the publicist's pleasure.

Government

The government is online, though not as prominently as you might think. The U.S. Defense Department built the Internet to serve as a decentralized communications system. The Net spread to academic users next, and finally opened to commercial traffic. The government has been slow to take advantage of the amazing capabilities of the Internet, which businesses immediately jumped on.

Most of the people I know who access the Internet through government facilities lag behind in connection speed, equipment, and software. Part of the slowness is due to a desire to protect confidential information maintained by most government agencies, though strained budgets and the government's incredibly slow acquisitions processes are factors, too.

Still, there are many government agencies using the Net, and it's best to consider them in whatever activities you're undertaking. Law enforcement has shown a willingness to monitor Internet transactions and intercept private e-mail. The amazing ability of Internet search tools to quickly sort through vast amounts of data has not been lost on government agencies. In particular, the Internet offers many possibilities for violating fair trade legislation, consumer protection laws and antidiscrimination laws. If you are conducting contests or similar promotions online, you should subject them to the same legal review required for offline contests and games.

Educational Institutions

At the backbone of the early Internet was a network of colleges and universities that used the Net to facilitate research. Now it's not just the professors who are getting online, but the students, too. Many schools are thoroughly wired and provide free access to the Net to students, who make up a large portion of the online audience, though their relative importance is declining as the Net continues to grow at a rapid pace.

The Internet provides many opportunities for influencing educators and students. There is a large commercial market out there for textbooks, computers, supplies, uniforms, multimedia—anything that might be used in school systems. There are also many people working on research papers and books that might benefit from your publicity efforts.

Investors

Investors are another group of computer-savvy people. The Net is a natural for them, giving them the ability to communicate with foreign markets without any transactions costs. Information moves at a lightning pace online, and most investors make decisions based on these information flows. The Net has search tools that can quickly sift through vast quantities of information. As you'll see in Chapter 11, Firefighting and Follow-Up, it's also possible to monitor the online activities of companies and key individuals.

You should consider how your online activities will affect current or potential investors. You may want to make more information available to them, such as your annual report. Or you might want to curb some of your activities because of the way they could impact investors. For example, you might not want the CEO of your company to use a recognizable e-mail account for his or her online activities.

Employees

The recognition that one's co-workers are also online is sorely absent in most businesses. As an outsider, I am able to learn more about some of my clients than their own employees know. For example, I know when book publishers are holding author chats online or putting excerpts on the Net, even though their own marketing departments sometimes seem unaware of these activities.

The Internet provides an easy, low-cost way of keeping staff informed about what is happening within the company. Distribution of a company newsletter over the Net is one excellent but overlooked publicity activity. Intranets are becoming popular ways to share information between departments, but don't forget the Net itself.

Custom-Tailored Promotions

One of the most attractive aspects of Internet publicity is that you can reach an audience whose demographics look nothing like the Net at large. When you place a magazine ad, the characteristics of the magazine's readership is more important than the characteristics of the general reading public. On the Internet, people reveal their special interests by the Web sites they visit and the discussion groups they participate in. You can gear your promotions to the characteristics of these smaller groups instead of the demographics of the Internet at large.

The Internet audience may be two-thirds male, but not the people using the Moms Online forum at America Online or the Women's Wire Web site. In the next chapter, Basic Tools and Techniques, you'll learn how to build a road map of all the discussion groups, forums, Web sites, and other Internet resources where you are likely to find a specific target audience. By carefully constructing your promotion, you can use the Internet to attract your target audience without annoying people who have no interest in your subject.

Many Web sites keep track of the people who visit, and you can use this information to help you reach a desired demographic. For example, Yahoo can sell you an advertising banner that appears only when someone does a search containing certain words (Figure 2.10). If you are in the car rental business, you could buy a banner that would appear only when someone ran a search using the words "travel," "tickets," "airlines," "fares," "vacation," "hotels," "rental cars," "Avis," "Hertz," and so on.

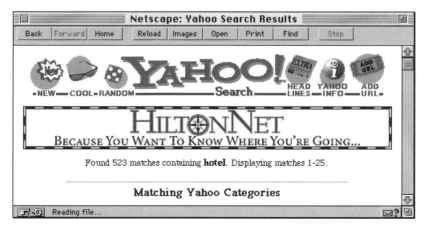

Figure 2.10 When I did a Yahoo search for "hotel," an ad for Hilton hotels appeared at the top of my Results page.

While this example deals with advertising, the same capabilities are important to the publicist. Many Web sites collect a great deal of information about their users. If you know the characteristics of HotWired's readership, you can craft a promotion that appeals to them. You can also search for Web sites that appeal to your target audience and partner with them in developing content that supports your company or clients.

In the next chapter, I'll show you how to find your target audience and how to create campaigns to appeal to them. I'll introduce the tools you'll use to conduct Internet publicity and show you how they differ from offline tools. After we cover the basics, we'll take a close-up look at news releases, announcements, chat tours, contests, and other promotions, and give you the detailed information you need to create and deploy irresistible Internet publicity campaigns.

CHAPTER 3

Basic Tools And Techniques

This chapter introduces you to skills and tools used in online publicity campaigns. You get a cinematic view of the big picture before going in for the close-ups in later chapters. We set some reasonable goals for your online efforts, recommend a good set of hardware and software tools, describe the basic building blocks of publicity, and show you how to assemble them into impressive campaigns. No matter what your background, there's a little something here for everyone.

You may have built a Web site and wonder why it gets so little traffic. Welcome to the club. You no doubt have heard about sites getting "millions of hits" a day, and despair to see that your site got 12. Put those big numbers out of your mind and focus not on attracting millions of people, but on one person, the *right* person; then give that person a rewarding experience. This chapter outlines several Web site publicity campaigns, which demonstrate when to bring people to your site and when to take your show to someone else's site.

If you're a veteran publicist, you'll be familiar with most of the materials used in Internet campaigns: the news release, the newsletter, the public appearance, the gala event. What may be new to you are the tools used and the need to modify your standard publicity pieces to suit the fussy online audience. You'll find some advice in this chapter that will help you adapt your hard-earned skills to the digital arena.

For the enthusiastic entrepreneur, the hustler, the marketer, the person who "makes things happen," this chapter introduces you to the subtle ways of the publicist. Many marketers have gotten scorched online, because the potential audience of millions is too difficult to resist and they plaster ads around cyberspace before they know the unwritten rules. Marketing online is more about publicity than advertising. This chapter helps you learn how publicists get results without getting into hot water.

If you are a manager or a technology expert and you just want to know what works online so that you can better direct the efforts of others, you've come to the right place. This chapter gives you an overview of the publicity activities that are most effective online. You learn what hardware and software a publicist needs to be effective, how much lead time they require, and which activities will need to be coordinated with other people or departments.

Subjects covered in this chapter include:

- **Basic Skills:** A systematic approach to Internet publicity will help you locate the target audience and effectively distribute your message. We talk about setting up a successful ongoing publicity operation without getting bogged down with information overload.

- **Getting Started:** We talk about the different types of online services available to you and recommend some hardware and software configurations. We introduce you to some of the important skills you'll want to develop, and help you organize the materials you'll need to get the job done.

- **Publicity Vehicles:** Brief descriptions are provided of the materials publicists use to call attention to their clients. I refer to these throughout the book, so it's a good idea to become familiar with them here. They include the news release, announcement, link, newsletter, library, public appearance, promotion, and event.

- **Publicity Campaigns:** We take the publicity vehicles described and join them into campaigns to promote a Web site, a product or service, a chat, an event. I tell you how long these campaigns take and how you should organize them. I also cover ongoing public relations activities that are not event-driven.

- **Top Tips:** These are a fistful of one-liners for getting started in Internet publicity.

Basic Skills

In the remaining chapters of this book, I talk about how to execute specific Internet publicity campaigns. In this chapter, the focus is not on an individual effort, but on your goals for your presence online. What are you hoping to accomplish on the Internet? What is your strategy for achieving these results? In this section, we talk about five general goals to shoot for:

1. Locating the target audience
2. Cultivating avenues for message delivery
3. Mastering the tools used to deliver your messages
4. Gathering information and feedback
5. Reducing time-wasting online

First you need to find your target market among the millions of online users. Then you need to find out where they're going online and how you can reach them. This book will help you master the techniques used to get your message in front of the target audience. As you work the Net, you'll be in position to gather valuable information for your organization as well as gauge the response to your promotional efforts. A key ingredient in your success online will be the ability to use search tools and filters to reduce the amount of time wasted chasing worthless leads. Now let's take a closer look at each of these fundamental skills.

Locating the Target Audience

To reach your target audience on the information superhighway, you need to draw a personal road map. The demographic information in Chapter 2 gave you a strong idea of who is online and what they like to do. Now you need to start charting specific places where you are likely to find receptive audiences. A good road map of discussion groups and online publications will save you a great deal of time wandering the Web wilderness.

You can start your road map with Usenet newsgroups and Internet mailing lists. Chapter 12, Resources, lists several Web sites where you can search for newsgroups and mailing lists by keyword, subject, or title. You can find descriptions of the content of these groups, including their charters and FAQ (Frequently Asked Questions) files to help determine whether your target audience is to be found there. You can then visit the newsgroups and subscribe to the mailing lists to verify the kinds of people they attract.

You will also want to locate newsletters and other e-zines that reach your target audience, and Web sites where they congregate. For every subject you can think of—from dog grooming to astrophysics—there is probably a Web site that catalogs all the Internet resources available on that subject. I call these SuperSites. Find the SuperSite, and you've found a road map. Chapter 12 has a section on finding webzines and SuperSites that will help you locate these valuable sites. Figure 3.1 shows one of the best Internet marketing supersites, from Singapore of all places.

One problem with a lot of SuperSites is that the links are not kept up to date. Some sites are so old that more than half the links no longer work. Instead of being time-savers, such sites are time-wasters. Look for a recent revision date and consider maintaining your own SuperSite of resources.

Each of the commercial online services has its own unique demographics and specialties. CompuServe attracts a more scholarly, businesslike and professional audience compared with America Online, which has a younger, more entrepreneurial, fun-loving audience. Prodigy is attractive to parents with home computers, and so has an unusual mix of conservative, older adults and a lot of young children.

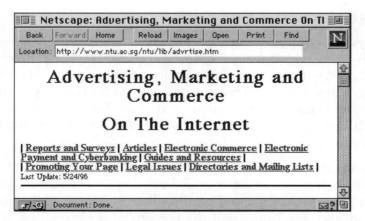

Figure 3.1 A SuperSite with links to thousands of resources for people doing marketing on the Internet.

There are also many regional online services that might be popular with your target market, such as The WELL in the San Francisco Bay area and Panix in New York.

Within each online service, there are forums that act as meeting places for people interested in special topics, and these forums are where most of your publicity activities will take place. Consequently, you want to find active forums that get a lot of traffic and those that appeal to your target audience. Each online service has resources for finding good forums, and these are covered in Chapter 7, Announcements.

As you locate the target audience online, you'll begin to chart your personal road map containing the names and locations of newsgroups, mailing lists, e-zines, Web sites, and forums where that audience is found. Figure 3.2 shows a road map for children's literature sites that I prepared for a customer. Note that you don't have to build a road map like this before you get started; it can be an ongoing part of your online publicity work.

Figure 3.2 A road map of discussion groups, e-zines, and Web sites where people interested in children's literature might be found.

Road map for Children's Literature

Usenet Newsgroups:

misc.kids	alt.parenting.solutions
misc.kids.info	alt.support.single-parents
rec.toys.misc	alt.support.foster-parents
rec.arts.books.childrens	alt.support.step-parents
rec.arts.books.marketplace	k12.chat.elementary
alt.books.reviews	k12.chat.teacher
soc.libraries.talk	k12.library
misc.consumers	bit.listserv.edtech
misc.kids.consumers	misc.education
rec.arts.comics.alternative	misc.education.home-school.misc
rec.arts.comics.marketplace	comp.infosystems.www.announce

Mailing Lists:

BOOKTALK - Childrens literature and classroom use

KIDLIT-L - Children and Youth Literature List

(continues)

Figure 3.2 (*Continued*)

ffk - Families for kids & Kellogg Foundation Project

KIDS-PT - Kids - PreTeen discussion list

KIDS-TE - Kids - Teen discussion list

KidsPeak - Announcements

KIDZMAIL - Kids Exploring Issues and Interests Electronically

FICTIONCHAT-L - Fiction Chat List

YAFICT-L - Young Adult Fiction Writers List

America Online:

Web Diner/Diner Chat/Fave Web Sites

Internet Connection/Exchange/Fave Web Sites

Family Computing Forum/Resources/Kids on Computer

Parent Soup/Parents Pick/On-line sites

Parents Exchange/Family Comp. Resources

Exchange/Family/Stay at home parents

Homeschooling Forum/HS Connections/Learning to read

Mom's Online/Ma'Zine & misc/Moms Online book Club

Nat'l Parentling Ctr/Parenting Forum/CHildrens Books

Family PC Mag/Community Center/Fave places online

Home PC Mag/Bookstore/

CompuServe:

INTERNET NEW USER FORUM/Internet Coffeeshop

INETRESOURCES/Web Hot Spots

INETCOMMER/Internet Events Topic/Great Sites

EDUCATION FORUM/Early Childhood Education Topic/Parents & Reading

KIDS & STUDENTS FORUM/Reading & Writing

YOUTH DRIVE FORUM/Computers & Internet

BOOK PREVIEW/Children's Books

Prodigy:

Books & Writing BB/ Children's Books

Computer BB/ News & Announcements/New Web Sites

Education BB/ Parent Exchange

Games BB/ Other Games

Parenting BB/ Web Pages

Web Sites:

Children's Book News For Parents and Teachers
  <http://community.Net/~ben_chun/bookafair>
Family Planet
  <http://family.starwave.com/>
The Great Glorious and Gandorious...Dr. Seuss!
  <http://www.freenet.ufl.edu/~afn15301/drseuss.html>
Online Children's Stories
  <http://www.ucalgary.ca/~dkbrown/stories.html>
Shelves Of Children's Books
  <http://www.users.interport.Net/~fairrosa/cl.index.html>
Educational Resources Info. Center - For teachers and parents -
  <http://www.indiana.edu/~eric_rec/index.html>
The Kids on the Web: Children's Books
  <http://www.zen.org/~brendan/kids-lit.html>
Welcome to Kids' Web
  <http://www.primenet.com/~sburr/index.html#literature>
Kids' Page
  <http://gagme.wwa.com/~boba/kids.html>
Berit's Best Sites for Children
  <http://www.cochran.com/theosite/ksites.html>
Children's Pages at WombatNet
  <http://www.batnet.com/wombat/children.html>
KID List "Kids Internet Delight"
  <http://www.clark.Net/pub/journalism/kid.html>
CyberKids/Cyberteens Launchpad
  <http://www.woodwind.com/cyberkids/Launchpad.html>
Kids.Com
  <http://kids.com/>
Education, Schools, and Young People Related Links
  <http://www.cs.uidaho.edu/~connie/interests-education.html>
The Ultimate Children'S Internet Sites!
  <http://www.vividus.com/ucis.html>
Internet Public Library
  <http://ipl.sils.umich.edu/ref/RR/ENT/Books-rr.html>
Special Sites for Kids
  <http://www.ipswichcity.qld.gov.au/eetint1a.html>
The Parenting Resource Center on the Web
  <http://www.parentsplace.com/>

(continues)

Figure 3.2 (*Continued*)

Internet Sites
 <http://www1.trib.com/CUMBERLINK/Net.page.html>
ON THE WEB...
 <http://www.ocps.k12.fl.us/kidsw.html#TITLE>
Kids Web: A World Wide Web Digital Library for Schoolkids
 <http://www.npac.syr.edu/textbook/kidsweb/>
Friendly Pines Camp
 <http://www.amug.org/~fpc/links.html>
Internet and World Wide Web Resources for Parents and Children
 <http://www.foundation.tricon.com/2f/children.html>
Electronic Resources for Youth Services
 <http://www.ccn.cs.dal.ca/~aa331/childlit.html>
Read Aloud! A Guide to Reading Children
 <http://funnelweb.utcc.utk.edu/~epling/readaloud.html>
Children's Literature Sampler
 <http://funnelweb.utcc.utk.edu/~estes/estes2.html>
Kelbie's Presto Print
 <http://www.libby.org/Presto-Print/>
Books for Children and More
 <http://www.users.interport.Net/~hdu/>
The BookWire Electronic Children's Books Index
 <http://www.bookwire.com/links/readingroom/echildbooks.html>
Children's Book Publishers
 <http://weber.u.washington.edu/~jabourne/projects/pub.html>
Pre-School Learning Fun
 <http://gatecom.com/~geraldd/apple.html>
Children's Hour Book Emporium
 <http://www.childrenshour.com/store.html>
CHILDRENS BOOKS Nerd World Media
 <http://www.nerdworld.com/users/dstein/nw171.html>
Our Kids Books
 <http://www.sunscape.com/kids/>
The InterLink KIDS' ZONE
 <http://www.spokane.Net/kidzone/index.html>

Cultivating Avenues for Message Delivery

As you collect a list of outlets for your messages, you'll develop a good feel for the online side of your industry. And because these forums and publications can make or break your online marketing efforts, you should try to develop relationships with the people who manage these discussion groups and Web sites.

Each Web site, newsgroup, mailing list, e-zine, and forum is a potential channel for your message. Behind every channel is a person or group of people who created that channel. Whether they still maintain it or have passed those responsibilities to a new group of people, it's their baby, sometimes their life's work, and you would do well to honor their efforts and cultivate their help.

When you move into a channel and post an inappropriate message, you do a disservice to the creators and maintainers of that channel, to the audience and participants, to yourself, and the people you represent. Posting inappropriate messages is not an effective strategy for promoting your goods and services online. It angers people, sometimes to the point of retaliation. That's why you should make an effort to understand the audience for each channel and to respect that channel's hosts.

What kinds of postings are inappropriate? Chapter 7 (Announcements) and Chapter 11 (Firefighting and Follow-Up) discuss this issue at length. In general, blatantly commercial sales pitches and announcements that are off-topic are not welcome in most forums. For example, you can rationalize that some people reading the *alt.books.reviews* newsgroup might be interested in your announcement about adult diapers, but good netiquette suggests that you confine such announcements to forums discussing incontinence, the problems of aging, or similar closely related topics.

These channels did not appear by accident—with rare exceptions, lively forums do not erupt spontaneously. Someone labors over them; encourages contributions, engages people in discussion, chases away disruptive people; keeps the channel clean and inviting, free of commercial clutter or ugly, insensitive comments. Sometimes this maintenance happens almost invisibly, so it's hard to tell there's a hand steering the course of discussion. But almost always, someone is back there. Try to find out who.

Figure 3.3 shows the hosts of the Rolling Stone forum on CompuServe. Most online forums and Web sites credit people who developed the content and designed the programming to put it online. But you may have to dig to find these credits. A lot of people never

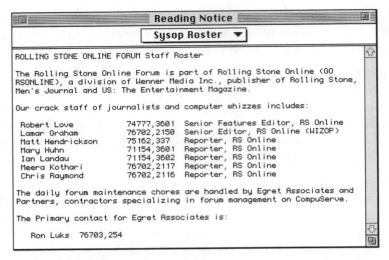

Figure 3.3 The sysops for the Rolling Stone forum on CompuServe. Look for the names of the people behind Web sites and forums.

acknowledge the efforts of the folks "behind the screens." When you identify these people, drop them a line, a kind word, a suggestion, a thank-you note. You will be surprised at how much it means.

They say a publicist is only as good as his or her contacts. When you develop a good set of contacts and get to know the *people*—not just their *names*—you will be much more effective in your work. Your postings and promotions will move more smoothly when you've already introduced yourself to the moderators or hosts. It's like sweeping the ice in a game of curling: you smooth the pathway so that your message will reach its target.

Every forum host, Webmaster, e-zine editor, and discussion group moderator is looking for good content to add to their channel. They want to have stimulating conversation and attractive files to give away. As a publicist, you can be a pipeline into good content for them. You can provide them with chat guests, news items, and help files. When you prepare the content properly, it is always welcomed.

Master the Tools Used to Deliver Your Message

When I first came online, I had to learn a lot of Unix commands to retrieve my e-mail and dispatch my messages. Then I made the switch to

Eudora for my e-mail, and my work became much simpler. When Mosaic came out and the World Wide Web appeared before my eyes, my life online went through a complete transformation. I had spent years learning to manipulate computers with a series of cryptic, arcane commands and suddenly all that knowledge was obsolete.

To be an effective publicist, one of your goals must be to master the tools needed to prepare and deliver your message. Unfortunately, some of these skills do not come easily and will likely become obsolete by the time you master them. To work the Internet requires mastery of a dozen different software programs, which seem to be completely redesigned every six months. But take a deep breath. Relax. The pace of change is slowing as the technology matures. The most important online skills are the ability to write and think clearly. If you have those, you can muscle your way through the technical part until the software matures.

I'll talk about specific software tools a little later in this chapter, many of which are available for free online and come with little or no documentation. You should try to build a library of books, training manuals and magazine subscriptions that will help you learn how to use these tools. In particular, you will be using e-mail and Web browsing software all the time. It pays to get the best software available and master it.

Gathering Information and Feedback

Not all of the publicist's work involves distributing information to the target audience. It's also important to gather information about the online environment and your company's position and image there. It's only natural that, while you are out delivering your messages to people, you're also gathering intelligence useful to the company.

As you work the Web and visit discussion groups, you'll see opportunities to promote your company's business. You are in position to bring those opportunities to the attention of your sales department, or to follow up on them yourself. No matter what business you're in, you will come across people in need of your services. You'll also uncover a great deal of information about your competitors. You can assist your organization by collecting this information and disseminating it to others. Chapter 11, Firefighting and Follow-Up, has instructions for doing *competitive intelligence* online; that is, tracking the activities of your competitors and gathering information about what they're doing or planning to do, online and offline.

As a publicist working the Web, you're also guardian of your company's reputation. You may come across damaging rumors that you can correct or bring to the attention of the proper people in your organization. You might be getting flamed or libeled online. Some companies use professional "firefighters" to put out such flames, correct misinformation, and protect their company image on the Internet. You will find more detailed information about this in the Firefighting chapter.

One of your goals should be to gain facility with the search tools and news filters available online so that you can find references to your company and its competitors. You may want to set a weekly or monthly schedule for "sweeping" the Net. You can automate the process of finding useful tidbits of information and dumping them into a readable report that can be circulated within your organization.

Reducing Time-Wasting Online

One of the biggest problems anyone faces on the Internet is reducing the amount of time wasted chasing bad leads. You can easily suffocate under the avalanche of data available on the Net. It's not uncommon for someone like Bill Gates, president of Microsoft, to get 300 e-mail messages a day. If he spends just one minute on each message, that's *five hours* processing the day's mail! It is a struggle to climb such a mountain of messages.

One of your biggest goals will be to use your time online efficiently. There simply won't be enough hours in the day to follow every lead, to reach every discussion group, or read every valuable e-zine. There are a variety of services you can use to make your life easier on the Net. Figure 3.4 shows an Infoseek Personal Page. You can program Infoseek (http://www.infoseek.com) to search all of its resources for those items that interest you and present them in a readable fashion. It's like being able to program your own television newscast.

The Infoseek Personal Page is just one of many similar tools for managing the information flow. These services—collectively called *filters*—allow you to track news stories by specifying the subjects you are interested in, the companies you want to follow, the people whose activities most intrigue you, the entertainment vehicles you most enjoy,

Figure 3.4 An Infoseek Personal Page brings a custom selection of news to your desktop.

and so on. Sorting through information is one of the tasks that computers perform very well. The trick is to specify your criteria in such a way that you get all the information that's most important without the superfluous stuff. That's not easy.

Throughout this book, you'll find many shortcuts I developed after years of pounding my head against the Internet. You will learn how to do more on CompuServe in 15 minutes than most members can do in hours. You'll learn how to move through the Web like a tornado, sucking up the valuable bits of information you need and quickly disgorging the debris. I'll even help you recognize when it's faster to look through a magazine or book than it is to search online, or when it's better to put down the mouse and pick up the phone.

The Net has become so large that unless you learn to use information filters, you will not be able to achieve your other goals. The enormity of the Web and the poor quality of many of the tools used to navigate it have turned a lot of people off the Net; they see it as a waste of time. After you spend two hours in an Internet directory following broken or obsolete links, you might agree. But there are so many opportunities for the publicist online that it seems worth the effort to learn the new technology.

Getting Started

It all begins with an Internet account. You have two basic choices: a direct connection to the Internet or an account with a commercial online service.

With a direct account through an Internet service provider (ISP) you will be able to use almost all the resources available on the Net, and to send messages to anyone else via e-mail. You won't, however, be able to access the proprietary content of the commercial online services, which means you can't access their forums and discussion groups, which may be important outlets for your marketing message.

With an account through a commercial online service such as America Online, CompuServe, or Prodigy, you can access all of your service's proprietary content and most of the resources available on the Internet. You can also send messages to anyone else via e-mail; however, your connection to services such as the World Wide Web and Usenet may be limited and slow. And you won't have access to the forums or discussion groups on competing online services.

An account with a commercial online service will run you about $10 per month plus $3.00 per hour for anything over five hours per month. A direct connection to the Internet starts at about $20 a month for an unlimited number of hours. If you're on the Net more than 10 hours a month, you'll most likely pay less with a direct connection than a commercial account. If you use the Net only to check your e-mail, you'll pay less with a commercial service account.

If you are doing publicity on the Internet, you're going to be spending a lot of time online. And to reach the millions of people using the commercial online services, you'll need multiple accounts. At one time, I had accounts with seven different online services (America Online, CompuServe, Prodigy, GEnie, Delphi, The WELL, and a direct connection). Keeping track of all the different software proved too confusing, and I had to hire people to handle some of these services for me.

For a beginner, I recommend an account on America Online or CompuServe. They make it easier to get started, and their discussion groups are more friendly than those on the Net. But once you start racking up some big bills, consider switching to a direct Internet connection.

For any company serious about online marketing and publicity, multiple accounts are necessary. I recommend accounts with America Online, CompuServe, any major regional services, and a direct Internet connection. You may want to set up your own domain name and Internet server (for example, www.mycompany.com) so that people have round-the-clock access to your Web site and marketing materials.

Be aware, too, that you don't have to run all your campaigns from your own Web site. One of the best things about Internet publicity is that you can often do your work through other people's Web sites. You don't need a big server and you don't need to do all the programming if you can place your promotions on other Web sites.

Hardware

You probably already have all the equipment you need to get online: a computer and a modem. You also need an account with an Internet provider. Table 3.1 lists some alternative hardware configurations. More is usually better, as in more memory, more disk storage, a faster modem, a bigger pipeline to the Net.

Table 3.1 Hardware Configurations

	Good	**Better**	**Best**
Phone Line	dedicated	ISDN	T-1
Modem	14,400	28,800	ISDN or Cable
Monitor	Color	15" color	21" color
CD-ROM	2-speed	4-speed	8-speed
RAM	8 megs	24 megs	32 megs+
Hard Drive	100 megs	300 megs	1 gig+ or Zip Drive
Multimedia	speakers	plus microphone	plus camera

One of the problems with the Internet is that people want it to work like a TV, but it doesn't. Viewers want a quality experience with excellent graphics, good writing, video, audio, and animation; but right now, that kind of experience can't be delivered through the pipe. That doesn't stop Webmasters from trying, though. Consequently, the Web is weighted down with heavy graphics that take forever to load. Just running a trapline of your favorite sites could take hours, even with a fast modem. The faster the connection to the Net, the easier your work will be (although paying your phone bill could be a very unpleasant experience indeed).

Software

Table 3.2 lists some of the software you'll need to do your work online. Most of this software comes bundled in easy-to-use kits such as *Internet In A Box* and *The Internet Starter Kit*. Once you're used to being online, you can update your software and find additional helper programs at the vast shareware and freeware archives on the Net. The Resources chapter has pointers to the best of these sites.

E-Mail

E-mail is still "the killer app" in my book—the most important piece of software you'll use online. As a publicist, your job is to distribute information to those who are likely to want it or need it. Your main distribution tool is e-mail. You'll use it to send news releases, to post messages to mailing lists, to transfer files, to send follow-up materials when you get inquiries, and to communicate with your co-workers, suppliers, and customers.

Your job also involves gathering information, and, once again, you'll be doing a lot of this with your e-mail program. You'll use your e-mail to read e-zines, newsletters and mailing lists. E-mail is the most powerful tool in your kit, so get the best software available and spend some time learning to use the fancy features.

Web Browser

Second in importance to e-mail software is the Web browser. You'll use your browser primarily to search for information. Through your browser, you have access to the Net's most powerful and easy-to-use

Table 3.2 Families of Software to Use Online

FAMILY NAME	Brand Names	Functions
Communications	Microphone, Z-Term	Dial in to bulletin boards.
Web Browser	Netscape, Mosaic, Lynx, MacWeb, Internet Explorer	Retrieve and display files stored on the World Wide Web.
Gopher	TurboGopher	Retrieve and display files stored on Gopher servers.
Telnet	NCSA Telnet, Trumpet Telnet	Log in to remote computer systems.
FTP	Fetch, Anarchie	Retrieve/deliver files from/to an FTP server.
News Reader	NewsWatcher	Read Usenet newsgroups and post messages to them.
E-Mail	Eudora, Pine, Elm, Microsoft Exchange	Send and receive messages and files to/from other people online.
HTML Editor	HoTMetaL, Pagemill, HTMLEditor, Web Weaver, BBEdit, Aracnid, Hot Dog, GNNPress	Create HTML files for the World Wide Web.
JPEG Viewer	JPEGView, LView Pro	View and edit JPEG images.
GIF converter	GIF Converter	Change file formats images are stored in.
Transparency	Transparency	Make a GIF image "transparent" for web.
Compression	Zip, Stuffit, MacBinary II, DiskDoubler, DropStuff, Gzip	To compress files before uploading.
Uncompression	Unzip	To uncompress downloaded files.
Phone		To send and receive realtime voice over the Internet.
TCP/PPP	TCP/IP, FreePPP, TCPack	Various communications programs enabling you to connect to services over the Internet.
IRC Chat	GlobalChat, IRCle, Palace, Microsoft V-Chat	Client software for participating in Internet Relay Chat (IRC)
Audio Player	Real Audio, True Speech, Sound Machine	Allows you to play audio files as they download.
Video Player	QuickTime Player, Sparkle	Allows you to play video files retrieved from the Net.

search tools and information filters. These will help you locate your target audience online and track important periodicals, without wasting a lot of time on dead leads.

Word Processor

A lot of your work will involve the plain, old-fashioned word processor. For messages that are going out to large audiences, it's better to polish them in your word processor, then, when they're perfect, import them into your Internet applications. Most of the spell-checking programs built into Internet applications pale in comparison to word processor spell checkers.

If you're creating Web pages as part of your work, you may also need a separate HTML program, although these functions are now bundled with most word processors.

Other Software

A lot of the other software you'll need is being integrated with Web browsers so that it's invisible to the user. For example, downloaded files automatically uncompress, audio files start playing when you click on them, and so on. Netscape 2.0 includes e-mail and a built-in news reader, but I've never found them as easy to use as the standalone programs.

If you're preparing content for the Web, you'll probably need graphics editing software. Preparing images for online use is a subtle art form and takes a variety of tools. You'll need a program like Photoshop for creating or touching up images, and then converters to transfer the images into formats that work well online.

The Resources chapter has the addresses of popular software archives on the Net where you can find almost any type of software for free. The chapter also lists sites that will help you learn to create successful Web pages.

Familiarizing Yourself with the Territory

Start your Internet experience by quietly listening as you design your road map of Internet resources. This phase could take a few weeks to a few months, depending on how comfortable you are with communicat-

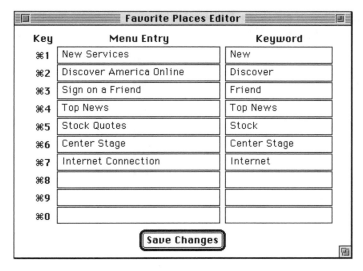

Figure 3.5 You can keep a list of Favorite Places on most online services and use the list as a shortcut to the forums.

ing via computer. This activity is called *lurking*; you just read and don't contribute much. But, feel free to pipe up, especially to encourage someone who has contributed something of intelligence or value. Too many people only post messages to complain or ask questions. It's nice to support people who are making positive contributions.

Look for forums and add the good ones to your hotlists. Figure 3.5 shows a Favorite Places list from America Online. You can create similar lists of your favorite forums on CompuServe, Prodigy, and other services. Building these lists is part of the process of developing your personal information highway road map which will save you a lot of time online.

On the Web, you add popular sites to your Bookmarks list. Figure 3.6 shows some of my bookmarks in Netscape 2.0. You'll want to quickly install bookmarks to the major searching tools (Yahoo, Infoseek, and so on.). Learning to use bookmarks and search tools will prove valuable skills indeed.

It is also essential to learn how to read and post to Usenet newsgroups. You can access these groups from any major online service, but be forewarned that they can be intimidating. They are open discussion

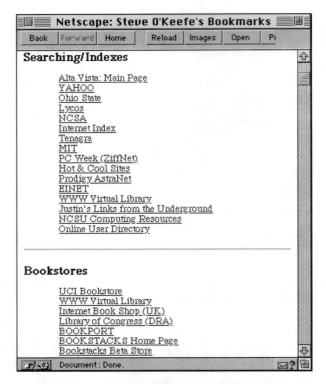

Figure 3.6 Part of my Netscape Bookmarks folder, with hyperlinks to my most frequently visited Web sites.

forums, during which people contribute messages, often in response to previous messages. A long string of messages on the same subject is called a *thread*. Forums on commercial online services tend to be more welcoming and comfortable, whereas Usenet tends to be provincial and even hostile. Lurking is definitely the best approach for the beginner, unless you are anxious to learn about flames, those angry messages from those who disagree with you.

Following a Usenet newsgroup is confusing at first, and posting a message is a bit intimidating, but you'll get the hang of it. You'll often hear people refer to *FAQs* on Usenet, which stands for Frequently Asked Questions. Many newsgroups maintain a FAQ file that supposedly answers just about anything you might want to know about the newsgroup or the subjects it covers. I suggest you try to locate and read one of these, just so you know what all the fuss is about.

You should also subscribe to a few mailing lists to get used to receiving them and using them. Mailing lists are a lot like newsgroups, except they're sent by e-mail to subscribers. When you join a list, you receive every message sent to the list, and everyone on the list receives the messages you send. You can subscribe to mailing lists no matter which online service you're using. Promising lists are named in almost any book about the Internet. The Resources chapter in this book lists tools you can use to find mailing lists on just about any subject.

You might want to play with some of the mailing list options to see how they work. You can usually set your list to Digest so that you get one e-mail a day containing all the messages, instead of getting them one at a time. Mailing lists are calmer than newsgroups and tend to have a higher "signal to noise ratio," or more bytes, less bites. They can help you get up to speed quickly with the current state of affairs on the Net.

Of course, you'll be sending and receiving e-mail right away. You should set up a *signature file,* a bit of text automatically appended to all your outgoing messages. It's sort of like letterhead, telling who you are and how to contact you. My signature file is shown in Figure 3.7. You'll find that having a good signature and being a thoughtful contributor to discussions will get you plenty of business on the Net.

I also recommend that you practice setting up your e-mail address book. In particular, learn how to group names so that you can send messages to the whole group. In Eudora, you can set-up *nicknames* with up to 2,000 e-mail addresses each. Other online services have similar features. You can set up a *family* group, an *employees* group, a *customers* group, and so on. Its very easy to maintain address books, and it's important that you learn to do so quickly.

Figure 3.7 A good signature file goes a long way toward establishing your company on the Internet.

After a few weeks of surveying the scene, you'll be ready to start putting some of the high-powered techniques you learn in this book into action. Don't worry about being new to the scene; *everybody* is new to the Internet. A veteran refers to someone who was around before the Web, which most people saw for the first time in 1994. If you make mistakes, remember, you'll learn from them. And keep in mind, no one owns the Net, no one controls it, and your unique way of doing things is probably what has been missing all along!

Preparing Materials for Online Publicity

Once you're comfortable online and are ready to get started promoting your business there, you can begin preparing the materials you'll need to run successful publicity campaigns. The online environment moves very, very fast. When I finally am ready to launch a campaign, it's usually all over within a matter of days. People either respond or they move on. You may spend quite a bit of time setting up the campaign, but when you flash that URL on the screen, people either visit or they don't.

Therefore, you want to have as much information at your fingertips as possible, and you want it prepared for electronic delivery so you can dispatch it instantly. You should be collecting news releases, reviews, endorsements, news articles, announcements, URLs, catalog copy, and just about any document you can get your hands on that's not a company secret. You may want to put your newsletter online, your annual report, your corporate phone book. Gather up as much of this kind of information as you can find.

When you're doing online publicity, you use a multilevel approach to releasing information. Most of your public messages—news releases and announcements—will be very short, usually only a few paragraphs. This is unlike the traditional news release, which may go on for a couple pages. News releases online are more like *an invitation to receive a news release* rather than the release itself.

The writing style you must use to produce such a piece is explained in much more detail in the upcoming chapters of this book. Right now, it's important to understand that you can't just cram your existing publicity materials onto the Net. You need to alter them for this new environment, and that means a layered approach, with the first layer being an invitation. After people respond, you can send them the whole nine yards—every document they could possibly use.

Before you send them the kitchen sink, however, you need to learn to format documents for electronic delivery. Most companies spare no expense to make their printed promotional materials look good. In contrast, when you're sending documents online, most of the struggle is to make them *readable*. In fact, good-looking documents with loads of artwork and fantastic display type don't transfer well online. You have to prepare most of your documents as text files, stripping out all formatting commands, and taking care to be sure the file will be compatible with whatever equipment your audience is using.

It's not easy learning to format documents for delivery online. It goes against everything you've been taught as marketers. Instead of making things look better, you're making them look uglier—but universally readable. This feels uncomfortable professionally, and in the future you will be able to send documents that look as good to the audience as they do to you. But for now, that's not possible, and you need to heed the advice given throughout this book to make your promotional materials accessible to your audience.

Another issue to address before embarking on any of the ambitious campaigns outlined in this book is streamlining the approval pipeline. Set up procedures for getting quick approval for your campaigns. Delays caused by not addressing this issue literally have cost companies millions of dollars, as you will see. For almost anything you put on the Net, some approval will be required, and you should automate the process as much as possible.

Don't forget, also, that all text and artwork is covered by copyright, and you need permission from the copyright owners to put such material online. You may think you have permission, but the owners might not agree. Electronic rights were not covered in most contracts prior to recently, and even now they are seldom addressed in a straightforward manner. Never forget, whenever you put something online, you're giving the whole world access to it.

There are also internal layers of approval to go through, and it is wise to consider these from the get-go. If you run a contest or giveaway or treasure hunt or anything that involves a transfer of goods with material value, plan some time for consulting attorneys. There's a lot of confusion about applying laws to online activities, and that confusion usually translates to delays. You should also cultivate relationships with the people who can provide the artwork, editorial content, and computing resources you need to pull off an online promotion.

Publicity Vehicles

There are certain items you will use over and over again while doing online publicity. We'll take a quick look at each of them in this section, then talk about how they are combined into campaigns in the next section. Although the following descriptions are brief, throughout this book you will learn exactly how to prepare and deploy these items in a variety of situations.

The News Release

The most basic of all publicity tools, the news release is used to inform the media of anything that could possibly warrant press coverage. On the Internet, news releases are delivered by e-mail and should be much shorter than their offline counterparts. A good suggested length is one screenful, or about three or four paragraphs (see Figure 3.8). Most online news releases aren't news releases at all; rather, as noted earlier, they're offers to *send* a news release upon request, or solicitations to visit your Web site for the full story.

Online news releases are sent not just to Internet journalists; e-mail is an excellent way to reach *anyone* in the media. Your news release arrives at the journalist's personal desktop computer, unlike faxes or snail mail or phone calls, which are often screened. Many of my customers have found that online news releases result in a higher percentage of inquiries and stories than news releases sent in more traditional ways.

The Announcement

An announcement is posted to online discussion groups, including Usenet newsgroups, Internet mailing lists, forums on commercial online services, and discussion threads built into many Web sites. The audience is the "general public" participating in these special-interest

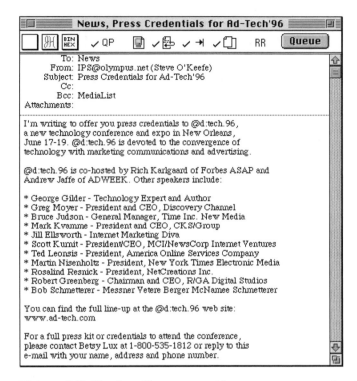

Figure 3.8 Most online news releases are very short and entice the reader to request further information or visit a Web site.

discussion groups. Figure 3.9 shows a sample announcement for a major Web promotion.

An announcement is similar in structure to a news release. It's usually short—just a few paragraphs—and is most likely an attempt to get interested parties to visit a Web site or to request further information. Announcements are used to promote Web sites, events, chats, and other promotions.

The Link

Links put the hyper into hypertext. On the surface, a link can be an image or a word; beneath is an address to a file available somewhere online. When a person activates the link by clicking on it, his or her computer retrieves the specified file. When you activate a link to a Web

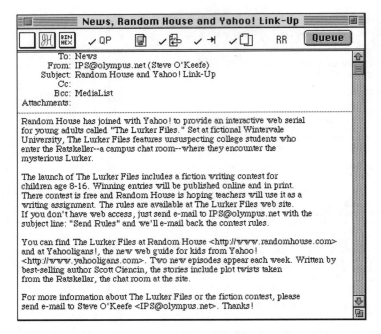

Figure 3.9 Like news releases, announcements should be kept very short. They usually offer a giveaway file of some sort.

site, it feels like you're being taken to that site; in fact, the site is being brought to you. Figure 3.10 shows some graphical links or *hot buttons*.

Links may not seem like publicity vehicles, but they're some of the most important elements in an online marketing campaign. Most promotions involve getting people to visit a Web site or at least to request a giveaway file. Links are the simplest way to travel the Web or retrieve files, therefore, seeding the Net with links is a critical ingredient in most publicity campaigns.

The Newsletter

A regular staple in the publicist's cupboard, a newsletter is used to keep various audiences up to date on new products, services, employees, issues, events, etc. Newsletters are easy and cheap to set-up online. Using list server software, people can subscribe to your newsletter and have it delivered via e-mail at no cost on either end.

Figure 3.10 Providing Webmasters with a cute button might help persuade them to install a link to your site.

An online newsletter can be longer than a few paragraphs, but you should still try to revamp any offline newsletter for your online audience. Online newsletters are often composed of several one-paragraph news items instead of longer stories. By subscribing to a few of the successful Internet newsletters, you'll get a feel for the prevalent style on the Internet. The most important difference is that you won't be able to use standard design elements to make the newsletter a more enjoyable reading experience. At the present time, you have to be as creative as possible with plain ASCII text.

The Library

One of the great advantages of doing publicity on the Internet is the ability to cheaply store vast quantities of information online. You can backup every announcement and news release with a whole arsenal of support files, including product brochures and descriptions, full-length news releases, press clippings about your company, answers to frequently asked questions (FAQ files), customer support documents, street maps and directions, newsletters, calendars of events, transcripts of interviews, help files, audio sound bites, video clips, just about anything that can be squeezed into two dimensions.

These support materials can be stored at your Web, Gopher, or FTP site where anyone can view or download them as needed. You can also use autoresponder software to deliver these materials at any time of the day or night. You may choose to keep frequently requested materials in a special folder on your computer where you can attach them to outgoing e-mail with a couple of keystrokes.

A well-structured library of support materials adds depth to your online publicity efforts. It also helps you save precious time responding to inquires. As you'll quickly discover, time management is a major problem for anyone working on the Internet.

The Public Appearance

What publicist hasn't had to arrange an appearance for a client? Whether your boss is making a presentation at a trade show or you're booking a celebrity's world tour, these activities you perform offline are similar to online appearances. *Chats*, where guests take questions from online audiences, are just one type of online appearance. There are also *dead chats*, where questions are solicited in advance and the answers are posted as an interview; and conferences, forums, and just plain old "schmoozing" with no scheduled event.

Good advance work will turn a sparsely attended chat into major event reaching literally millions of people. As a publicist, you may be called upon to secure a venue for an online appearance, drum up an audience, host the appearance, hawk the transcripts, and do other follow-up work to expand the impact of the event. I'll even show you how to put a client on a cheap world tour without leaving his or her desk.

The Promotion

People just love a good giveaway. Net users are nuts about contests, maybe because they're so easy to enter online. Other popular promotions include treasure hunts, trivia tests, sales, coupons, quizzes, surveys, and what I call "stupid Web tricks," such as a hyperlink that sends you to a different, random Web site every time you click on it.

Promotions are often tied in with other online activities, such as the launch of a new Web site or a major Web event. But there are many pitfalls that can hamstring an online promotion, and I cover those in detail later in the book.

The Event

At the top of the publicist's tree is The Big Event—a major online happening that attracts the media, the public, and anyone else wandering within shouting distance. Popular events include movie sneak previews, concerts broadcast online, debates by candidates for public office, roundtable forums, Web site grand openings, conventions and trade shows, and other large projects.

As the Internet audience has grown, online events have become concomitantly bigger. A new Web site is no longer worth media coverage—unless its debut is accompanied by some gala event, such as an exclusive interview, a simulcast, a contest, or a limited edition giveaway. In fact, the entire Internet is moving toward an event-oriented culture with cynical browsers looking for the next big thrill.

Publicity Campaigns

Those are the tools you'll be working with. The following chapters explain exactly how to create each of them and unleash them on the Net. They can be combined into powerful marketing presentations, especially when bolstered by offline activities. Let's look at some typical Internet campaigns and see which tools to use and which to avoid.

Promoting a Web Site

Web site promotions can combine any or all of the preceding publicity elements, but it's best to move slowly. Until you develop "webbed feet," you should take care that your promotion doesn't sink. I've been hired to promote many new Web sites, and I don't think a single one was completed on time. And, when they are done, they often don't work: links are broken, you can't chat in the chat room, the home page takes so long to load that most people bale out.

Guess what happens when you invite all the media on the planet to a Web site that doesn't work? It's not pretty. Directories refuse to link to you. Pundits make fun of you. Maybe some journalist devotes a chapter of her or his book to your monumental failure? Then just try to persuade all the press to come back a month later, when you've fixed all the problems. And yet companies still insist that I invite people to their Web sites before they've been tested.

You might find this hard to believe, but you can have a Web site up and running for weeks, months, or even *years* before having a Grand Opening promotion. And you'll get just as much press coverage as you would have in the first two days—maybe even more. And the media coverage will likely be favorable since you've had plenty of time to fix any bugs, develop good content and graphics, and learn what's special about your own site. The upcoming subsections detail some of the tools you'll use to launch your Web site.

Registration Campaign

To get your site listed in all the directories, indexes, and catalogs on the Internet (Yahoo, Lycos, WebCrawler, etc.), allow yourself four to six weeks for your listings to appear, and don't start until your site is up. This is not a campaign for temporary promotions: it's meant for semi-permanent sites. Refresh the campaign at least once per year.

Linkage Campaign

Getting other sites to install a link to your site is a slow but fruitful process that can help you become the dominant Web site in your subject area. Many of the people you approach will ask for a link back, so be sure to build a "cool links" page into your Web site. And remember, requesting and testing links should be an ongoing part of Web site administration.

News Release

A news release is sent to people who review and rate Web sites, and to your local publications and trade press. Most newspapers and magazines now routinely mention Web sites of interest; and, if the story is big enough, broadcast journalists get into the act. News releases should be sent only for your grand opening or when you have installed a major revision to the site. Don't forget: send the news release only when the site works!

Announcements

Announcements are posted to appropriate discussion groups to make people aware of your Web site. It's a good idea to have a help file or giveaway at your site to make it worth announcing to the general public. You can place follow-up announcements, but be careful not to post the same message to the same groups over and over again.

Promotions

A lot of Web sites debut with a promotion to help introduce the site to a wide audience. If you're holding a contest, plan some time in your schedule for legal review—most contests are regulated by state and federal laws. One good promotion is a treasure hunt to get people to work their way through the whole site in search of clues or answers. Try to craft a promotion that appeals only to your target audience; otherwise, the promotion just gums up the Web site with prize seekers.

Events

Events are dangerous to hold during a Web site premiere, because so many things can go wrong. If you must make a big splash, consider partnering with a popular Web site that has the expertise to pull it off. Consider instead using an annual event to unveil revisions at your Web site or to promote a new product line. An annual event gives you plenty of time to develop and test new content.

Promoting a Product or Service

Be very careful about promoting a product or service on the Net, as these can be difficult to differentiate from advertisements, which are big no-nos on the Net. Most campaigns like this are tied to a Web site, anyway so the product promotion actually becomes a Web site promotion.

The Soft Sell

Perhaps the most effective way to promote your goods and services is by participating in discussion groups. When you make intelligent comments or provide helpful advice, people come to know you and respect you. If your signature contains instructions for getting more information or for visiting your Web site, you probably won't lack for good, solid prospects. The soft sell takes time, but produces quality results.

News Releases

E-mail is an excellent way to inform the press about your new products or services. Try to collect the e-mail addresses of all your regular media contacts and any influential outlets that cover your business. You won't believe all the techniques described in Chapter 6, E-Mail News Releases, for ferreting out e-mail addresses of the media.

Co-Branding

It's nice to have your own Web site to service the business-to-business trade, but always take the time to work through other sites to reach the consumer audience. There are many big Web magazines and SuperSites that are constantly looking for fresh content. You will reach a much larger audience by installing your promotions on a popular Web site rather than only trying to entice the audience to your site. If you are an expert in your field, offer yourself for a chat, or write an article or help file for a popular Web site to install.

Announcements

Announcements promoting a product or service are risky, unless they are tied to an event. Only use announcements if you have a chat or a giveaway file or some Web promotion to which to invite people.

Publicizing a Chat

Chats are one of the more fascinating online phenomena. Many people who visit them find them chaotic and frustrating; guests often find them shallow and frustrating. Nevertheless, chats are extremely popular, both with celebrities and the online audience. At the same time, they are one of the most underused publicity vehicles available. Chats are truly perplexing.

From a publicity standpoint, a chat is a low-cost excuse to plaster messages all over the Net. If the advance work is done correctly, the announcement for a chat may reach millions of people, having an impact far greater than the small audience that attends. Give yourself about one month to book a chat and do the advance work. Here are some of the tools you'll use.

News Releases

Send news releases to Web sites, newspapers or other outlets that have chat calendars. Most chats aren't scheduled far enough in advance to promote to magazines or trade journals. You'll get better coverage if the guest is well known, or if some significant announcement will be made at the chat.

Announcements

Chats are perfectly suited to discussion group announcements. You shouldn't post more than a week in advance, though, because the human attention span is short. Even a disastrous chat can be a major marketing success if you run a good announcement campaign. Be sure to offer transcripts to those who can't attend.

Co-Branding

I've seen several companies struggle to install chat facilities at their Web sites. Why, when so many existing auditoriums are looking for guests? It is difficult and expensive to build your own chat facilities. This is definitely one area where you should try to book yourself into a large chat auditorium where the producers have experience putting on a good show.

Transcripts

If you're doing your publicity work right, more people will see the transcripts than attend the chat. You need to get permission from the chat venue to circulate transcripts. Once you have permission, install them on your Web site and promote them on the Net.

Promoting an Event

A substantial event should be promoted just as hard *offline* as *online*. Those who understand the power of a major event to attract attention have begun incorporating Web sites into all their promotions. One of the early successes in this area was the Web site for the Disney movie, *Toy Story* (Figure 3.11). Television and print ads all contained the URL for the Web site: http://www.toystory.com/.

Major events can also be major headaches. Contrast the *Toy Story* promotion with Apple's *Mission Impossible* companion Web site, which wasn't available when TV ads started airing. When it finally did appear, the site had technical problems. The main lesson here is to give yourself plenty of extra time for product development and testing.

Figure 3.11 Disney's Toy Story site was one of the early successes in movie companion Web pages.

News Releases

Of course, a news release is warranted for a major Web event; in fact, multiple releases: one for the traditional media and one for people who review and rate Web sites. You can also include ancillary releases to announce partner promotions or significant content developments. You might want to invite the media to preview the site before the grand opening (and promise to fix any problems they find before opening day).

Announcements

It would be nice if you could string the hype out over weeks or months the way Microsoft did with the release of Windows95, but most of that sort of advance publicity is best done offline. When you make announcements to discussion groups open to the public, the site should be accessible or you will lose hits.

Chats

A lot of companies fail to take advantage of the power of chat announcements. As noted, a chat is an excuse to get your product name before millions of people. Look for any excuse to hold a chat. If your Web event is clever (and it should be), host chats with the programmers, the designers, the illustrators—even the publicist— about how to market events online.

Promotions

Most major Internet events now contain some sort of contest or other promotion to draw people to the site. But take care to allow enough production time for legal review and to work out the kinks. Also be sure the promotion doesn't upstage the site's content, which should be the focus of the media attention you get.

Offline Efforts

Many publicists don't do a good enough job promoting their Web events offline. Direct mail is an excellent way to bring traffic to the site. Send invitations to customers, prospects, suppliers, employees, the media, and others. Postcards make a handy reminder to visit a Web site at a specific date and time. You can even mention the event on your voice-mail system. There's a certain cachet to having a major Web event, and your offline publicity should capitalize on that.

Ongoing Public Relations

In addition to all the event-oriented campaigns described, anyone with a significant presence online should maintain basic public relations functions on the Net. If you employ good search tools and filters, these duties will require half a working day per week, more or less, depending on the size of your organization.

News Releases

The development of a database of e-mail addresses of the media should be a major priority for your online public relations person or team. Also, cultivate a list of publicity services you can hire to expand the reach of special announcements or in case of a public relations disaster.

The Resources chapter provides you with a good starting list of online marketing services.

Newsletters

A quarterly or monthly newsletter should become a regular part of your online efforts. You can distribute it through e-mail or using one of the popular list server programs. You can use the newsletter to help employees keep track of what's happening with your Web site, not to mention prospects, customers, suppliers and others who work with you on a regular basis.

Libraries

Make an attempt to transfer important documents into electronic format for delivery on the Net. McGraw-Hill was one of the first companies to make its phone book available online. Many companies have started compiling customer service libraries on their Web sites. Publicists should have all the tools they need to respond to media inquiries, including a news release archive, transcripts of speeches or interviews, text from news stories, endorsements, artwork such as photographs of products or key people, and more.

Firefighting

An important part of online publicity is gathering information from the Net and relaying it back to others in the organization. As you'll see in the Firefighting chapter, several large companies have had public relations nightmares on the Internet. Obviously, it's important to know if your company is being attacked, and there are several tools that will automatically search newsgroups, mailing lists, e-zines, even e-mail for references to you or your company. You can preserve your company's reputation by dousing any flames before they spread.

By now you should be familiar with the basic campaigns and tools used in Internet publicity. The remaining chapters of the book will give you step-by-step, detailed instructions for carrying out successful campaigns. You'll find plenty of real-life examples learned in the school of hard knocks, and an occasional glimpse into the crystal ball to help you prepare for the road ahead.

Top Tips

- **Lurk and Learn:** Take a tour of cyberspace and spend a few weeks listening and chatting and getting to know some of the players and how the systems work. Don't start posting promotional messages until you're familiar with norms of behavior.

- **Invest in Education:** Most Internet software is poorly documented. Buy some books—they'll save you time online. Subscribe to a couple magazines—they're great for finding site lists for special-interest topics.

- **Turn Your PC into a Vending Machine:** Have your promotional materials prepared in advance, in a format everyone can read, in neat little folders on your computer or Web site, ready to serve those who respond to your messages.

- **Search and Sift:** Learn how to use the major search engines on the Net. You'll be amazed at some of the tricks they can do. Setup news filters, robots, or intelligent agents to sift through the infostream and bring you golden nuggets of data.

- **A Little Laziness Is a Good Thing:** There are Webmasters all over the Net desperate for good content, so why not run your promotions through their sites? You eliminate a lot of technical headaches, and they get a free publicity campaign for their site. Everyone wins.

CHAPTER 4

The Registration Campaign

Registration is the process of listing your Web site in all the appropriate Internet directories, catalogs, and search engines. This is one of the least expensive ways of attracting visitors to your site; at the present time, very few directories charge a listing fee. As traffic on the Internet grows and directories such as Yahoo! become saturated, however, you can expect to pay for higher-quality listings or premium placements. Even then, the registration campaign described here will be the start of all your Web site publicity efforts.

This chapter steps you through the registration campaign. You'll gain valuable insights when you understand a little of the colorful history of Internet directory services. You'll learn what information you need to assemble in advance, how to launch a registration campaign that will work now *and* later, and how to get the most from paid registration services.

Like any "free" service, unfortunately, the registration process is plagued with problems. But I'll show you'll how to deal with everything from very slow registrars to broken links. There are also opportunities for the savvy marketer and you'll get expert advice on making your directory listings more powerful and effective. Let's take a quick look at the topics we'll cover:

- **Spiders, Worms, and Night Crawlers:** Internet indexes work in strange and mysterious ways. Learn the basics of Internet registration and how to avoid the minefields awaiting the novice.

- **The Major Directories:** Meet the Net's most popular directory services; learn some of the Voodoo behind Yahoo!; get the gist 'a Alta Vista.

- **One-Stop Registration:** The easiest, cheapest way to register your Web site. But there's always a catch. Find out how to use one-stop registration sites such as Submit It! and why you might want to register individually with each directory.

- **A Sane Strategy:** From do-it-yourself to hiring a firm, there are many ways to approach the registration campaign. Weigh the alternatives, and I'll recommend a tried-and-true system.

- **The Registration Form:** If you can complete this form, you're ready to start your campaign. If you can't, you need to collect the missing information.

- **Coding Your URL:** One of the most powerful information-gathering tricks available. Does your Internet service provider let you code?

- **The Registration Report:** The form you'll use to keep track of your campaign. If you hire someone to do the work for you, you'll want to receive a report like this.

- **Registering Multiple Pages:** Once your Web site has achieved critical mass, you can start registering subpages. This is the cutting edge of Net registration—careful you don't get hurt.

- **Registration Responses:** How to take care of the paper(less)work that results from a registration campaign.

- **Fixing Registration Problems:** If you prepared well, your biggest problem will be waiting for your listings to appear. The rest of us might have to fix anything from a busted URL to a category calamity.

- **The Future of Registration:** Expect to see more specialized catalogs on the Internet and plan to start paying for position and prompt service. I'll help you prepare.

- **Top Tips:** My best bits of wisdom for a successful and spiritually rewarding Internet registration campaign.

Spiders, Worms, and Night Crawlers

The Internet is a vast and marvelous place. In the fall of 1995, there were an estimated 8 million documents on the World Wide Web alone. Tens of thousands of companies have Web sites, each of them crammed with descriptions of products and services, and hundreds of new sites are added to the Internet every day. How can you keep pace with this mind-blowing information overload? Fortunately, you don't have to. There are services that do it for you. They catalog all the Web pages, Gopher sites, Usenet newsgroups, mailing lists, and other Internet offerings, sorting everything by form and content. They're the librarians of the Net, with names like Yahoo, Lycos, and Alta Vista, and they're heroes; we would be hopelessly lost without them.

Unfortunately, it's not that easy getting around *with them* anymore either. Directories such as Yahoo are choked with so many listings that it's hard to know where to begin. Many of Yahoo's links lead to dead or disappointing Web sites. Powerful search tools such as Alta Vista bring up so many matches to a simple inquiry that you have to narrow your search to obscurity in order to get a manageable number of hits.

You can't blame the Net librarians—they're more overwhelmed than anyone by the explosive growth of the Internet. The major search sites have tried to make it easier for browsers to find the newest or most valuable links, and they've attempted to catalog sites in more tightly focused groups. Then they start cross-referencing listings and before you know it, it's all a mess again.

While major directories dominate the Web-searching business, more small competitors are challenging them. In the spring of 1996, I counted more than 100 general-interest directories. Do you remember when they deregulated telephone service? All of a sudden you were getting five phone books instead of one. Well, the Internet has always been deregulated and there are dozens of "Yellow Pages" to choose from. How do you know which are worth using and which are important to be listed in? There are two major kinds of guides to the Internet: *spiders* and *directories*. Spiders work like a phone call to "Information"—someone searches for listings that match your request. Directories work like your Yellow Pages—a self-serve listing of every site, sorted into categories.

Spiders

Spiders search the Net in response to your query. Two popular spiders are Lycos and Alta Vista. When, for example, you ask to see all the references to "grand pianos" on the Internet, they will search for any Web page or Usenet newsgroup that contains both the words "grand" and "piano" or either of them.

Lycos and Alta Vista don't actually search the Web with every inquiry. Instead, they fan out across the Net once every three days or so and cache everything out there. When you use these services, they search through their databases of cached documents rather than actually scanning the Net.

It's not necessary to register your home page with a spider; the spider will find it on its regular rounds. However, if the spider allows you to register, go ahead and do it. They don't catch everything, and it's a simple process to tell them about your Web site. Also, if your Web site is seated on someone else's server, spiders may miss you on their caching missions.

Directories

The other major type of Internet guide is a directory, such as Yahoo. Directories are simply large catalogs of Internet items. They don't search the Net for you; rather, they organize sites by subject or form and present you with a list of entries or categories that meet your search criteria. If you search for "grand pianos" in a directory, you're only going to get a list of sites that asked to be cross-referenced by those words. You'll likely get piano makers, sellers and enthusiasts; with a spider you'd get any page on the Web that had either the word "grand" or "piano" on it.

Directories don't automatically list new Web sites, so it's important that you ask for your site to be listed. This is usually accomplished by filling out a registration form, although sometimes it can be done through e-mail. Unlike a spider, where a listing is automatic, someone must decide whether to list your site in his or her directory. There might be criteria you must meet to qualify; for example, a directory might refuse listings for sites deemed obscene or poorly created.

There are many other nuances to dealing with directories. Who decides into which category to put you, and whether you can be cross-referenced to other categories? Must you have a Web site, or can you register an e-mail address? Can you register an infobot—an automatic mailer? The answers to these questions are in constant revision. Internet catalogs have grown to be big businesses. Competition among them is intense and drives them to improve their services. We'll look at some of the big players and how to work with them to gain exposure for your Internet sites.

The Major Directories

Many Internet directories and search engines started as hobbies or school projects. Today, they're some of biggest and most successful businesses online. In this section, I'll examine the backgrounds, strengths and weaknesses of some popular sites. When you understand a site's history and place in the market, you're better able to create an effective listing for that site.

Yahoo

Yahoo is the grandparent of all Internet directories (Figure 4.1). It started out with a couple of guys, Jerry Yang and David Filo, fooling around and putting up a page of links to their favorite places on the Net. They were engineering students at Stanford University at the time; but I suspect they're quite wealthy now that Yahoo has gone public.

Yahoo was just a fun and funky pile of links when I first visited in 1994. Then it became a database. Then Filo and Yang set up a registration page enabling anyone to list his or her Web site at Yahoo for free. After a few influential stories about Yahoo appeared in the trade papers, the site exploded. But no good deed goes unpunished on the Internet, and Yahoo was soon swamped by "index spammers," who try to register their Web sites in hundreds of different categories. The staff at Yahoo had to sort through the link requests and weed out duplicates. Then they had to visit the sites to be sure they existed. Soon it took weeks to get listed at Yahoo. The delay resulted in a deluge of e-mail asking when a site would be listed. What a headache!

The folks at Yahoo have dealt admirably with the onslaught. A partnership with Netscape provided them with faster and larger computers; advertisers helped Yahoo pay for extra staff to deal with all the link requests. In addition, Yahoo has consistently improved its interface and

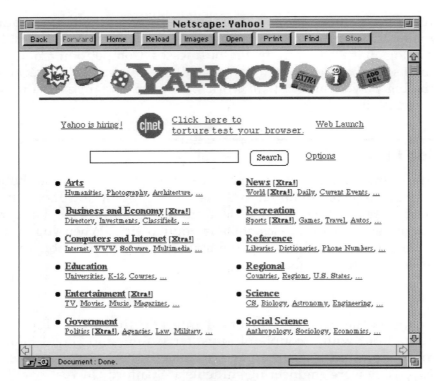

Figure 4.1 Yahoo! is the grandparent of all Internet directories.

ease of use, even helping people submit their searches to competing directories if they're dissatisfied with the results at Yahoo.

In mid-1996, Yahoo added a second directory called Yahooligans, for kids. This was Yahoo's first public attempt to build a special-interest catalog. You can expect to see many more of these subcatalogs very soon.

Lycos

Lycos is another pioneer Internet search engine (Figure 4.2). It was the first large spider on the Internet. Developed at Carnegie Mellon University by Dr. Michael ("Fuzzy") Mauldin, Lycos was extremely popular in the early days of the Net, that is, before the release of Mosaic and the growth of the Web. It organized the results of its spider-style searches

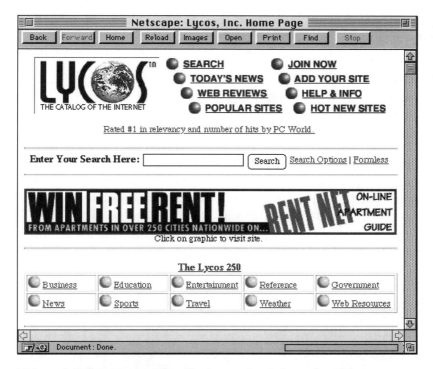

Figure 4.2 Lycos was the first popular Internet spider.

into fastidious categories that were dear to the hearts of librarians everywhere.

Lycos is an amazing tool. Its searches cover the entire Internet, including FTP and Gopher sites, as well as Web sites. It then builds a database of every address found and a description of the material contained at that address. Lycos is out there searching the Net every day and every night. It uses self-teaching techniques (*heuristics*) to determine the most popular sites and to correct faulty addresses and remove bad ones.

Like Yahoo, Lycos has both prospered and struggled with growth. It is now a private, for-profit venture. Advertiser support has helped Lycos keep pace with the huge growth of the Net. At this writing, the Lycos catalog has more than 10 million URLs, with 50,000 changes per day! Lycos is trying to update its somewhat fussy image with better graphics and more pedestrian categories. It has also added easy-to-use subcatalogs containing the newest and most popular sites.

Alta Vista

Yahoo and Lycos may have been the first catalogs of the Net, but they'll have to work hard to stay the best. Alta Vista (Figure 4.3) is a major new challenger to Lycos' reign as top spider. Sponsored by Digital, Alta Vista is an awesome search engine. Its Web index contains more than 16 million pages, and it can sort through them at speeds measured in milliseconds. The variety of search strategies available at Alta Vista make it one of the most powerful tools on the Internet for researchers, marketers, or plain old pleasure seekers.

On Alta Vista, you can easily craft searches that are difficult or impossible elsewhere. For example, the search string "link:mysite.com"

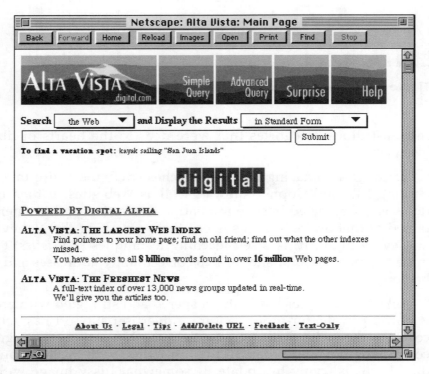

Figure 4.3 Alta Vista is an awesome search engine.

will return a list of Web sites containing a link to your site. This report can be extremely valuable when you have moved to a new URL and you need to correct all those old links out there. Alta Vista also searches virtually every newsgroup on the Internet. This is a handy tool for Internet firefighting—correcting misinformation about your company. Firefighting is detailed in chapter 11.

There are many other popular catalogs, directories, and search tools on the Internet. Some of the major players are listed in Table 4.1, along with comments on their structure, strengths, and weaknesses. It's important that your Internet offerings to be listed in all of these directories and many others. Most of them have submission forms which you can use to get your site listed. But an easier approach is to use one of the one-stop registration services available on the Internet.

Table 4.1 A Comparison of Top Internet Directories and Indexes

Name & Address	Type	Description
Yahoo! *www.yahoo.com*	Directory	A huge hierarchical directory of web sites. Easy to use and popular, the listings would benefit from a little editing.
Alta Vista *www.digital.altavista.com*	Spider	Extremely fast and comprehensive search engine. Scours the entire web every three days. Also offers newsgroup searching.
Lycos *www.lycos.com*	Spider	Another comprehensive search engine which claims more content than any other database. Can be slow or hard to connect to due to popularity.
Point *www.pointcom.com*	Directory	Evaluates web sites and awards "Top 5% of the Web" to selected sites. A good tool for finding well-made or popular web sites.
InfoSeek *guide.infoseek.com*	Spider	A free searching tool that also offers a variety of paid services. Very highly regarded. Searches the web and Usenet.
WebCrawler *www.webcrawler.com*	Spider	A no-frills search engine returns a list of links without descriptive text. Includes searches of FTP and Gopher sites.
EINet Galaxy *galaxy.einet.net*	Directory	This large, hierarchical directory is a bit academic compared with Yahoo. Scholars and librarians may prefer its more orderly structure.

Figure 4.4 Submit It! is a free, one-stop registration site.

One-Stop Registration

As more people signed onto the Internet, more directories sprang up, and the most popular directories became overcrowded. It began to be a real chore to register a Web site with all the different services. Then came Submit It.

Submit It (Figure 4.4) is a self-promotion site that gives you the opportunity to fill out one registration form and automatically submit it to over a dozen major directories and indexes. Figure 4.5 shows the list of Submit It sites in the spring of 1996. The environment on the Internet is so dynamic that it's stunning to watch how quickly solutions develop. When a given task becomes a chore, bam!, someone comes up with a better way of doing it. It's partly the chase for advertising dollars that spurs such innovation, and those people who condemn the commercialization of the Net should take a close look at the amazing, time-saving tools that have resulted from the Internet feeding frenzy. Advertising runs on hits: no hits, no sponsors; no sponsors, no money. Thus, the Internet audience moves like a school of sharks, always looking for fresh sites, then descending on them en masse. It wasn't long after Submit It started offering one-stop registration that it found a sponsor. Submit It was then subsumed into Promote-It (see Figure 4.6). By the time you read this, Promote-It will probably have been gobbled up by Microsoft or Netscape. So it goes in the wild waters of the Internet.

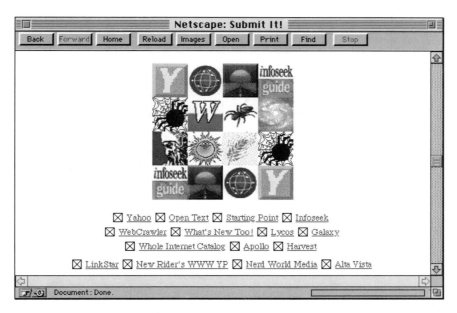

Figure 4.5 A list of the sites serviced by Submit It! in early 1996.

There are now dozens of self-promotion sites on the Internet, many of which are listed in the Resources chapter. Many of these sites offer both free and fee services; that is, you can register your Web site using their free links, or you can pay them to do the work for you. But there are some problems with one-stop registration sites that you should be aware of before entrusting your promotional campaign to their care.

One-Stop Problems

I'll say it again, no good idea goes unpunished on the Internet, and one-stop registration is a *great* idea. That said, word on the Net is that some directories and indexes are prejudiced against anything coming in from a one-stop registration service, reportedly stacking these registration requests in a virtual pile, to be cataloged "later." In the overburdened world of the directory Webmaster, later usually means never. This partly is due to the hits situation. Some directories want you to come to their sites to register so they can count the hits from your visit. They can't attract sponsors without hits. Many directories also sell promotional services, and they want the opportunity to market to you. They want you to visit the site so they can pitch their services.

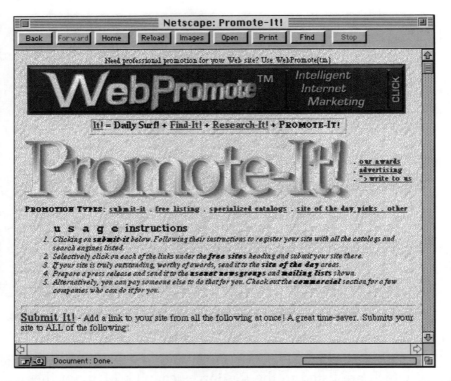

Figure 4.6 Promote-It is the parent site for Submit It. It also offers fee-based promotion services.

Another problem is *index spamming*. The folks who brought you Usenet spam realized that Yahoo and other directories had become critical to attracting browsers to their Web sites. Since registration is free at most directories, they figured there was no cost to registering in multiple categories. They ruined a good thing by jamming the works at places like Yahoo and Infoseek.

One solution to index spamming is to check each and every registration request. But this takes time, and time is money. Another solution is to charge a nominal fee, thereby generating the money needed to pay for verification. Since Yahoo does not charge a fee, it's hard to demand service. You can wait for months for your Web site to get listed. When directories start charging for listings, index spamming will be dramatically reduced.

Another problem with one-stop registrations is purely functional: not all directories want the same information. With one-stop, you fill out one form and submit it to everyone. But some sites allow you a paragraph of descriptive text and others allow only a bare link. If you approach the directories one at a time, it will take a lot longer, but you'll be able to customize each submission. Eric Ward at NetPOST is a master of Internet registrations (http://www.netpost.com). He doesn't like one-stop registration services and insists on registering individually with each directory. He finds that the listings appear more quickly and are more in tune with the subtle character differences between directories. Eric is a great publicist, and like all great publicists, he realizes that there are *people* behind those directories, and he has taken the time to get to know them personally. You may not have the time to get so involved in the registration process, but you can appreciate that there are human beings dealing with your registration requests and you can make it easier on them.

A Sane Strategy

For most Web site registrations, the best strategy is to submit individually to the largest directories and supplement this with a one-stop or paid service to list in the smaller directories. It's worth taking the time and effort to make sure that Yahoo and WebCrawler get a quality registration request. After you've serviced the best, you can use a one-stop or paid service to take care of the rest.

Figure 4.7 is a Registration Checklist you can use to help you keep track of your campaign. Use the blank lines to make notes, such as dates, that you can refer to later.

Figure 4.7 Use the Registration Checklist to track the progress of your campaign.

Registration Checklist

Registration Form:

❑ Complete Registration Form _____

❑ Spell check/Print/Proofread _____

❑ Approved by Customer? _____

(continues)

Figure 4.7 (*Continued*)

❑ Verify that URL Works _____

❑ Verify E-mail Contact Address _____

Registration:

❑ Submit Individually to Top Directories _____

❑ Blanket Submission with One-Stop Service _____

❑ Submit to Topic-Specific Sites _____

❑ Submit to Free Malls _____

❑ Paid Registration Service: _____

Date Service to be Completed: _____

❑ Paid Registration Service: _____

Date Service to be Completed: _____

Follow-Up:

❑ Prepare Registration Report _____

❑ Archive Registration Responses _____

❑ Check Directories in Two Weeks _____

❑ Send Inquiries for Missing Registrations _____

A simple approach to registration is to go to a one-stop site such as Submit It, find the page with links to all the directories and indexes, then save this as "source." Print out the page and use it to keep track of your registrations; it's important to know when you requested a listing and what category you asked to be in. Prepare your Registration Form (see Figure 4.8) and submit the information individually to the major sites. Then go to a one-stop site or paid service to submit to sites of lesser importance.

The Registration Form

Figure 4.8 shows a generic Registration Form that will help you collect the information you need to register your Web site. When the form is complete, you'll have all the facts at your fingertips, ready to register your page in most directories and indexes.

Figure 4.8 The Registration Form.

Registration Form

Company Name and Address:

Company Name
Mailing Address
City, State, Zip Code
Country

Contact Name; E-mail address, Toll-Free, Phone, Fax Numbers:

Web Site Administrator
E-Mail: Webmaster@mysite.com
Toll Free: 1-800-555-1212
Voice: (212) 555-1212
Fax: (212) 555-1212

URL to be used in postings:

http://www.mysite.com

The Title of the Site

My Site

Categories/Headings:

1. Widget Manufacturers
2. Widget Industry
3. Fictitious Products
4. Businesses
5. Awesome Web Sites

Keywords for Automatic Search Engines (Limit 10):

Widgets Tools Fake Web Business

Description of Service (10 words or less).

What's long, smooth, rigid and reliable? Come see our widgets!

Description of Service (25 words or less).

Widgets are the most versatile of tools. They're long and strong, smooth and sleek. We make 'em and sell 'em. Come see for yourself!

Some of the items are more important than others, and there are some subtleties involved. Let's look at each of the sections individually.

1. Company Name and Address: This is the company represented in the Web site, *not* the company that built the site or the one doing the registration.

2. Contact Information: This is the person to contact about technical difficulties with the site, usually the site's Webmaster. The directories request this information in case there's a problem with the registration or difficulties connecting to the site.

3. URL to be Used in Postings: The address of the Web page you are registering.

4. Title of the Site: Some sites have fancy names, such as ESPN SportsZone. Others use simply the name of the company.

5. Categories/Headings: Most directories want to categorize your site, so it's best to have a list of your preferences ready. Many of the sites will decide for themselves which category to stick you in.

6. Keywords for Automatic Search Engines: Spiders and bots scan the Web looking for these words when deciding to fetch a page. You're limited to about a dozen words (not phrases).

7. Description of Service (10 words or less): This is the text that will accompany your link in the directory. Many directories only give you a bare link—no description permitted.

8. Description of Service (25 words or less): A slightly longer description. This is the most common length allowed by directories. However, you might want to prepare a longer description, up to a full news release, in case you have the opportunity to use it.

Each time you register your page, you'll be asked for some or all of this information. The most important items are the site name, the URL, and the 25-word description; these are what will show up in most directories. The other stuff is mostly administrative and not worth laboring over.

Registration Subtleties

There are some subtleties that hard-core marketers will want to know about, so let's take a look at them.

Categories

When choosing categories, it's best to think about how someone *unfamiliar* with your business would look for you. People who regularly do business with you should be able to find your URL on your business cards, letterhead, or in ads, but you'll attract new prospects primarily from your directory listings. For important directories such as Yahoo, look over the categories carefully and try to identify a way to stand out from the crowd.

Some sites, such as Yahoo, will allow you to register in multiple categories. But go easy; I've heard on the grapevine that registering your site in more than six categories will get your submission placed at the bottom of the queue. Other sites allow only one listing and eradicate duplicate URLs, and if you try to put your site in several places, the registrar might eliminate your preferred categories and leave you stuck in virtual Siberia.

Keywords

For the Keywords section of the registration form, start with your best words in case the list gets truncated after the first few. Note: You can only use single words, not phrases. If you submit "online marketing" as your keywords, your listing will be lumped together with all the "online" listings and all the "marketing" listings, two huge categories.

Description

Rare is the Web site that benefits from a lot of traffic. The more visitors you have, the more server you need, and that can get expensive. Tailor your registration to narrow the audience to your best prospects. The point of your listing is *not* to describe your site; it is to attract your target audience and to entice them into activating that hotlink. Write something that pushes their hot buttons if you want them to push yours.

You should consider crafting a different description to fit the character of each directory you apply to. For example, you might want your Yahoo description to appeal to the general audience and your Galaxy description to appeal to a more scholarly audience. This is one more reason why a one-stop registration service is not the best choice for listings in the major directories.

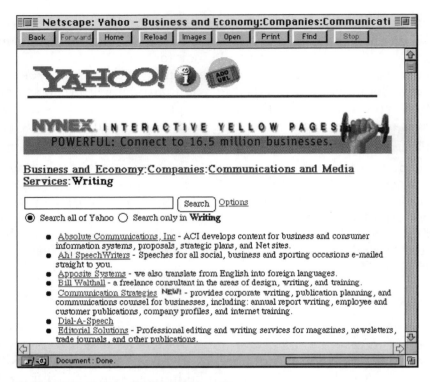

Figure 4.9 Yahoo listings for writers.

In registration, words are precious. If the title of your Web site is My Site, then don't start your description with the words, "My Site is a . . ." Also, don't duplicate words found in your URL. If the URL for My Site is www.company.com, then you might not want to use the word *company* in your description or keywords. Always include some description of your site—browsers tend to prefer annotated links.

Let's look at a couple examples.

Figure 4.9 shows some Yahoo listings for writers. Dial-A-Speech is a bare link, wasting an opportunity to lure browsers to its site. Ah! SpeechWriters, on the other hand, mentions social, business, and sporting events, and tells you they deliver by e-mail. If I were looking for a speech writer, I'd start with Ah!

Figure 4.10 shows the results of a Yahoo search for "piano." Carl's Music qualifies its entry with the geographical area served: northern

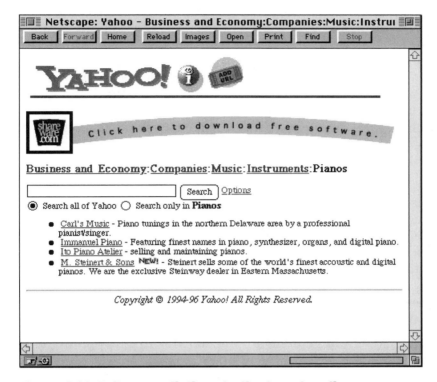

Figure 4.10 Tailor your listings to the target audience.

Delaware. This should cut down on the number of hits from unlikely customers across the planet. M. Steinert & Sons does the same thing, attempting to attract an audience in eastern Massachusetts while specifically mentioning the Steinway brand. Note that none of the piano listings is particularly lyrical or clever. It's worth taking some time to think about who you want to attract to your site, and then write some powerful prose to draw them in. Look in any direct marketing book for a list of power words that trigger a response: new, hot, fast, free, low-fat, sex, and so on. These words can be overused, but you get the general idea. Just remember, you are trying to entice, not describe.

One more thing: exercise care that your description doesn't include some temporary feature of your site. If you're running a contest offering a free trip to China, you'll have to change your registration as soon as the contest is over, and it can take weeks if not months to update or correct a listing.

The Challenge

I did the registration for an advertising agency's Web site with the tag line, "Ideas worth stealing." The Net is rampant with copyright infringement—it's one of the reasons the Net is so popular. People love free stuff: freeware, shareware, a celebrity photo, a game, whatever. As a consequence of the piracy, many Web sites are crammed with copyright notices warning of dire consequences for thieves. I went against the grain with the ad agency registration, in an attempt to lure people looking for clever ideas.

The point is, it's a challenge to prepare a registration that's mysterious, intriguing, irresistible, descriptive, timeless, *and* brief. This challenge should be met in an entertaining fashion. It's one of the reasons you might want to hire a professional firm to handle your Web promotion. At the very least, you'll have someone responsible for getting the listings up correctly in a timely manner.

Coding Your URL

Okay ladies and gentlemen, time to come in a little closer and learn one of the neatest tricks of the online marketer's trade: registration coding. Wouldn't it be nice if you could determine where all the hits on your Web site were coming from? Well you can, and I'll show you how.

Direct mail folks are always preaching to code your address for every ad and every mention of your company in order to identify where your inquiries and sales are coming from. In the real world, this is not always practical and certainly not easy. On the Net, it's easy as pie. Every week I get a Hit Report from my Webmaster that provides me with all kinds of information about activity at my Web site. Contact your Webmaster and ask for the same kind of report. There are programs available for Webmasters that automatically tabulate this information. I'm not a Webmaster, so I refer you to one of the many books on building Web sites for more information about these programs. You can also find information on the Internet by searching for "hit counters" or similar terms.

Figure 4.11 shows the domains my hits came from, including the country of origin. This week, I had 13 from South Africa. If nothing else convinces you of the amazing international reach of the Internet, your own Hit Report should do the trick. Ask yourself how easy would it be for you to market your services around the world without the Net?

Figure 4.11 Hit Report by Client Domain.

```
Total Transfers by Client Domain

Bytes Sent    Requests    Domain
-----------   --------  | --------------------
       6952          2  | au      Australia
      37798          7  | be      Belgium
       8461          2  | br      Brazil
      50160          9  | ca      Canada
      18421          3  | ee      Estonia
      10048          2  | il      Israel
      10048          2  | it      Italy
       2618          1  | se      Sweden
      25676          6  | uk      United Kingdom
      91278         13  | za      South Africa
     618228        121  | com     US Commercial
     311600         70  | edu     US Educational
     664483        117  | net     Network
     736676        151  | unresolved
```

Figure 4.12 is my Hit Report by subdomain. You really have to love the way computers can just crunch these kinds of numbers. After unresolved, my next highest hit source is com.aol.proxy, otherwise known as America Online. CompuServe is right up there, too. A lot of marketing people ignore the commercial online services, thinking they've got the Net covered if they promote in newsgroups or mailing lists. But the numbers do not lie. Ever since I did a live chat on America Online, I get thousands of hits from AOL every month. We'll look at how to promote on these services in Chapter 7, Announcements.

Figure 4.12 Hit Report by Subdomain.

```
Total Transfers by Reversed Subdomain

Requests    Bytes Sent   Reversed Subdomain
--------  -----------  | --------------------------
     151       736676  | Unresolved
       2         6952  | au.com.next
       7        37798  | be.vum
```

(continues)

Figure 4.12 (*Continued*)

```
     2         8461 |  br.org.undp
     3        15082 |  ca.direct
     3        17790 |  ca.mb.freenet
     3        17288 |  ca.nstn
    36       174039 |  com.aol.proxy
     3        12765 |  com.cais
    10        53376 |  com.compuserve
     2         9472 |  com.dsmnet
     2         4684 |  com.gwis
     1         2731 |  com.inch.dialup
     1         4099 |  com.interlog
     2        11489 |  com.loop
     8        38835 |  com.mcp
     3        12780 |  com.netcom.ix
    14        99731 |  com.netconnect-inc
     1         6932 |  com.oeonline
     2         5236 |  com.okeefe
     1         2730 |  com.primenet.phx
     5        23911 |  com.prodigy
     9        32056 |  com.sirius
     9        52990 |  com.teleport
     6        46222 |  com.usa1
     2         6491 |  com.utc.corphq
     4        17659 |  com.well
    18        89499 |  edu.berkeley.cs
     1         2731 |  edu.berkeley.hip
     2         6324 |  edu.colorado.cs
     2         8460 |  edu.cord
    22       103885 |  edu.dcccd.201.144
     1         2729 |  edu.harvard.student
     1         2730 |  edu.luc.it
     2         8463 |  edu.mscd
     5        32074 |  edu.rhodes
     1         2730 |  edu.sru.dorm.patterson
     1         2730 |  edu.stanford
     1         2729 |  edu.uci.hnet
     1         2729 |  edu.uoregon
     8        29438 |  edu.utexas.ots
     1         4099 |  edu.washington.cs
     1         3760 |  edu.washington.ee
     2         6490 |  edu.wednet.ptsd
```

```
  3       18421 | ee.digit
  2       10048 | il.net.netvision
  2       10048 | it.mclink
  1        6195 | net.access.dialup
  2        5460 | net.bluefin
  4       20673 | net.charm
  1        4099 | net.cic.dial
  4       19654 | net.earthlink
  1        2731 | net.gulf
  2        8460 | net.houston.com3
  1        2733 | net.ici
  1        4099 | net.iquest
 15       87772 | net.leonardo
  1        8316 | net.mbay
 21      143383 | net.mich.dialip
 13       80547 | net.micron.boi
  2        8463 | net.mo.dialip
 10       54616 | net.olympus
  1        2730 | net.port
  1        3760 | net.realtime.ip
  3        6797 | net.show
 16      113033 | net.slip
  2       14826 | net.tiac
  6       24410 | net.usa.den1-annex
  1        2733 | net.uu.ms.ma.boston.max5
  3       12159 | net.uu.ms.ma.boston.max7
  5       26834 | net.wis.vcr
  1        2618 | se.kth.nada
  4       20216 | uk.ac.lancs
  1        2730 | uk.co.easynet
  1        2730 | uk.co.indus
 13       91278 | za.co.global
```

The subdomain report is very useful. When I see one, two, or three hits, I figure someone just wandered into my site or is mildly curious. When I see double-digit hits, I know I'm being seriously scoped. I usually get a phone call or e-mail about a week later.

Figure 4.13 shows which pages (URLs) at my site were accessed most often. This is where the coding comes in. Any hit to /welcome/ okeefe/??? is a hit to my home page, where the ??? stands for the codes I use to determine the source of the hits. Some of the sources are shown at the top of page 94.

URL	Source of Hit
/welcome/okeefe/new	My signature on Usenet and mailing lists
/welcome/okeefe/IPS	My letterhead and business cards
/welcome/okeefe/trade	The trade section of Bookport
/welcome/okeefe/fyi	Link at the bottom of pages we designed
/welcome/okeefe/bpol	Book Publishers Online link

Figure 4.13 Hit Report by URLs.

```
Requests by Page for URLs containing okeefe

Requests     Archive Section
--------  |  --------------------------
      47  |  /Trade/okeefe/pixOkeefe.gif
      35  |  /Trade/okeefe/Services.html
      30  |  /Trade/okeefe/Samples.html
      25  |  /Trade/okeefe/index.html
      21  |  /welcome/okeefe/new
      20  |  /Trade/okeefe/clients.html
      19  |  /Trade/okeefe/Who.html
      18  |  /Trade/okeefe/Power.html
      16  |  /welcome/okeefe/trade/
      13  |  /Trade/okeefe/news.html
      13  |  /welcome/commons/okeefe/
      13  |  /Trade/okeefe/flyer.html
      12  |  /Trade/okeefe/dud.html
      10  |  /welcome/okeefe/IPS
      10  |  /Trade/okeefe/posting.html
       9  |  /Trade/okeefe/seinfeld.html
       9  |  /Trade/okeefe/bone.html
       8  |  /Trade/okeefe/Bone.gif
       8  |  /welcome/okeefe/chp/
       6  |  /Trade/okeefe/seinfeld.GIF
       6  |  /welcome/okeefe/fyi
       5  |  /welcome/okeefe/ips
       5  |  /welcome/bookfair/okeefe/
       3  |  /welcome/okeefe/dc
       1  |  /welcome/okeefe/bpol
       1  |  /welcome/okeefe/trade
       1  |  /welcome/okeefe/Ids
```

When you submit your registration to a directory, you can place a code at the end of your URL. For example, you might code your Yahoo listings with this URL:

http://www.mysite.com/yahoo

But first make sure that your Webmaster can accommodate URL coding and determine the proper format. You don't want to fill all the directories with URLs that don't work! You might be required to use a code word like "welcome" in your URL so the server knows that anything after "welcome" gets sent to the home page. This can get fairly technical—beyond the scope of this book—but now you have some idea of what's possible. If this kind of detailed information is important to you, insist on a service provider who can give you a good hit report.

If you use a one-stop registration service, you can't code for each different directory. Therefore, you might want to use a blanket code for all directories, such as:

http://www.mysite.com/dir

Following our sane strategy of registering individually with important directories and using a one-stop service for the rest, you can individually code your major registrations and use a generic code for the balance. Definitely code any link you paid for, to see if it generates an acceptable amount of traffic.

As just noted, coding your URL can get very complicated. I recommend you wait until you are comfortable on the Web before you start putting codes in all your listings. Consider saving the coding for the second edition of your Web site. Why? Because I've seen a lot of botched coding jobs out there. A lot of the dead links I click on from directories are due to coding problems. Maybe you moved to a different server, or your service provider moved to a different server, or you switched from a Unix server to an NT server? I'm not a tech guy; I just know that you have to work with top-flight Webmasters to code successfully.

Some people are obsessed with codes. They use four-digit numerical codes and change the code in their signatures on a daily basis. My advice is: don't code anything you don't need to track. A lot of people don't care where the hits come from, just so long as they're getting enough. Finally, be sure to keep a list of the codes you've assigned and their sources. I'm embarrassed to admit I can't remember some of the codes on my own Hit Report. I forgot to write them down when I assigned them. Fortunately, they don't account for very much activity at my site. You can use the Registration Report in the next section to keep track of your codes.

The Registration Report

The Registration Report represents both the beginning and end of the registration process. It's a list of the places where you plan to request a listing. When you're finished, it's a complete record of where you went and what you did. Figure 4.14 shows a modified version of the form we use at Internet Publicity Services to register our clients in the top 25 directories, catalogs, and indexes. For each directory, we list the name of the site, the main URL for the site, and the code for that site. Other information you might also include:

- The date you submitted
- The category you asked to be put in
- The password assigned to you for changing your listing

Figure 4.14 The Registration Report.

Internet Registration Report.

Site Name: My Home Page   **Date Started:** Today's Date
Site URL: http://www.mysite.com   **Password:** mysite

About Your Internet Registration Report:

We requested a listing for your Web site in all the directories, indexes, and catalogs listed below. We have no control over how long it takes for any site to list your site. If you can't find your link within 30 days, please notify us and we will resubmit your information to that site at no charge.

Major Directories and Indexes:

Name of Site:	URL:
Alta Vista	www.altavista.digital.com
BizWeb	www.bizweb.com
CERN's list of Web Servers	www.w3.org/hypertext/DataSources/WWW/Servers.html
EINet Galaxy	galaxy.einet.Net

Excite Netsearch	www.excite.com
Explorer	www.rtis.com/explorer/default.htm
I-Guide	www.iguide.com
Infoseek	guide.infoseek.com
Inktomi	inktomi.berkeley.edu
Internet Mall	www.internet-mall.com/imall.htm
Lycos	www.lycos.com
Metroscope	isotropic.com/metro/scope.html
NCSA/GNN What's New	www.gnn.com/gnn/wn/whats-new.html
Nerd World	www.nerdworld.com
Net-happenings	www.mid.Net/NET
Netcenter	www.netcenter.com
New Rider's WWW Yellow Pages	www.mcp.com/newriders/wwwyp
NetSearch	www.netmall.com
Open Text Web Index	www.opentext.com
Point	www.pointcom.com
Pronet	www.pronett.com
Starting Point	www.stpt.com
The Huge List	thehugelist.com
WebCrawler	www.webcrawler.com
WEBula	www.eg.bucknell.edu/cgi-bin/webula/tree
What's New Too	204.33.23.2
WWW Worm	wwww.cs.colorado.edu/wwww
Yahoo	www.yahoo.com

Publisher Directories:

Name of Site:	URL:
Book Stacks Publishers Place	www.books.com/scripts/place.exe
The BookWire Publishers Index	www.bookwire.com
Internet Book Fair Publishers Index	www.bookfair.com/Publishers/index.html
The Faxon Publishers Index	www.faxon.com
WWW Virtual Library of Publishers	www.edoc.com/ejournal

(*continues*)

Figure 4.14 (*Continued*)

Northern Lights Publishers Index	www.lights.com/publisher
AcqWeb Publishers Index	www.library.vanderbilt.edu/law/acqs /pubr/alph.html
Carnegie-Mellon Publisher Catalogs	206.101.96.68:8001/bookstores
WebWise Library	webwise.walcoff.com/library/ index.html

It's important to keep track of your registration requests, even if it's just on a piece of scrap paper tucked away wherever you keep your password list. What happens if you change domain names or servers? What if a directory botches your listing and you need to correct it? What if you want to update the description of your site? The Registration Report will prove very helpful at these times. Believe me, stuff happens. Many people register their Web pages without thinking about the process or the future. Then they regret it, since it can take months to correct a mishandled registration campaign.

At Internet Publicity Services, we try to do the entire registration campaign in one day, so we don't have a separate column for the date on our Registration Report. But you will want to keep track of the dates so you have something to refer to if the listing never appears. If you complain about not being listed, the registrar will often ask for the date you requested the link. At this writing, most directories are taking two to six weeks to list a new site.

You can quickly design a form like the Registration Report by going to a one-stop registration service and printing its registration page. Then just make notes on the printout. To save time, save their one-stop registration page and do your work off the saved page rather than having to reconnect with the Web site for every listing. Some of the one-stop sites get a lot of traffic and it can take hours to complete your registration campaign.

If you're doing many registrations for many different people or departments, consider building your own custom one-stop service. You can start with an HTML version of the Registration Report. On our in-house form, we have three hotlinks for each directory: one to search the site, one to submit a listing, one for help. The advantage of building your own registration page is that you can delete the directories you don't care about and add places important to your particular business.

We specialize in handling book publishers, so our registration page includes all the major publisher directories on the Internet. We call it *linkage* when you request listings at special-interest sites. A linkage campaign requires a different approach, and so it is covered in more detail in Chapter 5.

If you don't want to mess with the HTML, you can build your registration page in a bookmark folder or file in your Web browser. When you do your first registration, just bookmark every submissions page you hit. When you're done, put all the bookmarks in one folder and you've got an in-house registration service.

And if your need for registration services is infrequent, don't even bother trying to maintain your own in-house registration page. About one-quarter of the entries on our registration service disappear every month! They are replaced by an equal number of outstanding newcomers. The speed of change on the Internet is slowing, but it will be a few years before the directory business settles down. The upkeep on your own registration page will be more trouble than it's worth unless registration *is* your business.

Registering Multiple Pages

Once your Web site reaches critical mass, you can start registering subpages. This is the cutting edge of Internet registration, but be careful you don't get hurt. Just as directories like Yahoo started as one big list and split into categories, so many Web sites start to divide, hydra-like, after they grow beyond a reasonable browsing experience. In large companies, different departments will want to control their own Web sites. Banks that used to have one Web site now have separate sites for loans, investments, day-to-day banking, small business services, and others. Managers responsible for the results of the Web sites want control over the content. And the registration business has followed this curve of seeking links for sites within sites.

The first thing you have to decide when registering a subpage is, is it worth the effort? When you have something of a temporary nature to promote, such as a conference, chat, event, show, exhibit, or tour, it is best to use announcements and news releases rather than registration. Remember, it can take two weeks to two months for your links to appear. Trying to promote an event this way is an invitation to high blood pressure as you wait for what seems like an eternity for your links to appear.

Registration should be undertaken only for permanent portions of your Web site, or at least something with a digital life of over one year. I work with a lot of publishers, and they often want to register each imprint separately. Some of the imprints also have divisions (college, juvenile, trade, etc.) which require separate registration. But I tend to draw the line when they want to register a separate Web site for each book they publish. By the time the listings hit, the book might be out of print. And most directories don't accept advance listings; the page must be up and running or they won't add a link to it.

One of the problems with subpage registrations is dead links. If you register some temporary offering all over the Net, you must consider what happens to all those links when the page you registered goes down. Dead links reflect very poorly on the company people are trying to reach, and yet, for you, it can be a real pain to go back and ask for all those links to be changed or removed. If you're registering a temporary page, I suggest you hit just a couple key directories, then ask for the links to be removed as soon as the page goes down.

Currently, registering subpages is tricky business. It would be nice if you could set up a directory of your site and submit a whole list of URLs for registration at once. Unfortunately, you have to register URLs one at a time unless you cut some sort of special deal with the registrars at Yahoo and the other major directories. Of course, the spider-style search services will automatically add your new pages to their databases, so it's not impossible for people to find your subpages. If you're registering a mountain of subpages for one site, try to make e-mail contact with the registrars before unloading an avalanche of URLs on them. They will probably prefer a method of registration that is not described anywhere in the instructions on their sites.

When you are registering subpages with URLs that branch off a larger site, check the rules for each directory to see if this kind of registration is permitted. Some directories only allow you to register the "root" URL. That is, if you're trying to register a magazine at http://www.mysite.com/news/, they might only allow you to register the main URL, http://www.mysite.com. Or they might have special procedures for registering subpages. So check the help files before you spend a loft of time registering subpages that will never become links.

Registering subpages is a very attractive way of helping people quickly find the portion of your site of greatest interest to them. It also increases your exposure, allowing you to register in multiple categories without exceeding the limit for one URL. Your Web site needs to be designed with this sort of usage in mind. As your site grows, you should start thinking of it as a cluster of sites, and design your navigation accordingly.

Registration Responses

When you register with different directories, you often get feedback mail informing you that your request has been received. Sometimes this mail comes with set of instructions to follow if your link does not appear, or if there's a problem with your link. Figure 4.15 shows a typical e-mail response for a listing at LinkStar. Often the feedback mail gives you a password to use when requesting changes to your listing. If you lose the password, however, you may have a difficult time changing your listing, so it's a good idea to write your password on your Regis-

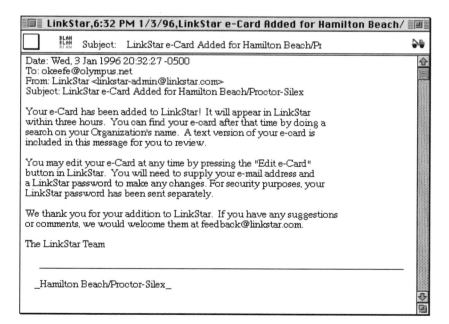

Figure 4.15 Confirmation e-mail from a registration request at LinkStar.

tration Report. If you get to choose the password, don't get too fancy; unless you're Disney, your listing at LinkStar is probably not a major security item. We try to decide on a simple password, eight characters or less, before we start the registration campaign. Then we use the same password at every site.

Some of the instructions for changing Web listing are quite complicated. I recommend that you set aside a separate e-mail folder and transfer all your registration responses there, in case you need them. Depending on your back-up procedures, you might want to print the responses and keep a paper archive. You almost never need to look at these, until there's a problem, at which point you want to find the instructions *immediately*.

Many directories use the registration response to try and sell you something. Your listing usually doesn't hinge on buying anything, but a cynical person might suspect that paying for a *bold listing* in a directory might get your link to appear faster. If your Web site is a major investment, you might take a look at some of your paid registration options. Prices range from ridiculously cheap to outrageously expensive. Maybe the first listing is free, but you have to pay for multiple listings? Maybe you can pay a little more to be placed in a "new links" section for a month? When offered value-added options, try to get the site to quantify the extra exposure you'll get. Does a bold listing make any difference in people's usage patterns? How many people visit the new links or hotlinks section each day or week? Is there a way for you to get a report on how many people click on your various links each month? Without a way of measuring the results, it's difficult to know whether you're getting ripped off. I've tried all sorts of cheap value-added services, and I've been disappointed by the results of most of them.

Fixing Registration Problems

Suppose your site has been up for *three whole days* and your listing in Yahoo hasn't appeared! What are you going to do? Take a deep breath and relax. Remember that your site has timeless content, and no matter when the Yahoo link appears, people will love your site. Wait two weeks, then you initiate the following procedures if your link is still among the missing:

1. Double-check your Registration Form. Did you spell your URL exactly correctly? If not, you may have to fix your registration everywhere.

2. If you kept a copy or printout of your registration request, double-check for errors, especially in the spelling of your URL.

3. Go to each directory on your Registration Report and see if your listing has appeared. If not, look for a "help" link and try to find a form or an e-mail address to use to track the status of your listing.

4. *Be polite*!!! I don't care if it has been three months and you're frustrated beyond belief. From a tactical standpoint, a flame is not a successful way to fix a registration problem. Unless you paid for the listing, kindness is the fastest road to satisfaction.

5. Have your registration information handy, including the date you submitted your request and all the information needed to resubmit it.

6. Once you are in this troubleshooting mode, continue to follow up every few days until you get some sort of satisfactory response.

I sit on pins and needles after I do a registration campaign, waiting for my listings to appear, waiting for the problems to surface. The waiting is terrible, but most listings actually appear in the time frame advertised. When there's a problem, I try to remember that most registrars are poorly paid interns, completely overwhelmed with the work and discouraged by the immense number of flames they receive from people who expect service in 60 minutes. I try to remember the human beings behind the e-mail address and connect with them. How many times do they get thanked for a job well done?

The Future of Registration

Time to Windex the crystal ball and see what's headed your way. If you look in the Yellow Pages, you'll get a good idea what Yahoo will look like in a couple of years. There will be a huge variety of registration options, ranging from a plain free listing to some of these services:

- Multiple listings across different categories (for which you pay extra).

- Instead of alphabetical listings for each category, there will be several tiers:

    New Sites

    Best Bets

    Regular Listings
- You will pay extra to be included in New Sites or Best Bets or similar premium areas.
- Lots more categories, broken into hair-splitting subject classifications.
- Lots more display ads. Eventually, the page will be a tiny little window of information surrounded hotlinked banners.
- Incredible cross-referencing, particularly by geographical area, but also by name, subject, product type, and contact person.
- More listings will include toll-free phone numbers so folks can bypass the Web altogether. These toll-free phone numbers will be Net-phone hotlinks: your computer calls my computer and we "do voice."

It's fun looking into the crystal ball, especially when you know some of the inside scoop and you're not really guessing at all. You can expect to see a lot more special-interest catalogs and a lot fewer all-purpose catalogs. These special-interest catalogs will be the source of most of the Web browsing, most of the advertising, most of the registration work. People looking for information online will follow a three-step pattern: (1) using general directories such as Yahoo to (2) find special-interest directories to (3) find good sites.

Special-interest directories will be more heavily edited, tighter, with fewer user-contributed listings and more annotated links. There will be many Web magazines devoted to nothing but critical reviews of Web sites. These will result in rampant conflicts of interest between raising ad revenue and providing honest evaluations of Web sites.

In the future, you can also expect to pay for everything except the tiniest little listing buried way down deep in Yahoo. You'll pay for listing, for position, for frequency, for formatting, for space. One of the most effective tools in registration will be the quality hot button: a tiny graphical link to your site that promotes your brand identity while helping you stand out in a crowded field. We'll learn more about the hot button in Chapter 5.

Top Tips

- **Prepare in Advance:** Complete your Registration Form, printout your blank Registration Report, choose your default password, have everything ready before you roll.

- **Entice, Don't Describe:** Your listing is not a news release. Meditate on your target audience and the profile of each directory's users, then write an irresistible invitation to your site.

- **Code Your Listings:** Ask your Webmaster whether you can code your URL, but only assign codes if you plan to track the results. Keep a list of the codes you've assigned.

- **A Sane Strategy:** Register individually with the directories most important to your success, then use a one-stop or paid service to reach the rest.

- **Explore Value-Added Options:** Some services are worth paying for, including multiple listings, better positioning, faster turnaround. Remember, though, only buy if you can quantify.

- **Document Everything:** Keep copies of all your work and all the responses you get. It is certain you will need them the minute you delete them.

- **Be Nice:** Until registration becomes a cash business, you are dependent upon the kindness of strangers. Sometimes the squeaky wheel gets a busted link.

CHAPTER 5

The Linkage Campaign

A linkage campaign involves seeding the Net with links to your Web site. This is one of the new marketing activities made possible by the technology of the Net. Through distance-obliterating hyperlinks, people are whisked to a Web site from anywhere in the world. You have to love this technology.

There's no secret to running a linkage campaign. You simply look for compatible Web sites and ask for a link to your site. However, advance preparation will help you increase the number of sites you reach and the number of people who say yes to your link. I'll show you a systematic approach for conducting a cost-effective linkage campaign. Topics covered in this chapter include:

- **Defining a Hyperlink:** We'll look at the anatomy of a hyperlink and discover what makes a hotlink hot.

- **The Linkage Campaign:** You'll learn the differences between the registration campaign and the linkage campaign, and the benefits of a linkage campaign.

- **Finding Sites for Your Links:** You'll find out how to locate compatible Web sites using print publications and Internet search engines.

- **Scoping the Sites:** You'll learn to look with linker's eyes, and what to look for when visiting a site in search of a link.

- **The Art of the Linkletter:** Most link requests are made via e-mail. It's a good idea to have your linkletter prepared in advance of your visit.

- **Tracking Your Link Requests:** When you finish your linkage campaign, you'll have a nice Linkage Report that you can use to market your goods.

- **The Link Button:** You'll get better results with a link request and a cute graphic hot button than you will with a link request alone.

- **Responses to Link Requests:** We'll discuss how to handle the flames, praise, or silence that follows your request for a link.

- **Top Tips:** One-liners of linkage.

What Is A Hyperlink?

A hyperlink is a time machine. Find the blue text on a Web page, place your cursor there, and click! Through the miracle of modern technology, you are transported to a new destination. You might go to another spot on the same page or to a completely different Web site. You could end up in New Delhi or New Orleans. On the Internet, all destinations are only a click away. That's the magic of hypertext.

A more boring description is that a hyperlink is a coded reference to a file available somewhere on the Internet. When you place your cursor on the link and activate it by clicking your mouse, you are directing your browsing software (Netscape, Mosaic, etc.) to retrieve the file and display it on your screen. There is an illusion that you're traveling to a Web site when in fact the site is traveling to you. Here's what the hidden part of a hyperlink looks like:

```
<a href="http://www.mysite.com/home.html">LINK</a>
```

The greater-than and less-than symbols indicate that the enclosed text is a set of instructions and should not be displayed. Only the word LINK would be visible on your browser, usually in color and/or underlined to indicate that it's "hot." The default color is blue and, although you can change the color scheme, most links on the Web are blue.

The term "href" indicates a link to a file somewhere. If "href" were changed to "name," the link would be to someplace else on the current page. The text enclosed in quotation marks is the destination. In this case, the text is a URL and the destination is a Web page. The URL begins with a file type: "http" stands for HyperText Transfer Protocol, and indicates a Web page; "ftp" stands for File Transfer Protocol; "gopher" indicates a Gopher site, and so on. The site address (www.mysite.com) is followed by a file name: home.html.

The word LINK is hot. Clicking on it will retrieve the file listed in the href. The hot text can say anything you want. It can be one word or ramble for pages. The text will remain hot until turned off by the closing command </a>. And note, not just text gets hot—images can also be hotlinked. Most of the buttons you see on the Web are hotlinks, also known as *hot buttons*.

The Linkage Campaign

In the preceding chapter on registration, we discussed how to get links in directories, indexes, and catalogs such as Yahoo. A linkage campaign is similar to a registration campaign, with these differences:

- The purpose of a directory is to link people to Internet resources. The sites you approach in a linkage campaign usually are not directories. They may have a page of links to other sites, but that's not their focus.

- When registering in a directory, you use a submission form. A request for a link is less formal and is most often done through e-mail.

- Most directories will link to anyone who meets the minimum criteria. Most nondirectory sites won't link unless your site is compatible with theirs.

The goal of the linkage campaign is to get hotlinks to your Web site (or Gopher or FTP site) from as many compatible sites on the Internet as possible. You start with the best locations and work your way down the list. Figure 5.1 shows what you're looking for. It's a page of links from a Web site for a trade show. Thousands of Web sites have link pages like this. You want your site to be added to the list.

At the end of your linkage campaign you should have a report similar to the one shown in Figure 5.16 later in this chapter. The Linkage Re-

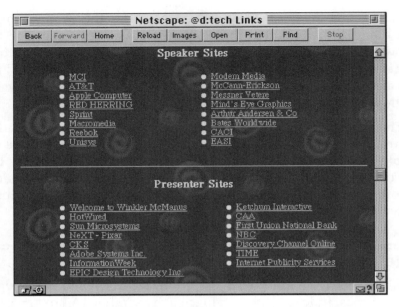

Figure 5.1 A typical links page from a Web site. These are called *bare*
links **because they don't contain any descriptions of the sites.**

port lists every place you asked for a link. It reads like a survey of the
best Internet sites devoted to your subject area and so can be a valuable
business asset.

Linkage is often approached as an afterthought to Web building.
Many Web builders now offer directory registration in their package
price, but few offer linkage campaigns. Most linkage requests happen
when you're browsing a site and think, "Maybe I should ask these people for a link to my site?" In this chapter, you'll learn to take a more systematic approach.

You can conduct a thorough linkage campaign in a couple of days if
you prepare in advance. You should have three things before you start
requesting links:

- **A Site List:** A list of promising sites or the location of a SuperSite
  that contains a comprehensive set of links to promising sites.

- **A Linkletter:** Form e-mail requesting a link, all ready to send.

- **A Button:** A graphical button used as a hotlink to your site, ready
  to send on request.

This chapter shows you how to find and make a good site list, what to say in your linkletter, how to make a good hot button. Read through this chapter first, then assemble the materials you need, and off you go. Some of the positive benefits of a linkage campaign will surprise you.

Benefits of a Linkage Campaign

Getting links is a much more hands-on operation than registering in directories. A linkage campaign is time-consuming, requiring a custom pitch for each request. For these reasons, many people forgo a linkage campaign, preferring to use one-stop registration sites or pay for links in hundreds of online malls. But a good linkage campaign brings great rewards.

When you conduct a linkage campaign, you learn more about your competition than you could imagine. Perhaps you've checked out what your main competitors are doing online? A linkage campaign gives you a much clearer picture of the overall market. You'll find not only competitors, but also trade groups, associations, suppliers, customer organizations, discussion groups, and a few individuals who have taken it upon themselves to catalog the online side of the industry you're in.

One of the major benefits of a linkage campaign is that it helps you secure a dominant position on the Net. You may not be able to build a better Web site than your competitor, but you can outlink them. If people see your links all over the Net, you are perceived as the market leader. Look at how effective Yahoo and Netscape have been getting people to link to their sites (Figure 5.2). These links don't appear by accident; someone asked for them. The cumulative impact of all those links is widespread name recognition and rock-solid market position.

Figure 5.2 Have you seen these links on the Web? They didn't appear by accident.

Many Webmasters have a low tolerance for links. They don't put up links for just anybody. Imagine starting a new Internet catalog and trying to get Webmasters to replace their links to Yahoo with links to your site. Good luck! The same scenario may be true for whatever business you're in. If you have links spread all over the Net, your competitors will be in the unenviable position of having to unseat your links in order to get links to their sites.

A linkage campaign also brings the rewards of connecting with your colleagues. Most of us never bother to acknowledge the work of the Webmasters whose sites we visit. A linkage campaign forces you to look behind the screens for the names of the people responsible for the site. A link request is usually a personal request. By connecting with the Webmasters of these sites, you open the possibility of a relationship that can be both personally satisfying and professionally rewarding.

Finding Sites for Your Links

One of the hardest parts of a linkage campaign is finding quality sites for requesting links. You wouldn't think this would be so difficult—after all, there are an abundance of Web sites to choose from. The problem is, it's difficult to know before you visit a site whether it has a page of links to other people's sites, whether it's professionally run, or whether it's even devoted to your subject area. I've wasted a lot of time working my way through Web sites only to decide not to request a link. Even with a fantastic site list, I only request links at about half the sites I visit. The other half either have no links outside their site, are inappropriate, or I can't connect to the site.

Before I started approaching linkage in a systematic manner, I wasted a lot of time bookmarking promising sites with the intention of returning later to request a link. That just doubled the amount of time I spent on each link. Now I have my linkletter ready before I visit, and as soon as I've determined that the site is a good prospect, I send the linkletter and move on.

So, finding a good site list will save you a lot of time. One good way of finding these lists is through the print media. That's right—old-fashioned ink on paper.

In Print

Magazines and newsletters that cover your industry probably have run articles about interesting sites on the Net. These articles can provide a good starting list for your linkage campaign. And using print publications cuts down on your research time—magazines and newspapers hire professional researchers to do the grunt work for you.

You can also search computer and Internet magazines for articles about your subject area. These articles usually include hotlists of good sites with descriptions of what you'll find there. The advantage of using magazine articles is that they've made value judgments about the quality of the sites they cover, whereas most online directories don't give you a good idea of what to expect when you finger that link.

You can also find excellent site lists in books. Visit your library and photocopy the appropriate pages from the many Internet directories that have been published recently. You can use these as your starting lists. Or there may be a book that covers your industry on the Internet, such as The Book Lover's Guide to the Internet. These books usually contain tightly focused, annotated site lists that can cut your linkage time and improve your results.

Many Internet magazines and books now come with CD-ROMs that contain hotlists of Web sites sorted by subject area. Pop these into your CD drive and hit the information highway at full speed.

The major problem with print publications is that their site lists are out of date almost as soon as they are published. The lead time for most magazine articles is three months, and for books, it's even longer. The pace of change on the Internet is so brisk that many of the links will be obsolete by the time you reach them. To compile the freshest site list, you have to go to the Net itself.

On the Net

Let's begin with Yahoo. If you go to the Yahoo category for accounting, for example, you'll find a list like the one shown in Figure 5.3. The trouble with Yahoo categories is that they're sketchy. Some of these sites will be very important to your campaign and others will be worthless, and it's difficult to know which is which without visiting each one.

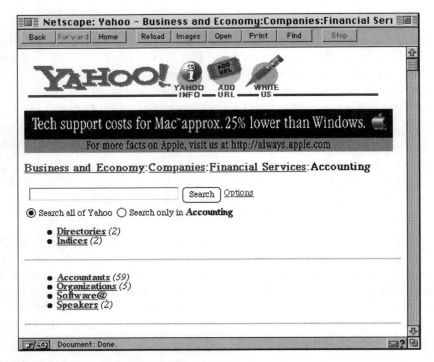

Figure 5.3 Yahoo accounting category.

Yahoo is a user-contributed directory: You see only the sites people register. Consequently, the quality of the listings is inconsistent. Figure 5.4 shows the Yahoo listings for accounting organizations. You see there's only one listing for a U.S. organization and only one state organization, but many states have accounting trade groups with Web sites—they're just not listed at Yahoo.

Let's go to Alta Vista for a more comprehensive search. Figure 5.5 shows the results for a search for "accounting." If you examine the fine print, it says that more than 200,000 matching entries were found! If Yahoo is sketchy, Alta Vista is impossibly broad, with dozens of hits leading you to the same page.

Fortunately, there are many ways to craft a more focused search at Alta Vista. You can find suggestions in the help section. Figure 5.6 shows the results of a tighter search, this time for the phrase "accounting organizations." Still, we found 400 listings, including many dupli-

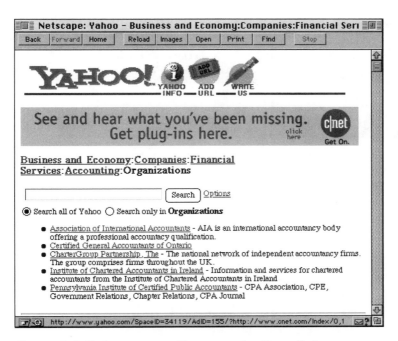

Figure 5.4 Yahoo accounting organizations list.

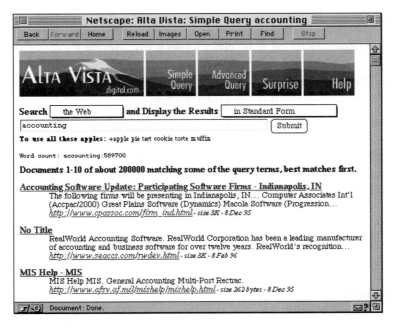

Figure 5.5 Results of an Alta Vista search for "accounting."

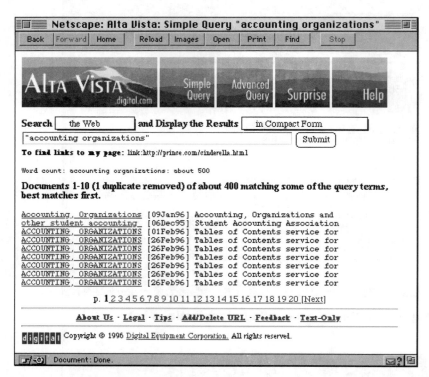

Figure 5.6 Results of an Alta Vista search for "accounting organizations."

cates to the same site. If you continue to narrow your search though, you run the risk of excluding quality sites.

A better approach to is to use the major Internet search sites to find *quality directories*, not sites. Yahoo, Lycos, Alta Vista, Galaxy, Infoseek are all too broad for this sort of work. What you need is a special-interest directory or catalog, put together by someone who knows the field. This is really the goal of your searching strategy: to find *the* SuperSite, the one mega-directory put together by an ardent fan. Luckily, for every subject you can think of, there's probably a SuperSite out there that has all the links you need in one place. Find the SuperSite and you can grind out the links like a sausage factory.

Finding the SuperSite

The following subsections detail some good tricks for finding the SuperSite.

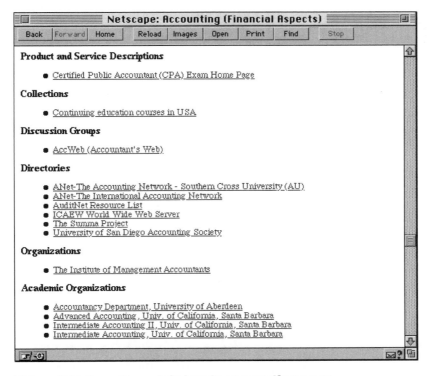

Figure 5.7 A portion of Galaxy's accounting page.

Start with Galaxy

Galaxy (also known as EINET) is more library-like than most Internet directories. If you can find the category your business fits into, Galaxy will return a page of links showing you, among other things, directories devoted to your subject. Figure 5.7 shows Galaxy's accounting page. Halfway down the page there's a Directories category containing six links. Any one of these could be the SuperSite for accounting.

Try Infoseek Next

Figure 5.8 shows the results of an Infoseek search for "accounting." On the left side of the page, you see links to related topics. You can use these to focus your search. On the right side of the page, at the end of each entry, there is a link to Similar Pages. This is another way to tighten your search in hopes of finding the SuperSite.

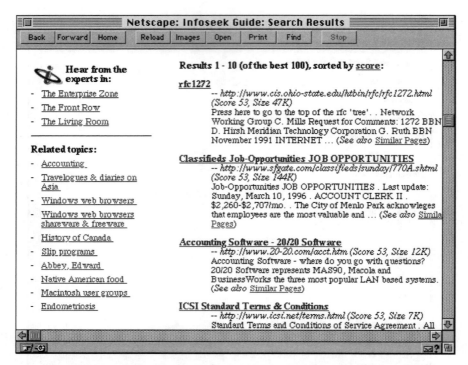

Figure 5.8 An Infoseek search for "accounting" offers many alternatives.

Do an Alta Vista "Link" Search

If you know the URL of a popular Web site similar to yours, you can ask Alta Vista for a list of all the pages linking to that site. This is a powerful tool for finding out who has linked to *your* page as well as to your competitors' pages. The syntax for the search is as follows: link:mysite. This will deliver a list of all the pages with a link to mysite. You might find the SuperSite you're looking for this way, or you might choose to visit all these pages and ask for a link to *your* site.

The SuperSite

Using Galaxy, I eventually found the Rutgers Accounting Web—the SuperSite of the accounting world. It's so large that the screenshot in Figure 5.9 doesn't do it justice. This site has hundreds of links to accounting resources, all neatly classified and annotated. It became my firm's home base as we conducted a linkage campaign for an accounting services customer.

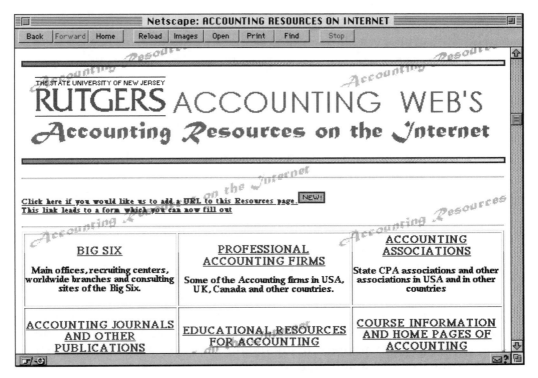

Figure 5.9 Rutgers Accounting Web—an accounting SuperSite.

We've found similar SuperSites for children's interests, business, travel—you name the subject and somewhere out there is a SuperSite devoted to it. Find the SuperSite and you can save it as source from your Web browser and use it to complete your linkage campaign. Some of these SuperSites may offer a fee-based service for handling your publicity needs, and this isn't a bad way to go. If they specialize in the subject areas of greatest concern to you, chances are they will be able to do superior work in a fraction of the time it would take to do it yourself.

Scoping the Sites

Once you've found your SuperSite (or other master lists of promising pages), it's time to visit each site and ask for a link to your site. As you browse the sites, ask yourself these questions:

1. Is this a good place for a link to my site?
2. If so, which page should the link go on?
3. Who is the person responsible for maintaining that page?
4. What is his or her e-mail address?

The first question may seem unnecessary initially. After all, you want as many links as you can get, don't you? Not always. Some of my clients are fussy about the sites they're associated with. They don't want links from places that contain sexually explicit imagery or otherwise may reflect poorly on them. Most of my customers would love a link from the Playboy site because of the traffic it generates, but a few don't want to be associated with the Playboy image.

You also don't want to request a link if the site is a fee-based service or if you suspect it's a scam. Some people use their Web sites to build mailing lists, then hound you with solicitations. Several companies have notorious reputations online and you might want to avoid sites associated with them. You might not want to ask a competitor for a link, either, and it's not always evident from the surface that the site belongs to a competitor. You might not want a link on a poorly designed site or a site that hasn't been maintained for a year or so. Even a free link takes time to request and maintain.

If you do a good job finding a SuperSite or site list, most of places you visit will be appropriate. The next question is, do they have a page of links to other sites? If so, that's probably where they'll put a link to your site. Link pages are often difficult to find because they can be called many things. Common names include Links, Cool Sites, Resources, and so on. Figure 5.10 shows a typical links page called Surfin' Safari.

Some Webmasters sprinkle links throughout the site, so be on the lookout for any page on which a link to your site would be appropriate. Once you've found the page, note the location (URL) and look for the e-mail address of the person responsible for maintaining that page. This is usually the Webmaster on smaller sites, but it's a lot nicer to get the person's name and individual e-mail address.

Some pages will tell you how to submit requests for a link. Other pages will include a copyright notice or credits at the bottom of the page, and you can often find contact names and e-mail addresses in these stock notices. If you can't find a contact name or address, try

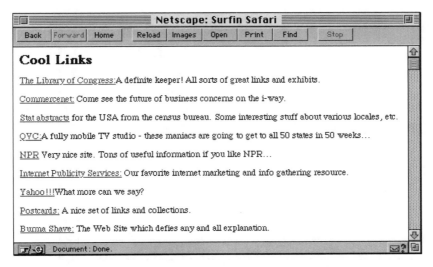

Figure 5.10 An annotated links page contains brief descriptions for each link.

webmaster@sitename.com and hope it is forwarded to the right person. But be careful about using a bare Webmaster e-mail address. Many Web sites are built by companies that have no say in the content. They might not even maintain the site, having turned over those responsibilities to the client. Sending e-mail to webmaster@digitalplanet.com, for example, is not likely to get you a link on one of the sites they built. So don't be lazy and just address 100 e-mail messages to Webmaster in hopes of getting a few good links. Go the distance and look for the appropriate contact.

The Art of the Linkletter

You found a good site. You found a page at that site where a link to your site fits perfectly. You found the name and e-mail address of the person responsible for maintaining that page. Time to make the pitch!

You should prepare a linkletter in advance of your visit and have it ready to send when you find good prospects. If your Web browser is equipped with e-mail, you can send linkletters right from there. Many of the contact names you find will be mailto links, meaning you can just click on the link to get a blank e-mail addressed to the contact person. Figure 5.11 shows the blank e-mail page that appears when you activate

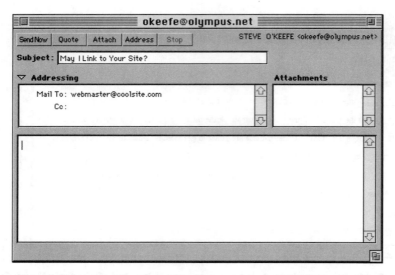

Figure 5.11 You may be able to send e-mail right from your Web browser. This is an e-mail screen from Netscape version 2.0.

a mailto link in Netscape 2.0. Copy your linkletter from your word processor and paste it into the blank e-mail screen. Tweak it a little and send it off!

Figure 5.12 shows the linkletter we used for the Dr. Seuss campaign. I like to start my linkletters with a compliment. Look for something on the site that genuinely stands out. Webmasters put a lot of effort into their sites and seldom get any recognition. If you can say something honestly praiseworthy about their site, so much the better.

When you ask for the link, it's important to *specify the page and its URL where the link should go*. Identify the exact location, to make it as easy as possible for the Webmaster to comply with your request. Keep in mind that the site may have been built by an expert then turned over to a novice for maintenance. If you tell him or her exactly where to put the link you're more likely to get a successful placement. It also proves that you visited the site and aren't just spamming the planet with link requests.

After you make a suggestion about where to place the link, furnish the linking text marked up in HTML and ready for installation. Inserting the HTML is oh-so-easy and makes it a snap for the Webmaster to install the link. I like to provide both the site name and a brief descrip-

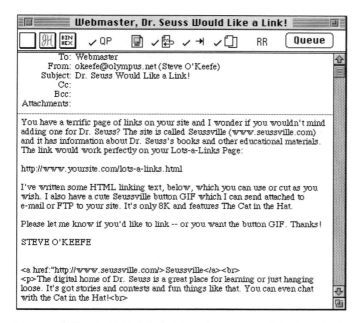

Figure 5.12 A typical linkletter, requesting a hotlink for Dr. Seuss.

tion, in case there is room for an annotated link. Here's what the HTML looked like for Dr. Seuss:

```
<a href:"http://www.seussville.com/">Seussville</a><br>
<p>The digital home of Dr. Seuss is a great place for learning
or just hanging loose. It's got stories and contests and fun
things like that. You can even chat with the Cat in the
Hat!<br>
```

The top line is the link, with a simple HREF to the URL for the site. By providing the Webmaster with the HTML, you can direct people to the proper page. If the Webmaster had to choose, he or she might link to a secondary page instead of the page on which you want people to start their visit. Providing the HTML also allows you to code your URL to track the source of hits to your site. For more information about coding your URL, refer back to Chapter 4.

It sometimes helps to offer a small, graphical button to go with the link as we did in Figure 5.12. These so-called hot buttons help your link stand out from the crowd and reinforce brand recognition. But don't send the artwork with the link request because few sites have graphical link pages. It's also considered rude to dump a file on someone without permission. Netscape and Yahoo (refer to Figure 5.2) are only two of the many successful link buttons. There's more information about preparing button graphics later in this chapter.

As you can see, the art of the linkletter is to make the connection with the right person and give him or her every reason to say yes to your link. I receive e-mail all the time asking for links, and sometimes the sender forgets to tell me where the site is! I've learned that you get a lot more links when you provide the text, the HTML, a cute button, and the exact location where the link should go. Some people think this is too much work, and maybe they're right. But one quality link that brings the target audience to your site is worth 500 links in all the lame malls cluttering up the Web.

Tracking Your Link Requests

It's a good idea to keep track of your link requests so you can follow up as needed. If you're sending e-mail through your Web browser, why not send a copy to yourself for archiving? In Netscape, you can set your preferences so that you're automatically sent a copy of any outgoing mail. In Eudora, you can adjust your settings to keep copies of all outgoing mail. You may never need to look at this e-mail again (unless you delete it, in which case it's certain you'll need it immediately), but it is best to be prepared.

Keeping copies of e-mail requests also will help you deal with some of the responses you'll get. Your e-mail contains the name of the contact person and the URL for the page on which you want your link placed. Sometimes your requests are forwarded to the person who deals with links, and you may not recognize his or her name in the response. A copy of the e-mail can refresh your memory. You can also resend the e-mail if you haven't received a reply in a couple weeks.

Along with copies of e-mail, track the names and addresses of the sites you visited. You can do this several different ways, but the easiest way is to "bookmark" the home page of the site. After you're done with a session of link requests, you can move all the bookmarks into one linkage folder. Or you can print your Web browser's bookmark list and track your responses on paper. Figure 5.13 shows a Netscape bookmark folder used in a PowerPC linkage campaign.

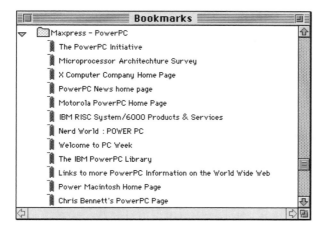

Figure 5.13 A Netscape bookmark folder used in a linkage campaign.

But be aware that there's a catch to bookmarking your sites. The bookmark references the title of the page you're on, not the title of the site. If you bookmark from the links page—not the home page—your bookmark may read something like "Links to Other Resources" instead of "Smart Business SuperSite" (or whatever the site name is). If you've used bookmarks a lot, you know it's not always easy to tell which site you bookmarked or why you marked it. You may want to go back to the home page at each site before bookmarking, or annotate your bookmarks using Netscape's Edit Bookmark command (see Figure 5.14).

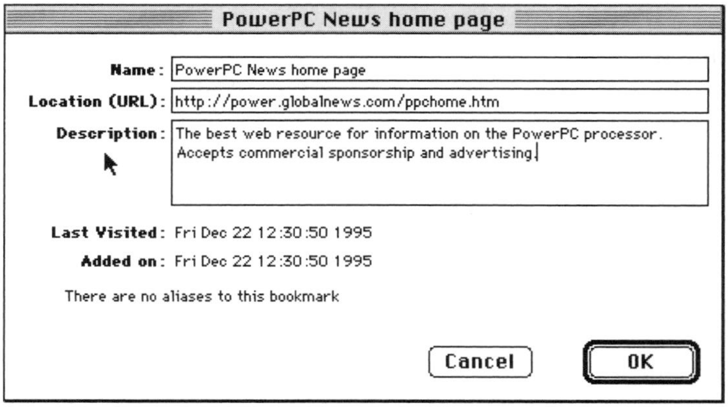

Figure 5.14 You can annotate your bookmarks using Netscape's Edit bookmark window.

Another way to track the sites you visit is with a Linkage Report that you keep in your word processing program. The report shown in Figure 5.15 is from our campaign to register Seussville, Random House's Dr. Seuss site. The report shows the name of the site followed by the URL. Even though we carefully prepared this report, some of the site names are a little cryptic.

Figure 5.15 Linkage Report, tracking the sites visited in a campaign for Dr. Seuss.

Web Site Linkage Report

Client: Random House   **Site Name:** Seussville
Date Started: March 19, 1996   **SiteURL:** http://www.seussville.com

About Your Linkage Report:

We visited each of the Web sites shown below looking for a place to add a link to your site. We sent individual messages to persons responsible for maintaining the link pages at these sites. We have no control over whether people will link to your site. The addresses of the sites are provided so that you can look for your link.

Name of Site and URL:

Children's Book News for Parents and Teachers
  <http://community.Net/~ben_chun/bookafair>
Family Planet
  <http://family.starwave.com/>
The Great Glorious and Gandorious...Dr. Seuss!
  <http://www.freenet.ufl.edu/~afn15301/drseuss.html>
Online Children's Stories
  <http://www.ucalgary.ca/~dkbrown/ stories.html>
Shelves of Children's Books
  <http://www.users.interport.nt/~fairrosa/ cl.index.html>
Educational Resources Info. Center—For teachers and parents
  <http://www.indiana.edu/~eric_rec/index.html>
The Kids on the Web: Children's Books
  <http://www.zen.org/~brendan/kids-lit.html>
Welcome to Kids' Web
  <http://www.primenet.com/~sburr/index.html#literature>
Kids' Page
  <http://gagme.wwa.com/~boba/kids.html>

Berit's Best Sites for Children
   <http://www.cochran.com/theosite/ksites.html>
Children's Pages at WombatNet
   <http://www.batnet.com/wombat/children.html>
KID List "Kids Internet Delight"
   <http://www.clark.Net/pub/journalism/kid.html>
CyberKids/Cyberteens Launchpad
   <http://www.woodwind.com/cyberkids/Launchpad.html>
Kids.Com
   <http://kids.com/>
Education, Schools, and Young People Related Links
   <http://www.cs.uidaho.edu/~connie/interests-education.html>
The Ultimate Children's Internet Sites!
   <http://www.vividus.com/ucis.html>
Internet Public Library
   <http://ipl.sils.umich.edu/ref/RR/ENT/Books-rr.html>
Special Sites for Kids
   <http://www.ipswichcity.qld.gov.au/eetint1a.html>
The Parenting Resource Center on the Web
   <http://www.parentsplace.com/>
Internet Sites
   <http://www1.trib.com/CUMBERLINK/net.page.html>
ON THE WEB
   <http://www.ocps.k12.fl.us/kidsw.html#TITLE>
Kids Web: A World Wide Web Digital Library for Schoolkids
   <http://www.npac.syr.edu/textbook/kidsweb/>
Friendly Pines Camp
   <http://www.amug.org/~fpc/links.html>
Internet and World Wide Web Resources for Parents and Children
   <http://www.foundation.tricon.com/2f/children.html>
Electronic Resources for Youth Services
   <http://www.ccn.cs.dal.ca/~aa331/childlit.html>
Read Aloud! A Guide to Reading Children
   <http://funnelweb.utcc.utk.edu/~epling/readaloud.html>
Children's Literature Sampler
   <http://funnelweb.utcc.utk.edu/~estes/estes2.html>
Kelbie's Presto Print
   <http://www.libby.org/Presto-Print/>

(continues)

Figure 5.15 (*Continued*)

Books for Children and More
    <http://www.users.interport.net/~hdu/>
The BookWire Electronic Children's Books Index
    <http://www.bookwire.com/links/readingroom/echildbooks.html>
Children's Book Publishers
    <http://weber.u.washington.edu/~jabourne/projects/pub.html>
Preschool Learning Fun
    <http://gatecom.com/~geraldd/apple.html>
Children's Hour Book Emporium
    <http://www.childrenshour.com/store.html>
CHILDREN'S BOOKS Nerd World Media
    <http://www.nerdworld.com/users/dstein/nw171.html>
Our Kids Books
    <http://www.sunscape.com/kids/>
The InterLink KIDS' ZONE
    <http://www.spokane.net/kidzone/index.html>

We use the printed Linkage Report to track favorable responses, noting the date we received a reply and whether they asked for a button graphic. Our clients can follow up to see if links were installed. These reports become valuable marketing tools, listing places that might be receptive to announcements or advertisements of future products or services.

The Link Button

As mentioned earlier, it helps to offer a graphical hot button for people to use when linking to your site. The button is a logo, which enforces name recognition, strengthens a brand, improves the visual presentation of a page, and helps you stand out in a sea of hotlinks. These buttons are one of our not-so-secret weapons to improve the quality and results of our linkage campaigns.

Point's Top 5% of the Web graphic, shown in Figure 5.16, illustrates the benefits of a good hot button. It seems that it's on about 25 percent of all the Web pages out there. This link button brings a lot of traffic to Point's site, no doubt pleasing Point's advertisers. It has helped position Point as one of the premium catalogs on the Internet, and therefore

Figure 5.16   Point's Top 5% of the Web button is all over the Net.

it will be difficult for a competitor to unseat its links; there's only so much space a Webmaster has for graphical links like these.

Characteristics of a Good Link Button

What are the characteristics of a good link button? The following sub-sections detail the answers to this question.

Keep It Small

Under 10K is best and with dimensions as small as possible. I've seen 100K buttons that are more like banners and take forever to load. Pare those buttons down to the bare essentials!

Keep It Simple

Aim for brand recognition. Don't try to cram too much information into one tiny little image. But simplicity is easier said than done. Point's button is crowded, but it works because they stress one image (5%). It also has a distinctive shape. This is part of the universal strategy, described next: the Point button is a transparent graphic.

Universal

Universality means the button should look good against any background color. Transparent graphics allow their background to show through. For this reason, transparent buttons often have a cookie-cutter quality: they look shaped, not square, adding to ease of recognition. Transparent graphics can backfire, though, if they get lost in the background color. Successful transparent buttons always include a border to ensure they're set off from the surrounding color.

Figure 5.17 Netscape's 2.0 button is guaranteed to go out of date.

Timeless

Timelessness is tricky, as every image will look dated at some point. Nevertheless, try to avoid text or images that won't wear well with age. Some people actually build obsolescence into their buttons! as Netscape did when it put a "2.0" banner across its popular button (see Figure 5.17). In my opinion, it ruined the button because now all the folks who have the plain old Netscape button look out of date, which is not the impression most Webmasters want to cultivate. I don't have to tell you how silly the Version 2.0 button is going to look years from now when Netscape is in release 7.5.

Maybe Netscape's revisions will cause people to upgrade their buttons more frequently? More likely, though, people will just not install the button in the first place. Creating buttons for contests, events, and other short-term projects is only going to clutter the Web. If you change your logo or look, you have to find all those old buttons out there and ask the Webmasters to install your new button. There's only so much patience a Webmaster has for such requests.

The Button

Figure 5.18 shows some of the buttons created at my firm, Internet Publicity Services. In most cases, the artwork was taken from the client's Web site. The Seussville button works well because the Cat in the Hat is universally recognized and is the main character at the Web site. Unfortunately, we had to clutter up the image with a trademark notice in order to please the attorneys. The Book Stacks button is shown at double its final size.

You can create buttons using your favorite graphics software. We make ours in Photoshop, and use a GIF converter to make them transparent. You can save your graphics as GIFs or JPEGs, although the GIF format is preferable for most link buttons because it does a better job re-

Figure 5.18 Link buttons from Internet Publicity Services.

producing line art or simple art. Also, you can make GIFs transparent, which you can't do with JPEGs. And there are still some Web browsers that can't view JPEG images.

On the other hand, JPEGs take up less disk space and result in higher-quality images when you're working with photographs or complex color graphics. But most link buttons are so small that the space you save with JPEGs isn't significant.

Responses to Link Requests

You can expect a wide variety of responses to your link requests. Some people will be enthusiastic and will install the link immediately. That's great! Others will tell you how lousy your site is. But most people will remain silent, whether or not they install a link.

We frequently get lengthy e-mails from people telling us about all the problems they encountered trying to visit a client's Web site. It's tempting to bury such bad news or defend the site. Resist that urge! These people are doing you a big favor. How many other people encountered problems with the site and didn't bother to send e-mail? How many people left the site with a bad impression and will never return? When someone tells you about trouble at your site, they're doing you a favor. You need to investigate the trouble and find the cause of the problem and determine whether it's worth fixing. But the first thing you should do is thank your critics profusely and let them know you're investigating.

When you pay someone to build a Web site, whether it's an employee or an outside firm, he or she won't always tell you the truth about your site. You could have a disaster in the making and no one says anything except what a terrific site it is. Then you launch the site, it flops, and no one seems to know why. So when an outsider comes along and gives you an unsolicited evaluation of your site, listen closely because that's your market talking.

Sometimes the criticism can be devastating. We had one site that Yahoo refused to list because the registrar couldn't connect. If you're not listed in Yahoo, you might as well not exist. One of the Webmasters we requested a link from gave us a detailed list of the difficulties using the site. As it turned out, the problems were due to the site being installed on a temporary server that couldn't handle the load. We thanked these people for their comments, investigated, and asked them to reevaluate the site.

The Web is a new world of communications. All of us are feeling our way in the dark, trying to build sites that work. It's hard to know you have a problem until someone tells you the bad news. There are companies (mine included) that charge hundreds or thousands of dollars to evaluate a Web site. When someone comes along and gives you an opinion for free—even if he or she lacks a gentle Webside manner—you should immediately thank them and follow up. When you do a linkage campaign, you may get several such responses.

Other responses are easier to handle. If someone asks for a link button, send it, along with a repeat of your HTML for the link. Figure 5.19 shows a typical letter we send in response to a button request. You want to make it as easy as possible to install the link. Repeating your HTML helps keep everything in one place.

You might have difficulty sending the graphic attached to e-mail. Eudora defaults to sending graphics using *binhex* encoding. (This is where my technical limitations show.) I'm not sure what all this stuff means, but I've had some success sending graphics using *uuencode*. You

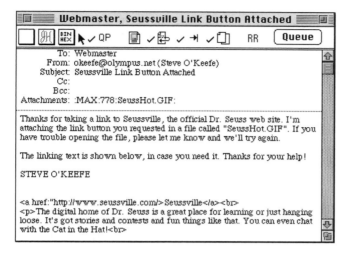

Figure 5.19 E-mail reply to a request for a button graphic.

can change Eudora encoding from binhex to uuencode using the pull-down menu at the top of your e-mail message. The cursor in Figure 5.19 (an arrow) points to Eudora's encoding menu.

Your linkage campaign should generate many quality placements and some good feedback about your Web site, but many people will not respond at all. In those cases, check their Web sites in two weeks; if they haven't installed a link, resend your linkletter with a gentle reminder note. One of the responses you'll see frequently is, "I'll install your link if you install mine." That brings us to our next topic.

Reciprocal Links

A lot of people will not install a link to your Web site unless you install one for them. This is only natural, and you should be prepared for such requests. In the biz, this is called *reciprocal linkage,* a variation on "You scratch my back and I'll scratch yours." It's the Web's little referral system, and it can work wonders for your site.

You might want to plan on reciprocal linkage when you build your Web site. It will come in handy if you have some sort of Cool Links page at your site. If you don't have a links page, consider adding one. You can take your Linkage Report (see Figure 5.16) and turn it into HTML for a ready-made links page for your Web site. If you're planning on asking other people to install a graphic link to your site, you should design your own links page to accommodate graphic hot buttons.

Top Tips

- **Prepare a Linkletter:** Have a script ready when you go looking for links.

- **Add Some Art:** A graphic hot button will help strengthen your brand. A good button is small, simple, universal, and timeless.

- **Find a SuperSite:** Somewhere on the Web, there's a site with links to every other site on any given subject. Find the SuperSite in your field and your linkage campaign will be easy.

- **Make It Personal:** Try to find the name and e-mail address of the person maintaining the sites you visit. Don't settle for the generic Webmaster unless you can't do better.

- **Give and Take:** If you're asking for a link, be willing to give one in return. Always include a page of links on your own Web site.

- **Listen:** When people tell you about problems at your site, thank them immediately and investigate. For every person who complains, there may be thousands who turned away.

CHAPTER 6

E-Mail News Releases

The news release is the seed from which most publicity grows. This chapter shows you how to cultivate the somewhat sterile soil of electronic information transfer, how to prepare the seed so that it will flourish in this environment, and how to spread the seed on to the most promising terrain so that it will blossom into media coverage.

Publicists should be dancing in the virtual streets over how easy it is to reach the media using the Net. Over the last few years, I can think of hundreds of nonstories that became "news" because they happened online. Michael Jackson talking with fans isn't really news, unless it's part of a *simulchat*. The release of a new Lands' End catalog isn't news—unless the catalog is on the World Wide Web.

When I started promoting books on the Net, my medialist consisted of the e-mail addresses of a few dozen journalists. Most of these writers worked for computer magazines or covered the technology beat for large newspapers. Today, my medialist contains more than 2,000 contacts. And it's no longer just technology writers. Now the online media is so thick they trip over each other looking for stories. Almost every newspaper in the United States has a reporter assigned to the Net. Every major magazine from *Playboy* to *Martha Stewart's Living* includes some coverage of interesting Web sites. Hip radio jocks hop on the Net in the morning. Screenwriters soup up their scripts with online bits. They say "dog bites man" isn't news, but if it happens online, it is.

This chapter shows you how to reach the media more effectively using e-mail. I'll help you write a good news release and format it for electronic delivery. I'll also give you a battery of techniques to use to get the e-mail addresses of the press. Topics covered in this chapter include:

- **The Power of E-Mail:** E-mail is best thing to happen to the publicist since the TV news magazine show.

- **Unsolicited E-Mail:** Is it wrong to send e-mail to people who don't ask for it? What happens when you do?

- **E-Mail Software:** It pays to get the best software you can buy and learn how to use it.

- **Why E-Mail News Release Work:** You can get substantially higher response rates from e-mail news releases than other methods—but only if you do them right.

- **E-Mail Style:** Nitty-gritty details about using e-mail news releases, including audience, length, content, and purpose.

- **Anatomy of a News Release:** All the parts of a news release—subject line, address, body, signature—and how to buff them up.

- **The Medialist:** How to find the e-mail addresses of the media, including some downright sneaky—but legal—methods.

- **Address Books:** The technical details about maintaining your medialist. How to use nicknames and bulk e-mail.

- **Top Tips:** A cheat sheet for the online publicist. Tape these tips to your terminal.

The Power of E-Mail

E-mail is nothing less than the best thing about being online. It eliminates the per-item charges associated with most forms of message delivery: telephone, fax, express mail. It provides a written trail of your communications (how many times have you wished for proof of some phone conversation you had?). Unlike a phone call, e-mail isn't an intrusion. People read their messages when they want to, or just delete them if they're not interested. E-mail is better than voice mail because the sender has time to intelligently compose his or her thoughts before committing them to paper.

E-mail is far superior to surface mail for many business communications, too. It has international and instantaneous reach, making it possible to have an exchange in a matter of minutes, which would take weeks by mail. You save money with e-mail, not only on postage, delivery, and fax charges, but on valuable time. It takes less time to compose a document, address it, and send it.

I used to have a 10-best list of reasons for getting online. As I became more familiar with the Internet, I realized that 8 out of 10 reasons were e-mail. How much do people use e-mail? There's no clear answer to that. Many corporations were using internal e-mail long before the Internet became popular. When you hear "40 million people are on the Internet," the reference is to the number of people reachable by e-mail over the Internet. These people might not know a Gopher from a hole in the ground and they might never have seen the World Wide Web, but you can reach them through e-mail.

It pays to get the best e-mail software available and master it. A publicist is only as good as his or her contact list, and for the online publicist, the contact list is a database of e-mail addresses. Every week, I send messages to thousands of media people. Many of my colleagues and customers believe I have the best e-mail medialist in the world. I am a fanatic about my list. I spend hours each week grooming it so that I only send messages to people who are likely to be interested in them. As a result, few people ever ask to be taken off my list.

As a journalist, I am also on the receiving end of other people's news releases. Most of what I get is amateur spam, inappropriate messages formatted so poorly they are tortuous to read. Look at the example in Figure 6.1. Would you venture very far into a message that looked like that? I have sympathy for people just starting in online publicity. The Internet is a crucible where the weak get vaporized but the strong are forged. People on the Net are not the least bit bashful about calling your attention to your failings. I know. I've made every mistake imaginable. I've been flamed enough to build up a pretty good layer of scar tissue. One by one, I've learned about all the hidden problems with e-mail promotions. I can help you look like a pro from the get-go.

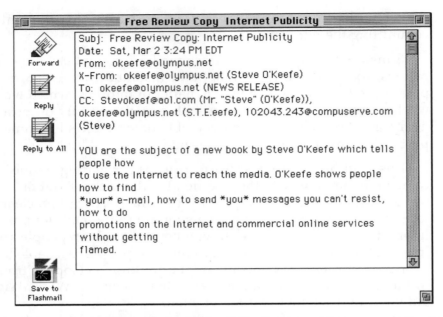

Figure 6.1 This news release is difficult to read because of the line endings. Most journalists would rather delete it than try to read it.

Unsolicited E-Mail

With apologies to all my Internet-correct friends and colleagues, don't let anyone tell you you can't send unsolicited e-mail over the Net. You can, and it's okay. Don't let anyone tell you it's immoral, impolite, or not good netiquette. Don't worry about the acceptable use policies you agreed to when you signed up for Internet service. What counts is your relationships with people, not the fine print of the contract. I wonder how many of the people citing acceptable use policies have violated the fine print that comes with every piece of software they own or use? A good friend of mine and a fellow Internet author says in one of her books, "Don't ever send unsolicited e-mail." I get a kick out of sending her notes now and then, knowing she has not asked me to. My sister Janet sends me unsolicited e-mail and I'm glad to get it. I send queries to magazine editors over the Net all the time. At least half of the mail I receive every day is unsolicited and I'm happy to get about 90 percent of it.

When people say, "Never send unsolicited e-mail," what they really mean is "Never send me anything I don't want to read." They like unsolicited e-mail if it's something they're interested in. People are funny that way. I have one of those great big country mailboxes at home, shaped like a barn and large enough to raise small livestock inside. I never know what I'm going to find in there: magazines, catalogs, solicitations, letters from friends, bills, merchandise, photos, sometimes small creatures. I like getting all the interesting stuff, and I throw away the stuff I don't care about. Simple.

But online, nothing is simple. Some people take offense at junk e-mail and, instead of just deleting it or asking to get off your list, they carefully compose hate mail to you, your Internet provider, and anyone else who will listen. Sensitive people, like myself, are often so turned off by the one pyromaniac on their mailing list that they ignore the "thank you" notes from other people. Fortunately, tempers have cooled a little online, and following some standard operating procedures should keep you in the good graces of the Net cops.

As I said, I've received some nasty flames, but those days are mostly behind me. I wish I had archived a couple of the choicer ones, though, so I could accurately reproduce them here. On the other hand, recently I received this compliment in my mailbox; if you follow the advice in this book, you too could be getting fan mail from journalists:

```
I love the fact that I get your "pitches" by e-mail, rather
than "tree."  Much easier at this end.
.............................................
JACLYN EASTON
Host/Creator, Log On U.S.A. (Radio Show)
Weekly Contributor, Los Angeles Times
Author, "Shopping on the Internet and Beyond!"
```

Unsolicited e-mail is not the same as spam. Spam is the *indiscriminate* distribution of messages, without consideration for their appropriateness. Definitely don't spam. Only post messages to discussion groups when you're reasonably certain they're appropriate. Only send e-mail to people you believe are interested in your message. Remove anyone from your mailing lists who asks to be removed. If you follow these simple guidelines, while you may still get a flame now and then, they'll be few and far between. After a while, you'll get a good feel for what works and what doesn't.

News releases are sent to people in the media. In general, they're interested in hearing almost anything having to do with the beat they cover. I get their addresses from public sources, most often from their bylines. I look at it this way, if they don't want unsolicited e-mail, why are they publishing their e-mail addresses? Fan mail is unsolicited—do they flame their fans? Last week, I sent unsolicited e-mail to 700 Internet journalists (can you believe there are 700 Internet journalists?). One person asked politely to be removed from the list; 75 requested review copies of the book I was promoting. I can live comfortably with those numbers.

E-Mail Software

As I've said, I use Eudora for most of my e-mail needs. Most of the examples in this book are based on it. Of course, there are many other e-mail software programs, including Pine, cc:mail, Chameleon, MCI Mail, Lotus Notes, and others. I don't have enough experience with these other programs to give you specific instructions on how to use them; however, most e-mail programs contain features similar to Eudora. If you can't do some of the tricks covered in this chapter with your current software, you'll probably be able to with the next upgrade.

Some people have their e-mail program determined by their Internet provider. If you're using America Online, CompuServe, Prodigy, or another commercial online service, you're stuck with the software it offers. Since you don't have the choice of using Eudora with these services, I'll point out some important differences as I go. Rest assured, though, the commercial online services will continue to offer better e-mail as they compete with direct Internet access. The capabilities of your software should soon equal or surpass those of Eudora.

Eudora is manufactured by Qualcomm (Figure 6.2). It was initially available for free on the Internet, and you still might be able to get a free copy. For more information, send e-mail to eudora-sales@qualcomm.com or call toll-free, 1-800-238-3672. If it's still available, you can download the program via anonymous FTP from ftp.qualcomm.com, or look for it at other popular software repositories on the Net.

Until it became the dominant e-mail software on the Net, Eudora followed the now-familiar Internet strategy of giving away their prod-

Figure 6.2 Eudora is a popular brand of e-mail software.

uct, then started charging for upgrades or extended features, such as spell-checking. One benefit of this strategy for the publicist is that most of the audience can be reached using Eudora software, thus eliminating compatibility problems. Another benefit is that Eudora is such a darn good program.

Prior to the release of Eudora, I was using Pine for my e-mail. Pine is a Unix-based program, and I can almost hear the former Pine users out there groaning in sympathy. A publicist using Pine for e-mail is like a neurosurgeon using a flint for a scalpel. Eudora makes e-mail much easier. However, Qualcomm has been slow to improve Eudora, and other programs are starting to challenge it. As more companies hook their internal networks up to the Internet, there are more compatibility problems using Eudora, which means more formatting problems, and more work for the publicist.

Why E-Mail News Releases Work

I started sending e-mail news releases within minutes of going online. Since then, I have never been less than amazed at how effective they are. One customer didn't see the need for using my Electronic News Releases. He was using PR Newswire and spending a small fortune to do it. And PR Newswire is very good at reaching the media by wire, fax and mail (and now e-mail, too). Then my customer tried my service, and has been using my electronic news releases ever since—in addition to PR Newswire.

For years, my customer had been sending conventional news releases to the same people I have on my e-mail medialist. Yet when I sent the news releases via e-mail, I got many more responses than my customer could have imagined. Why was I getting better results through e-mail than he was through other channels? I don't have a magic wand—I'm also amazed at how responsive my list is. But I do have some theories as to why e-mail works so well.

- **E-mail is personal:** My list is built around the e-mail addresses of individual writers, reporters, producers, and journalists. When you fax something, more often than not it's going to a shared machine. When you mail something, it might be screened or it might land on a big pile of junk mail. But if you get a journalist's e-mail address, chances are your mail will be opened by the person you're trying to reach.

- **E-mail is instantaneous:** When the Kevin Mitnick hacking case broke in early 1995, HarperCollins asked me to promote a couple of their authors as expert commentators. Within two hours, virtually all the journalists covering the Internet had my news release in their in-box. There is simply no more efficient way of reaching large numbers of reporters with a breaking news story.

- **E-mail is easy to answer:** If journalists get a fax, voice mail or paper news release and they want to interview you, they have to call to set the whole thing up. Maybe they'll get to it and maybe they won't. With e-mail, it's just as easy to reply to the message as it is to delete it. E-mail is usually processed as it is read, rather than being placed on a pile somewhere to grow mildew.

- **E-mail is effective only if you use it well:** There are many factors that determine whether your e-mail will generate the desired response. We'll look at four of the most important considerations in creating a compelling e-mail news release.

Appropriate Audience

If you plan on doing repeat mailings to the media, it's important to target your audience carefully. Say you're announcing the premiere of a new movie and you send your e-mail news release to computer print journalists; obviously, you're not going to have much success. In fact, you'll probably be flamed and many of the recipients will ask to be removed from your list. Then, if next week you're promoting a movie such as *Sneakers*, which *would* be of interest to computer journalists, you will have lost credibility if not half your list.

As I've mentioned before, you always mail to people who are likely to have a strong interest in your subject. If they're not the natural target audience, then modify your news release so that it has some appeal to them. For example, if you're preparing a news release for an apparel maker, in most cases, computer publications couldn't care less. If the apparel maker has a new Web site, however, you could make that your lead when e-mailing to computer journalists.

I had a customer whose book was going to be excerpted in *The L.A. Times Magazine* and *Wired*. He wanted his electronic news release to include that information, in order to add legitimacy to the book. But if there's one thing a reporter doesn't want to hear about, it's a story that has been covered by the competition. So, since the audience for the news release was the media, I decided to use celebrity endorsements to get their attention instead.

As tempting as it may be to send e-mail to everyone on your medialist, this strategy often backfires. I sent a poorly worded announcement to my medialist once, and several prominent people asked to be removed from my list. For me, it was like losing a members of my extended family. And, if I refused to honor their requests and continued mailing to them, my messages would likely be deleted, unopened, or, worse, I might have been publicly flamed on the Net.

How do you know which addresses are appropriate? If you know the person at the other end of the e-mail address, you have a pretty good idea. But if the address is for a company or a department rather than an individual, unfortunately, you just have to guess. Many magazines have e-mail addresses for letters to the editor; don't send news releases to those addresses, as they just clutter up the mail. On the other hand, if the magazine has just one e-mail address for everything, then it's fair game to send news releases to it.

Later in this chapter, I'll show you so many ways to find good addresses that you will never lack for people to send your messages to. For now, let's continue with some other characteristics of effective e-mail.

Keep It Short!

In the good old days (say, five years ago) news releases were supposed to be "no more than two pages." That's what most publicity textbooks say. If you ask a working publicist or reporter, though, most will tell you to keep news releases to *one* page or less. In the world of online communications, however, anything more than a paragraph is suspect.

E-mail is best when brief. Brutally brief. I started out grafting standard one-page news releases onto the Net. Since then, based on instinct and improving results, I have whittled my news releases down to one screenful. I try to get to the point in three short paragraphs: the first for the hook, the second for the pitch, the third for contact information. Here's an example of a very effective release from early 1996:

```
Subject Line: Free Review Copy: KidNet

There's been a lot of talk lately about the dangers waiting
for children on the Internet and precious little discussion of
the benefits. If you're looking for balanced coverage,
consider KidNet, a new book by Debra and Brad Schepp that
explores the wealth of online resources available for
children.

Subtitled "The Kid's Guide to Surfing Through Cyberspace,"
KidNet offers pointers for parents and children aged 9-14.
KidNet covers the Web, America Online, CompuServe, Prodigy,
the Microsoft Network, and other online services. Subjects
covered include parental control, homework helpers,
international pen pals, games, music, sports, hobbies,
ecology, TV and movies, among others.

For a free review copy or an interview with the authors,
please reply via e-mail or contact HarperCollins Publicity,
(212) 207-7723.
```

One reason to keep your messages short is that they have a better chance of being opened. Most e-mail programs enable the receiver to see how big each piece of e-mail is before opening it. Every morning, I go through my in-box and transfer most large messages to a folder to be read "later." I either delete large news releases or put them in another folder to be read "later." Once a month, I go through these holding tank folders and delete almost everything. "Later" usually means "never."

I get hit with most of the major news releases that go out over the Net and like most journalists, I can usually tell a news release from other types of communications without opening it. You might fool me once or twice, but your name will sink in and I'll recognize you in the future. That's why it makes no sense to try and disguise your purpose. We'll talk about good subject lines later in this chapter. For now, the important point is to keep your news release short so you don't trigger automatic deletion.

The next reason to keep your message short is so that, if it is opened, it is then read. The first does not guarantee the second. Jill Ellsworth, co-author of *The Internet Business Book,* says she gets between 150 and 200 e-mail messages a day. I know several reporters who claim to receive 300 pieces of e-mail a day. Assume two minutes to read and process each message; that's *ten hours per day* just dealing with e-mail! If you want to gain respect with the press, you have to avoid sending them anything off-topic; and, when you do mail to them, get to the point fast!

Give Them a Story

The best news releases offer a relevant story idea as a hook into the product or service being promoted. If you can find a way to associate your message with some current news story, you'll improve your chances of success. If you look back at the example news release for *Kid-Net*, you'll see how we set the hook by tying the book to a wave of stories about the dangers awaiting children online. We offered another perspective, and many reporters went with the slant we gave them. In e-mail, you don't have time for a long setup. If there's an angle you can suggest in one or two sentences, then go for it. Otherwise, just make the best case you can and get out of the way.

In early 1996, I promoted the book *Finding Your Perfect Work* by Paul and Sarah Edwards. While I was preparing the campaign, AT&T announced the layoff of 40,000 employees. Robert Welsch, my contact at Tarcher/Putnam—himself a great publicist—mentioned that these soon-to-be-unemployed people would be surfing the Net looking for job opportunities. He planted the seed in my head. While preparing the materials for the campaign, I read a section of the book dealing with subcontracting. Some of the most successfully self-employed people got started when they were laid off, and the companies they worked for had to subcontract for the same work. I had my hook. The news release read:

Subject Line: Free Review Copy: Perfect Work

Two weeks ago AT&T gave pink slips to 2,000 of an expected
40,000 employees as part of a major restructuring and
downsizing effort. These people, and millions more like them,
are looking for work. Paul and Sarah Edwards are helping them
find something more.

Paul and Sarah Edwards are the self-employment experts.
Authors of the best-selling book "Working from Home," they
host CompuServe's Working from Home Forum and cable TV's
"Working From Home" show. Where some see the clouds of
corporate downsizing, they see a silver lining of self-
employment.

To celebrate the release of their new book, "Finding Your
Perfect Work," Paul and Sarah have contributed an article and
resource list to the World Wide Web's JobCenter
<http://www.jobcenter.com>. In the article, Paul and Sarah
point out that workforce reductions often result in
opportunities for former employees to become independent
contractors, thereby gaining more control over their work and
their lives.

For a review copy of "Finding Your Perfect Work"
(Tarcher/Putnam, ISBN 0-87477-795-X) or an interview with the
authors, simply reply to this e-mail or contact:

A lot of journalists were writing about the AT&T layoffs, and most
of the coverage was about how difficult it would be for the former employees to find work. We gave them another angle—some optimistic
numbers they could use in their coverage. A newsy hook is one way to
make your story valuable to the media.

Entice a Reply

The goal of most e-mail news releases is *not* to generate media coverage; it is to entice the journalist into requesting further information.
There is simply no way to successfully make the case for your product
or service or Web site in the space of an e-mail news release. This is one
of the most common beginner mistakes—which means that I've made

this mistake myself several times. You are much better off setting the hook, and providing the full story only when the journalist requests more information. If you can get the journalist to request a press kit, or ask for a sample of the product for review, or visit your Web site for more information, then you've done an excellent job. The rest of the work happens offline, in phone calls and through the mail, as you follow the lead to its conclusion.

John Wiley & Sons publishers wanted to promote a news conference they were holding in New York City. Several authors were involved, plus nonprofit organizations, sponsor organizations, educational institutions, and publicists on two continents. The printed news release was six pages long, and everything in it seemed important. So, when we sent it online, we decided to just try to get people to ask for the news release. Here's the message:

```
Subject Line: Criminal and Antisocial Behavior

No, I'm not talking about spam. I'm referring to a new book
that will be the subject of a major international news
conference in New York City next Wednesday, January 24.

"Genetics of Criminal and Antisocial Behaviour" is a landmark
study with serious legal and moral implications. The
controversial issues surrounding this book will be explored in
depth at a news conference chaired by Professor Sir Michael
Rutter of the Institute of Psychiatry, London, and including
Dr. Deborah Denno of the Law School, Fordham University, New
York, and Dr. Gregory Carey of the Institute of Behavioral
Genetics, University of Colorado.

You are invited to attend the news conference at the New York
Academy of Sciences, 2 E. 63 St, New York City, beginning at
10:30 a.m. on Wednesday, January 24. You are also invited to
request a copy of the news briefing, an interview with one of
the speakers, or a review copy of the book. Simply reply to
this e-mail with your RSVP or request, or contact one of the
following people:
```

Online publicity is a complement to standard publicity techniques—not a replacement. You can make a longer case in print than you can in e-mail. The e-mail release follows a pattern similar to other online communications: it is layered. You start with a sound bite. If people like the taste, you give them more. Most Web sites work this way. Everything happens very quickly online. Serious delving is done offline, through print or voice or video.

Time and again I've received 10-page e-mail news releases that include entire company histories, blah blah blah. As a journalist, I find this information useful only if I've *already* decided to do a story. It almost never entices me to pursue a story; in fact, a good story idea can get buried in so much verbiage.

Anatomy of an E-Mail News Release

E-mail programs may differ, but e-mail messages look pretty much the same no matter what software you use. There are two main parts to an e-mail message: the address section and the message section. Figure 6.3 shows a typical e-mail news release with the parts labeled. We'll examine each of these parts and I'll offer suggestions on how use them effectively. Let's start with the subject line, since it is unique to e-mail.

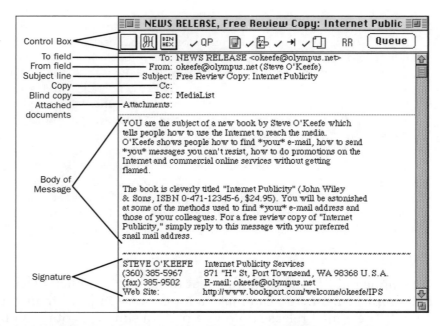

Figure 6.3 A typical e-mail message with its parts labeled.

The Subject Line

A subject line on your e-mail messages is like answering a receptionist who asks: "Can I tell Chris what this call is regarding?" If you have the right subject line, maybe Chris will open your message. If you use the wrong line, maybe not. I can't imagine Chris taking a phone call from someone who "wants to show you how to get rich fast." Yet that's exactly the kind of subject line many bulk e-mailers use.

When you're sending a news release, the subject line isn't as critical as it is with discussion group postings to the general public. (We'll talk about subject lines again when we get to Chapter 7, Announcements.) With a news release, the audience is known: you're mailing to media people. If you try to trick them into opening your news release, you won't have much long-term success. The best suggestion is to be straightforward and build up a reputation for honesty.

Most of my work involves book publicity, so my subject line usually reads "Free Review Copy: *Book Title*." That's a pretty good subject line; it has that magic word "free" in it, it tells people what I'm offering, and the title of the book usually gives some clue as to the subject matter. If they've heard of the book or are interested in the subject, they'll probably open the message. There's also enough information for them to decide to delete the message unopened if it's something they're not interested in.

Some publicists I know always identify their messages as news releases in the subject line, starting the line with the words NEWS RELEASE or just NEWS so the recipients know what to expect. This is not a bad idea. Once the journalists on your list know who you are, they'll have a good idea about the quality of your news releases. If you consistently provide timely information about the subjects they cover, they'll open your news releases.

Whether you're promoting a Web site or some other product or service, you should look for some unique characteristic to bring out in the subject line. Possibly the most worn-out subject line on the Internet is "Check Out My New Web Site!" I did a promotion for a Web site called At Home, by appliance maker Hamilton Beach/Proctor-Silex. When you visit the site the first time, you answer a few lifestyle questions after which the site deposits you in one of five different kitchens. Each kitchen is decorated and has appliances to match your lifestyle. We went with the subject line, "This Home Page Has Five Kitchens." The play on the term "home page" might have been lost on some journalists, but was perfect for reporters covering the Net.

"New" is one of those power words that advertisers like to use. But just because your Web site is new or improved doesn't mean reporters will want to visit it. You have to promote the unique characteristics of your site. Lots of sites have contests, or quizzes, or secure ordering. You have to go deeper, looking for an angle that will help you stand out from the crowd. Your audience is the media, and they're looking for a story. It might help to think of the subject line as a headline for a story, and you'll be well on your way to writing news releases that get opened.

One good way to get a feel for effective subject lines is to visit the Usenet newsgroup Net Happenings (comp.internet.net-happenings). It consists almost entirely of news releases, and there are dozens posted every day. Take note of which subject lines grab your attention. Why? Because they were clever, or because they mentioned a subject of great interest to you? You'll notice people making beginner mistakes, such as using ALL CAPITAL LETTERS or very long subject lines.

Figure 6.4 shows a sampling of subject lines from Net Happenings with three of the lines highlighted. The first says "USA Today Hot Web Sites." That line caught my attention—I'd want to know who compiles their list. But look at that second line. Doesn't it look inviting? It reads: "=?iso-8859-1?Q?WWW=3E_Background_Briefing=..." Makes you want to jump right in. The third highlighted line, "Michigan vs. Dr. Kevorkian—DAILY" works very well. It's probably about the trial against the infamous "Dr. Death." The subject line isn't cute or clever, just accurate and brief.

There's no hard and fast rule on subject line length, but you should be aware that long subject lines will be truncated by some e-mail systems. With Eudora and other e-mail programs, users determine how much of the incoming subject line to display. But shorter isn't necessarily better, either, because you want to provide enough information for people to decide whether to open the message. A good guideline is to shorten any subject line over 25 characters long, and never exceed 55.

Avoiding a Bad Beginner's Mistake

When you're sending bulk e-mail, it's advisable to put your medialist in the Bcc field rather than the To field or the Cc field. "Bcc" stands for

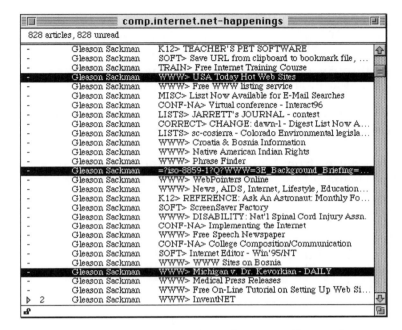

Figure 6.4 Sample subject lines from Net Happenings.

blind carbon copy even though no carbon is involved in the process. When you put an address in the Bcc field, the recipient will not see it. If you put your medialist in the To field or the Cc field, everyone receiving the message will also receive your entire medialist. This can be most embarrassing.

I put my medialist in the To field in one of my first mailings. As I watched the e-mail addresses fly across my screen and out over the Net, I thought, "This technology is amazing. With the press of a few buttons, I just sent a news release to 350 journalists." I went to bed feeling very smug. I eagerly checked my e-mail the next morning. I had more than 50 messages. Most of them went something like this: "You are a complete moron. Remove my name from your list immediately." I quickly realized the magnitude of my mistake. By putting the medialist in the To field, everyone on the list got a 19-page message consisting of a 350-line header and a 20-line news release. I suspect most journalists deleted it without opening it. I hope so.

Some good actually came of this fiasco. When I realized my mistake, I sent a note of apology to the same people (this time, putting the medialist in the Bcc field). After all, these people are my bread and butter. If I lose their goodwill, I lose my ability to promote my customers effectively. I explained what happened and promised not to foul their inboxes in the future. I offered to send the news release again—upon request—without the monster header.

Several journalists thanked me for owning up to my error. Many said, "Don't worry, Steve, it happens all the time." Still others said, "No need to apologize—you've just given me the best medialist I've ever seen." A reporter from National Public Radio bestowed upon me their "Longest Header of the Month" award. Now whenever I receive a news release with a huge medialist attached, I smile with sympathy. Then I see if I can steal any of the names.

I wish I hadn't made that mistake; it was embarrassing and cost me good contacts who asked to be taken off my list. But you're going to make mistakes in this business, too, and because everything is so automated, they'll probably be *big* mistakes. With e-mail, your message is gone in seconds. If you have the wrong date for an event, you'll have to send a second message to correct it. My best advice is that when your moment in the searchlight arrives for some boneheaded e-mail you sent, do your best to make it right. The online press corps won't mind watching you eat a little crow, and, who knows, you might ultimately earn some respect that will serve you in the future.

The Address Fields

If you can't put your medialist in the To field, what do you put there? Your own address. Eudora requires some valid address in the To field. Everyone in the Bcc field will see who you addressed the mail to, so you might as well make it yourself. I use the To field as a flag to let people know I'm sending them a news release. Here's how my typical address fields look:

```
        To: NEWS RELEASE <IPS@olympus.net>
      From: Steve O'Keefe <IPS@olympus.net>
   Subject: Free Review Copy
        Cc:
       Bcc: Medialist
Attachments:
```

You can call yourself any name you want as long as there's a valid e-mail address between the less-than and greater-than signs in the To field. Even though the To and From fields show the same address, the names I use help people understand why they received the message. Some people put their alternate e-mail address in the To field.

In Eudora, you can also use any name for yourself in the From field as long as the e-mail address is correct. You don't have to use the official name on your account, and that can help if you're mailing to several different lists. Sometimes, we use the name Electronic News & Reviews depending on the list we're mailing to.

It's best to leave the Cc field blank, to keep the message from getting cluttered. You can add last-minute names to your medialist in the Bcc field. The Bcc field contains the word "medialist." That's a nickname in Eudora, also known as a group name, mailing list, or distribution list. Figure 6.5 shows a portion of my medialist as it looks in Eudora's Nicknames folder.

You can have multiple nicknames in the Bcc field, or a mix of nicknames and individual names. Some commercial e-mail systems don't allow you to have group names or they severely limit their size. Eudora limits the length of a nickname to 2,000 e-mail addresses. If you want to send e-mail to more than 2,000 addresses, you must use multiple nicknames.

Figure 6.5 Some of the e-mail addresses in the Eudora nickname, medialist.

Some e-mail systems don't have a Bcc field or any way to send blind copies. On these systems, you're better off sending to each address individually (in the To field) rather than lumping people together in the Cc field. In fact, some publicists suggest you get better results if you send the news release separately to each recipient, because they won't feel like they're getting bulk mail. This might work fine for a short list of key media contacts, but it is unnecessary and impractical with a medialist numbering in the hundreds or thousands. And besides, as long as the medialist is in the Bcc field, the recipient may know they're getting bulk mail, but it will look almost identical to a personal pitch.

A better suggestion, if you can't send blind copies, is to get a direct SLIP or PPP Internet account so you can use Eudora or other high-quality software programs for your bulk e-mail. You can probably get a direct Internet account for $10 to $20 a month, which is what you'd pay in postage for a news release to 50 people.

It used to be advisable to send messages to CompuServe addresses *from* CompuServe, to America Online addresses *from* America Online, and so on. CompuServe charged people to receive messages from the Internet, so many folks deleted unsolicited messages without opening them. On America Online, the formatting always looked better when the message was sent from another AOL account. But CompuServe no longer charges for incoming Internet mail, and all e-mail systems have gotten better at receiving mail from other systems. You still have to be careful with your formatting, though, if you want the message to look good across platforms.

Finally, it's best to leave the Attachments field blank and put your entire news release in the body of the message. When you send file attachments to the many different e-mail systems hooked up to the Net, you're just asking for trouble. It's hard to know whether people will be able to receive the files or what the files will look like if they make it through.

The Body of the Message

The meat of your message is the few paragraphs of text found in the body of the e-mail. It would seem straightforward to put in your prose and send it. But you will quickly encounter the biggest bane of the Internet publicist: formatting problems. All Internet software has one common design flaw: the look of the message is determined by the user's software, not the sender's. While this makes it possible for so many people to share the benefits of connectivity, it makes it difficult to provide every viewer with a quality reading experience. Figure 6.6 shows what some folks see when they open their e-mail—and that's after wading through a header that looks like the instruction manual for your VCR.

As far as I know, every e-mail message sent over the Internet goes out as ASCII text. Consequently, what looked like perfect prose on your screen may look like very bad poetry on the receiver's screen. Eudora truncates every line at 76 characters. If the person reading the message has a shorter default line length (as most do on America Online), they will get the kind of jagged line endings shown in Figure 6.6.

Another problem is nonstandard characters, especially so-called curly quotes. Curly quotes are common in word processors, used to distinguish an open quotation mark from a closing one. The apostrophe is also a problem; and dashes are often changed to underscores. When e-mail is sent with curly quotes, they are changed into ASCII equivalents; that is, into meaningless gibberish. Dashes are also problematic, often changed into underscores.

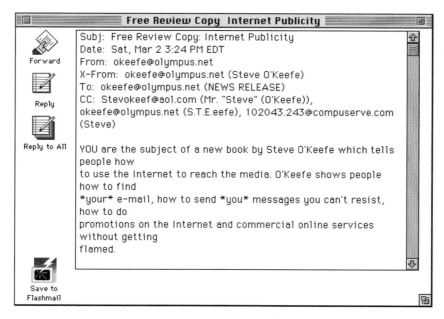

Figure 6.6 A poorly formatted e-mail message.

They way to deal with most formatting problems is to compose your message in a word processor with a 60-character line length. Save the file as ASCII text with hard returns at the end of each line. Then inspect the text file for problems before pasting it into your e-mail message. Obviously, this is more work than you want to go through for day-to-day e-mail, but for news releases going to a large medialist, it's well worth the effort.

Incorrect spelling is another notorious problem with e-mail. Bad spelling is commonplace on the Net because most e-mail programs either don't have spell checkers or they work so poorly. If you're sending bulk e-mail to the media, you don't want a news release littered with typos. This is one more reason to compose your message in a word processor and spell check it before using it in e-mail.

When you save text as ASCII, you lose a lot of your formatting. Tabs disappear, and are often replaced by space bands. Italics and bold drop out; as do larger point sizes, ruling, colors, and unusual characters such as dingbats. To add emphasis to your message, therefore, you must be creative. You can use *asterisks* or _underscores_ to highlight phrases. Using all uppercase letters, however, is considered shouting online and should be used carefully. You might have to rewrite your news release so that it works as ASCII text.

The Signature

A *signature* is a few lines of text you can automatically append to all your outgoing e-mail. The signature is often used like a letterhead, providing contact information for the sender. Like a letterhead, it can include some graphical element. For most news releases, however, it's completely unnecessary.

Your objective with a news release is to entice a request for further information. If the reporter is interested in the story, he or she will contact you by e-mail, replying to the message. I sent thousands of e-mail messages with my full signature before I realized that people always made first contact by e-mail. My signature was wasting six lines of precious cargo space that could be used to deliver a more potent news release. After someone contacted me, I used my full signature in all follow-up e-mail.

The header of your e-mail message already includes your name and/or company name and your e-mail address (in the From field).

There's no need to duplicate this information in the signature. If you want your recipients to visit a Web site or phone you for further information, you're better off including that in the body of the message instead of setting it apart in the signature where it may be ignored.

Formatting is also a big problem with signatures. Your signature may look perfectly formatted in the monospaced font you use, but it will probably look ridiculous in the proportional font of one of your readers (see Figure 6.7). The same goes for ASCII graphics: your replica

```
                              _____
                             |Agent Knowledgebase Associates, Inc.|
                                      P.O. Box 2502            |
            /  ) |     Virginia Beach, Virgina 23450     | (  \
          /  /   |           Phone:   804-495-1210        |  \  \
        _(  (_   |           Fax:     804-495-6319        |  _)  )_
       (((\  \>| /->       http://akainc.com        <-\ |</ /)))
       (\\\\ \ | / /        http://chatweb.com        \  \/ ////)
         \        /_____\        /
          \    _/                                   \_    /
          /   /                                        \    \
         /   /                                            \    \


           "Pioneering and Breaking Into New Paradigms"


                         _____
                        | Agent Knowledgebase Associates, Inc. |
                            P.O. Box 2502          |
           / ) |   Virginia Beach, Virgina 23450    | ( \
          / / |        Phone: 804-495-1210        |  \ \
        _( (_ |        Fax:  804-495-6319      |  _) )_
       (((\  \>| /->    http://akainc.com     <-\ |</ /)))
       (\\\\ \ | / /    http://chatweb.com     \  \/ ////)
         \     /_____\    /
          \  _/                          \_   /
          /  /                              \   \
          /  /                                \   \


           "Pioneering and Breaking Into New Paradigms"
```

Figure 6.7 The top graphic is a signature file in a monospaced font incorporating so-called "ASCII graphics." The same signature file looks messy in a proportionally spaced font (bottom graphic).

of the Starship Enterprise may look more like the garbage barge from Alien to a recipient. You never know where the signature will appear on other e-mail systems, or *if* it will appear; remember, some e-mail systems automatically delete signatures over a certain length.

One good use for a signature is to give instructions on how to get *off* your mailing list. I just take people off if they ask, but some publicists have an automated process (such as sending mail to remove@mysite. com). If you want to include the information from your signature, copy the text from your signature file and paste it into your message (rather than appending the signature file). That way, you have more control over how it looks to the receiver.

Testing

Until you get the hang of it, it's a good idea to test your news releases before embarrassing yourself in front of the media. Put different versions of your own name and e-mail address in the To field *and* the Bcc field. When you receive the Bcc copy, you shouldn't see the name you used in the Bcc field. This is what the release will look like to other recipients with the same software you use. How do the lines break? Does the release look inviting?

If you have multiple e-mail accounts, send the news release to yourself and pile all your other e-mail addresses in the Bcc field. Then check the mail at your different accounts. If you detect formatting problems, rework your release until you get it right.

Most of your mail will go to three distinct services: America Online, CompuServe, or other direct Internet accounts. Try to test your mail on all three. If you don't have accounts, see if you can get a colleague or friend to help you. It took me several tries to get my messages to look good across different platforms, and I still have to test from time to time as these services upgrade their software.

There's an easy way to tell if you're having formatting problems. When someone copies from your mail in his or her reply, and the quoted text looks choppy or contains unusual characters, you've got a problem. Check your formatting again. You may have upgraded your word processing software and forgot to turn off the curly quotes.

Figure 6.8 shows what can happen when a news release goes wrong. This was sent to me by my online friend, Art Kleiner, a talented writer

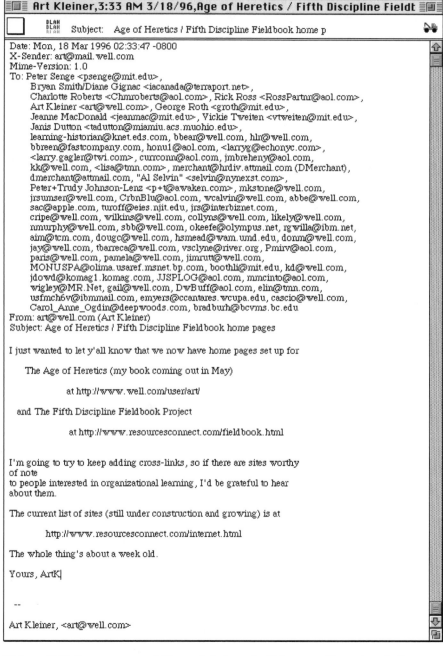

Figure 6.8 Can you spot the mistakes in this e-mail message?

with years of Internet experience. In it, he's promoting his books, *The Age of Heretics* and *The Fifth Discipline Fieldbook*. Imagine you're a reporter receiving this. The first thing you see is a wall of e-mail addresses; Art should have used the Bcc field for his mailing list. Second, the indentation seems somewhat random, and the line endings break poorly. The final mistake is not apparent: one of the URLs was incorrect and Art had to send a follow-up message correcting it. Unfortunately, the follow-up had the same wall of e-mail addresses.

The Medialist

"Where can I get the e-mail addresses of the media?" I see this question almost every day, in e-mail I receive or in discussion groups focused on Internet marketing. The best answer is: "Try your Rolodex."

There *are* lists floating around the Net, especially the famous E-Mail Addresses of the Media compiled by Adam M. Gaffin. The problem is, I haven't seen an update of Gaffin's list since October 1994, which is ancient history in Net life. Most of the addresses on that list are no longer accurate. And the people on that list have been pounded so hard with junk e-mail that if your message goes through, it probably won't get opened. There are a couple other problems with this and similar lists:

- They provide the addresses for publications or stations—not people. You need the addresses of individual journalists if you want to conduct effective online publicity.
- These lists are seldom in the proper format to be used in Eudora or other e-mail programs. By the time you clean them up, you realize you would have been better off starting from scratch.

Nevertheless, it probably is worth hunting down some of the medialists you hear about, just so you can pick a few names and add them to your own list. If you have a friend or colleague who has a good list, he or she might be willing to share it or trade for yours. Or you might find it easier to hire a professional firm to do your e-mail news releases. It can often be cheaper and more effective than trying to maintain your own list. The Resources chapter (Chapter 12) lists names of professional publicists.

The best approach to building your own list is to begin with the media you already deal with on a regular basis. To fill out your medialist, you have to be an e-mail address bloodhound. In the remaining part of this chapter, I'll show you how to sniff out the addresses of anyone you want on your list.

Finding Addresses Offline

Identify the media you want to get close to and start sniffing out those e-mail addresses. Are you in the music business? Pick up the latest copy of *Rolling Stone, Billboard, Guitar Player,* or whatever, and look for the @ sign—a quick visual clue that an address waits for you. Start with the staff box. There should be a generic address for the publication. You can use that address until you find the addresses for individual reporters, although you might find the e-mail addresses for the editors, senior writers, and staff writers there. Magazines like *Red Herring* and *Wired* have them nicely laid out for you. If you can't find the addresses you want in the staff box, fan out and look for them in the story bylines or at the ends of articles.

When the Internet just began to get popular, and an e-mail address was considered chic, many writers put their e-mail addresses at the ends of their articles—although most of these writers would never think of displaying their phone numbers. As magazines got more savvy—and writers were nailed with junk e-mail—the addresses started to disappear. But you may still be able to find writers' e-mail addresses in back issues of your target publications.

If you are after a large, broad-based medialist, you might have to spend a day with your portable computer in the periodical room of a well-stocked library. I've made several such trips and I always come back feeling like a miner who's hit the mother lode. A lot of people expect to find these addresses on the Internet, but hour-for-hour, your time is better spent doing research the old-fashioned way.

As you're no doubt aware, the trend in magazine publishing (as with other large corporations) is to fire everybody and contract out. Many magazines keep a bare-bones staff of managers and editors and hire freelancers to do the writing. No matter what field you're targeting, there's a cadre of freelance writers out there who make their living covering this turf. You probably won't find these people listed in the staff box; rather, look for their e-mail addresses in the writers' credits at the ends of articles.

It's a good idea to work hard to build a good list of freelance writers covering your area(s) of interest. They seldom change e-mail addresses, and they usually write for several publications. You may get their address from *Business Week,* but next week they'll be writing for *The Wall Street Journal* or *Chainsaw Age.* Unlike most editors, freelance writers actually write, therefore, your e-mail news release will reach the in-box of a journalist, *not* an administrator.

The broadcast industry is not immune to corporate restructurings either. If you want to make the news anymore, you have to connect with the producers, the hired guns who pitch story ideas and produce segments. You can send a great story idea to Dateline@NBC.com and wait for Stone Phillips or Jane Pauley to call. Or you can scan the credits for each segment and search the Net for the e-mail addresses of the producers. You'll find that producers move from program to program, but they never seem to leave the business or change their e-mail addresses.

One good way to collect the names of producers is to videotape news shows so that you can more carefully examine the credits. You can usually find a generic e-mail address for the program and the names of segment producers. Videotaping is especially helpful for programs you're never home to watch. You can then look up the producers' e-mail addresses on the Net using the techniques described next. I also keep pen and paper handy so I can write down those lovely e-mail addresses as they flash across my television screen.

For regional coverage, you'll want the e-mail addresses of local radio and television stations. Just call and ask for the e-mail address of the news director. As with the other media outlets, you can use a generic station address until you get a better address. Popular DJs may have their own e-mail addresses that they give out over the air. Rush Limbaugh's address is 70277.2502@compuserve.com, and you can reach Garrison Keillor at gkeillor@madmax.mpr.org.

More directories are starting to include e-mail addresses, too; in a couple years they'll be the best resources for starting a medialist. Three of the biggest media directories are Gale's, Uhlrich's, and Bacon's. They cost hundreds of dollars to buy, but you can find them at large libraries. Of the three, only the 1996 Uhlrich's had e-mail addresses, and these were spotty. These publications tend to give you company addresses, not the individual addresses you want. But they're a start.

A few books also list e-mail addresses. The most notorious is Seth Godin's *E-Mail Addresses of the Rich and Famous.* I grabbed a bunch of

Seth's addresses when the book first came out, but almost all the good ones have changed. In a few years, once the Net has settled down, you'll be able to use addresses you find in books with confidence. Right now, though, such information is usually out of date by the time it's printed.

Finding Addresses on the Internet

There are a few good resources for finding someone's address online. Four11's Online Users Directory has listings for about 11 million people. You can add your name to the list or search for someone else at the Web site: http://www.Four11.com. This is a voluntary directory containing only the names of those people who register. I've had luck finding several critical media contacts at Four11. Figure 6.9 shows its search form.

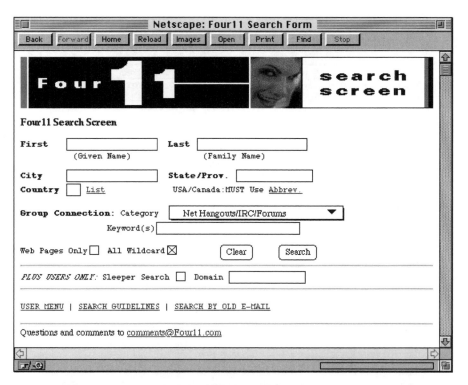

Figure 6.9 Searching for an individual at Four11's Online Users Directory.

If a writer has an e-mail address, there's a good chance he or she has contributed something online that can be tracked down. You can try to find that person through a spider-style search of the Net at Lycos http://www.lycos.com, or Alta Vista http://www.altavista.digital. com, or another spider.

The biggest problem with spider-style searches is that they bring back *too many* matches. If you're looking for one e-mail address, it could be buried in any one of the matching documents, or *none* of them. It's a catch-22: you have to narrow your search criteria to get an acceptable number of hits, but then you might screen out the one document you need. Figure 6.10 shows the results of an Alta Vista search for yours truly, using the Advanced search, which allows me to tighten the match criteria.

A few months ago, I was trying to find the e-mail address of Paul Wallich, who covers the Internet for *Scientific American*. His address

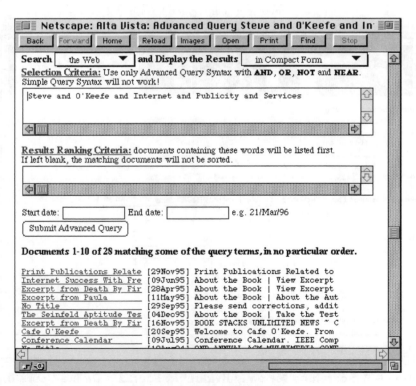

Figure 6.10 Search results from Alta Vista.

wasn't in the staff box or at the end of his articles. I went to Alta Vista and turned up about 20 Web documents, but still couldn't find his e-mail address. From these documents, however, I learned he was a frequent contributor to the Usenet newsgroup soc.feminism. At Alta Vista, you can search Usenet as well as the Web; a Usenet search easily located his e-mail address.

You can also get e-mail addresses by monitoring newsgroups, but be careful. If you get the brilliant idea to steal all the addresses of people contributing to alt.journalism, you should know this isn't an original thought. A lot of media people stay away from this group precisely because they are tired of all the spam. The journalists who still contribute to newsgroups covering media issues are probably very hostile to junk e-mail. Most media people have little time or patience for Usenet. A better strategy is to stick to the newsgroups that cover your areas of interest and watch for contributions by journalists.

One very sneaky way of getting the e-mail addresses of the media is to surf the feedback threads at various Web sites. You'll find discussion threads at HotWired, The San Jose Mercury News, GNN, Time-Warner, and many other newspaper, magazine, and television show Web sites. Journalists often get involved in these threads, either to defend their stories or because they've been asked to help drum up discussion. You may not be able to find their addresses in their bylines, but you can often find them in the threads. Figure 6.11 shows an example from HotWired's threads. Can you spot the staff writer's e-mail address?

Finding Addresses on Commercial Online Services

You can find e-mail addresses on America Online using some of the same techniques already described. You can note when members of the press reveal themselves in discussion groups. You can also search the message areas associated with media outlets. Figure 6.12 shows the staff box for *Atlantic Monthly* on America Online—it has a wealth of e-mail addresses.

America Online also allows you to search the entire membership directory by keyword. Many people do not fill out the membership "profile" used to compile the directory, but enough do to make a search worth the effort. If you're going to do this, though, I suggest you turn

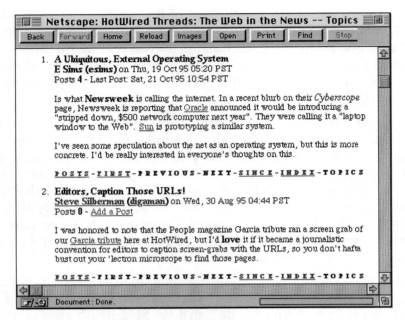

Figure 6.11 HotWired discussion threads.

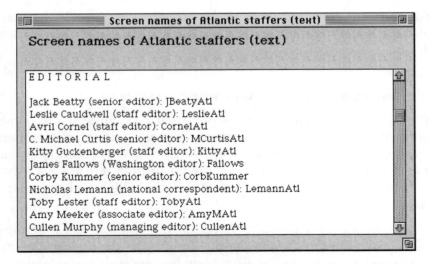

Figure 6.12 *Atlantic Monthly*'s staff box from America Online.

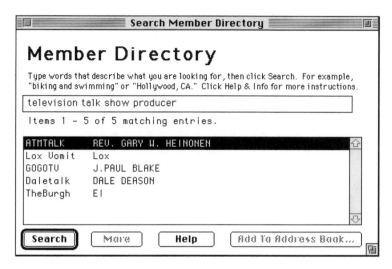

Figure 6.13 Membership search on America Online.

on your system log to capture your session and then edit it offline. Searching for words like "newspaper," "journalist," "TV," will give you a long list of matches, as shown in Figure 6.13. You can then quickly open and close the profile for everyone on the list, and their vital information will be captured in your log. Although you'll get a few premium e-mail addresses this way, most of your capture file will be junk. Why? Because if you searched for "newspaper," you get not only newspaper reporters but also everyone whose profile says they enjoy "reading newspapers."

Similar strategies work well on CompuServe. You can't do a keyword search of the general membership directory, but you can search individual forums this way. CompuServe requires people to "join" their special-interest forums if they want to fully participate in forum activities. Forum members can build little profiles for the membership directory, and you can search these by keyword. Figure 6.14 shows the results of a search for "newspaper" in one forum, revealing the address of a Swiss music journalist.

If you have something to promote to people in Marketing or Public Relations, you might want to search for journalists in CompuServe's excellent PRSIG discussion group. But remember, to search a membership

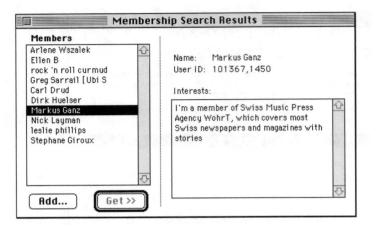

Figure 6.14 Searching a forum membership directory on CompuServe.

directory, you must first join the forum. But since there's never a cost to join, this is always recommended. Then you just use the pull-down menus under Members to search the directory. My version of Compu-Serve's software doesn't allow me to capture the information the way America Online does, so I just copy the names I want and paste them into my word processor.

You can also view the staff boxes of online media outlets that maintain CompuServe forums. Once again, you have to join the forums to access this information. Under the pull-down menus, you'll find one that says Sysop Roster or something similar. Open the roster and you'll be rewarded with some valuable e-mail addresses. Look what I found in *Rolling Stone* magazine's roster in Figure 6.15.

You can try these same techniques on other services, such as Prodigy and the Microsoft Network. The basic maneuvers are:

1. Search the membership directory by name or keyword.
2. Search discussion groups for contributions by journalists.
3. Look for the staff boxes of popular online publications.

You can also find canned medialists in the libraries on CompuServe, America Online, and other services. But beware of using these. I've downloaded several of them, only to find they contain the same hope-lessly out-of-date addresses as the Net's famous Medialist. Using the

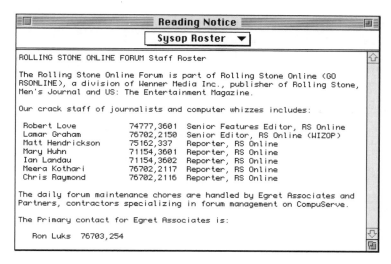

Figure 6.15 Sysop roster for the Rolling Stone forum on CompuServe.

search techniques just described will quickly yield a fresher, more personalized medialist.

Managing Your Medialist

The media is a moving target. TV producers change programs on a monthly basis. Magazine editors seem almost as fleet of foot. As noted earlier, most magazine content comes from freelancers who are mobile by definition. E-zines appear, get hot, fizzle and fold, all before they make it to your medialist. That's why you should focus on the *people* who write the stories, not on the outlets where the work appears.

Who do you think opens the e-mail at time@aol.com? Probably the lowest-level staffer on *Time* magazine's editorial ladder. There is a small chance your message will be forwarded to the appropriate person, so this generic address is worth keeping until you find something better. If you ever get a reply from *Time* magazine, it will probably come from a specific staffer, at which time you can capture his or her e-mail address and add it to your list. Use this pattern of working from generic addresses to personal addresses to slowly build a good medialist.

Definitely track the responses you get from your medialist to help you use the list more effectively. I keep my medialist in my word

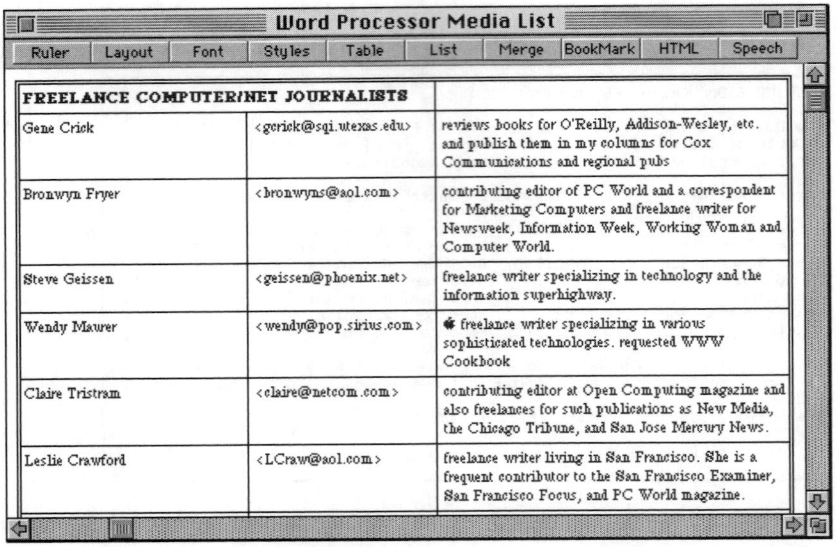

FREELANCE COMPUTER/NET JOURNALISTS		
Gene Crick	<gcrick@sqi.utexas.edu>	reviews books for O'Reilly, Addison-Wesley, etc. and publish them in my columns for Cox Communications and regional pubs
Bronwyn Fryer	<bronwyns@aol.com>	contributing editor of PC World and a correspondent for Marketing Computers and freelance writer for Newsweek, Information Week, Working Woman and Computer World.
Steve Geissen	<geissen@phoenix.net>	freelance writer specializing in technology and the information superhighway.
Wendy Maurer	<wendy@pop.sirius.com>	freelance writer specializing in various sophisticated technologies. requested WWW Cookbook
Claire Tristram	<claire@netcom.com>	contributing editor at Open Computing magazine and also freelances for such publications as New Media, the Chicago Tribune, and San Jose Mercury News.
Leslie Crawford	<LCraw@aol.com>	freelance writer living in San Francisco. She is a frequent contributor to the San Francisco Examiner, San Francisco Focus, and PC World magazine.

Figure 6.16 A sample of my medialist in WordPerfect.

processor because it's convenient. I use WordPerfect, which allows me to keep the list in a database format. A section of my list is shown in Figure 6.16. The first column is the contact name or publication. The second column is the e-mail address. The third column contains notes.

You might want to keep your medialist in a database program or a contacts program—whatever you're most comfortable with. Whatever you do, though, it's important to be able to isolate the e-mail addresses so they can be exported to your e-mail software. It's also nice to have notes about who has responded to previous mail and what topics people cover. These indicators will help you determine who to send messages to.

You may prefer to use a professional e-mail service rather than maintain your own list. My list is my baby. It's groomed constantly, updated at least once a week, expanded with religious zeal, trimmed as required by good netiquette. For some magazines I have the e-mail addresses of everyone on the editorial staff. I keep notes to remind me what kind of material they like, what they don't want—even what their hobbies are.

My clients could keep their own lists—and many of them do—but they like using my services as well because my list is so large and up to date. It's not practical for most people to keep such a detailed medialist. It's a better strategy to maintain a list of your most important, consistent media contacts, and rent a list or use a professional service when you need a broad-based push.

Formatting E-Mail Addresses

All e-mail programs are fussy about the way you format e-mail addresses. In Eudora, you can't use commas or colons; they are interpreted as the end of an e-mail address and will cause the mailing to abort. This problem always surfaces when dealing with CompuServe, which does use commas in their e-mail addresses, as follows:

Steve O'Keefe 102043,243

This address works fine when your mailing *from* CompuServe, but if you're mailing *to* CompuServe across the Internet, you have to change the comma to a period, as follows:

Steve O'Keefe <102043.243@compuserve.com>

The following addresses would also cause problems in Eudora:

Vinton Cerf, Father of the Internet <cerf@xxxx>
Wired: Louis Rosetto - Editor <lrosetto@wired.com>
NBC Nightly News nightly@nbc.com

The first e-mail address has a comma and the second has a colon; both will cause Eudora to abort the mailing. The third does not mark off the e-mail address with less than and greater than symbols. Eudora will interpret the entire line as an e-mail address and it will be undeliverable. Eudora will accept a plain e-mail address, or one marked off in different ways. Any of the following address formats would be acceptable:

ak@mecklermedia.com
Andrew Kantor <ak@mecklermedia.com>
(Andrew Kantor) ak@mecklermedia.com

Eudora is a pretty friendly e-mail program in other respects. As far as I can tell, it's not case-sensitive: you can mix lower- and uppercase letters. It also ignores space bands in e-mail addresses. You'll notice that many America Online addresses have capitalization and space bands, but they read in Eudora just fine. Here are some other punctuation marks that are acceptable to Eudora:

"   quotation marks

'   apostrophes

-           hyphens

_   underscores

.   periods

;   semicolons

*   asterisks

&   ampersands

Address Books

You can keep your medialist in whatever program you like—word processing, database, spreadsheet, contact, and so on—but you need to get the addresses into your e-mail software before you can send a message. Therefore, you will want to set up your medialist so that you can easily extract the e-mail addresses from the rest of the information. Then you can dump the addresses into your e-mail software's address book.

Eudora allows you to create a nickname for a large group of people and then mail to that nickname. Figure 6.17 shows the Eudora Nicknames window. I've highlighted the nickname SteveOkeefe which I use for testing my news releases. Three of my e-mail addresses are included in the nickname. (They contain some strange punctuation as a reminder to myself of what punctuation is acceptable to Eudora.)

When I first started sending news releases to the media, I would sometimes send two messages to the same address, like this:

Joe Cool - HotWired Surf Team <surf@hotwired.com>

Mary Hot - HotWired Surf Team <surf@hotwired.com>

I hoped that whoever processed the mail would forward my messages to the appropriate party. When you send mail using Eudora's Bcc field, however, everything except the e-mail address is stripped out of the message. Thus, the person opening the Surf mail at HotWired in the preceding example would see two copies of the same message, with no indication that one was for Joe Cool and the other for Mary Hot.

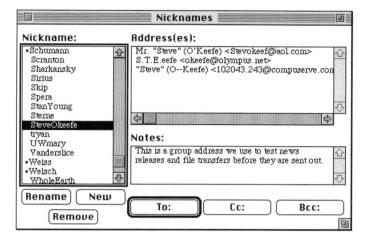

Figure 6.17 The Nicknames window in Eudora.

I'm mentioning this to you because there is no reason to include the recipients' names in the nickname you use in Eudora. If you mail using the Bcc field, all the names will be lost. You can't address a message to Peter Lewis <mail@nytimes.com> and hope someone at *The New York Times* will forward it to Peter, because his name will be stripped out when the message is sent. This is another reason it's so important to get the e-mail addresses for individual journalists rather than stations or publications.

When I am ready to e-mail a news release, I go through my medialist and select those people who would likely be interested in the subject. Then I copy their e-mail addresses and paste them into a Eudora nickname. Figure 6.18 shows a portion of my medialist as it appears in Eudora. There are no names, titles, publications, notes, or anything else—just the bare e-mail addresses of my contacts. When I'm ready to send my message, I just put the nickname Medialist in the Bcc field and off it goes.

Address books on America Online, CompuServe, and other services are not nearly as easy to use as Eudora's. CompuServe allows you to use group names, but everyone on the group list must also be in your main address book. That means your address book can get choked with names. And since names have to be added to your address book one at a time, it can be a slow, painful process to build a good medialist on CompuServe. Figure 6.19 shows an example of CompuServe's address book with the group name Journalists highlighted.

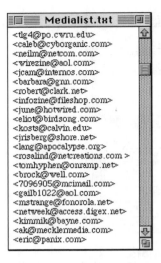

Figure 6.18 My medialist in Eudora.

America Online is even less friendly. You can't build group names
on America Online, and you can't blind-copy people. Prodigy allows
you to build group names, but you can't blind-copy people on the list.
It can be difficult paging through your Prodigy address book, though,

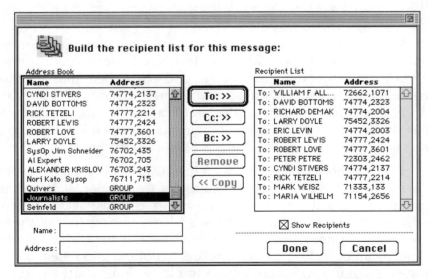

Figure 6.19 Using group names in CompuServe's address book.

Figure 6.20 Prodigy address book with message creation window in back.

with only a few names shown on each page. Figure 6.20 shows a Prodigy address book including a group name called Wholesale.

All the online services have restrictions on the number of e-mail addresses you can keep in your address book, how many group names you can have (at one time, Prodigy only allowed two), and how many addresses you can pile into a group name. At this writing, Eudora tops out at 2,000 names in a nickname file. All of these parameters are changing, though, so check with your current provider to find out your limits.

I have over 2,000 names on my medialist and I've mailed to as many as 800 at one time. But ramming that list through CompuServe, America Online, Prodigy, or other services would be a logistical nightmare, so if you're doing any kind of heavy e-mailing, it pays to get a direct connection to the Net and use Eudora or one of the other excellent e-mail programs available.

News Release Checklist

Figure 6.21 shows the checklist I use when preparing an e-mail news release. Most of the steps will apply to your work, as well. I use the lines following each item for notes such as the date the task was completed or the file names I used for important documents. Even with all my preparation and my checklist completed, I double-check the message just before I launch it to make sure the medialist is in the Bcc field.

Figure 6.21 Electronic News Release Checklist.

Electronic News Release Checklist

Writing:
- ❏ Write News Release _____
- ❏ Spell check/Print/Proofread _____
- ❏ Get Client Approval _____

Mailing List:
- ❏ Open Medialist File _____
- ❏ Save with New Name _____
- ❏ Delete Inappropriate Media _____
- ❏ Isolate E-mail Addresses _____
- ❏ Save as Text _____

Sending Release:
- ❏ Create New Nickname for Medialist _____
- ❏ Open the Medialist Text File _____
- ❏ Select All, Copy, and Paste into Nickname _____
- ❏ Create a New Message _____
- ❏ TO: NEWS RELEASE <my e-mail address> _____
- ❏ BCC: New Nickname _____
- ❏ Open News Release Text File _____
- ❏ Select All, Copy, and Paste into Message _____
- ❏ DOUBLE-CHECK: ❏ No Signature   ❏ TO: Field   ❏ BCC: Field
- ❏ Print Message _____
- ❏ Queue Message _____

Inquiries:
- ❏ Send Digital Flyers _____
- ❏ Forward Important Responses to Client _____

Returned Mail:
- ❏ Update/Delete Bad Addresses in Medialist _____

Troubleshooting

No matter how good your medialist is, you'll get some returns after each mailing. You have to open each returned message and try to figure out why it was not deliverable. We've covered too much material in this chapter to go into the details here, but Chapter 11, Firefighting and Follow-Up, will tell you how to troubleshoot returned e-mail. You'll also learn advanced techniques for medialist management in that chapter. For now, let's recap the most important points for preparing e-mail news releases.

Top Tips

- **Focus on Individuals:** Build your medialist with the e-mail addresses of individual journalists—not just the publications or stations they work for.

- **Pitch a Story:** No matter who or what you're promoting, try to tie into current events. Use your news release to present a story idea built around your client.

- **Keep it Short:** Anything more than a screenful is wasteful. Use your news release to entice a request for further information. Don't try to tell the whole story in one short e-mail.

- **Be Appropriate:** Just because you have a medialist doesn't mean you have to send mail to everyone on it. Only mail to those people who are likely to be interested in your message.

- **Remove on Request:** When someone asks to be taken off your list, remove him or her immediately. You will only anger that person and damage your reputation if you continue mailing there.

- **Format Carefully:** Be kind to your readers. Test your e-mail on different services. Try to format your messages so they will be readable by everyone.

CHAPTER 7

Announcements

When you're trying to reach the media online, you use a news release. When you're trying to reach the public, you use an announcement. Announcements are placed in discussion groups on the Internet and the commercial online services (America Online, CompuServe, etc.). You use these postings to tell people about a new Web site, an event, an appearance, a news item, anything that's appropriate.

Appropriate news items and announcements are welcome in most discussion groups. We'll talk about how to approach an announcement campaign, how to write a good announcement, how to find appropriate discussion groups, and the mechanics of posting your messages. We'll also follow up and see what good and evil can come from an announcement campaign.

Conversely, posting inappropriate announcements is what gets many newcomers to the Net in trouble. To avoid such a situation, keep in mind that these are *discussion* groups you're posting to, and most of them don't look kindly on ads. As defined earlier, the indiscriminate posting of messages is known as spamming. The angry responses to spam are called flames. We'll carefully examine ways to stay out of the battle between the spammers and the flamers.

Topics covered in this chapter include:

- **The Announcement Campaign:** The goals of the campaign, and how to organize the work, including checklists, distribution reports, and more.

- **Spammers versus Flamers:** Inappropriate announcements in discussion groups are the source of a great deal of vitriol on the Internet. We'll look at acceptable use policies and other guidelines for online behavior.

- **Writing Good Announcements:** It all starts with an irresistible subject line, then continues with a short message offering further information upon request.

- **Usenet Newsgroups:** The toughest audience online, and yet I've been posting to newsgroups for years with virtually no flames. I'll show you how reach this audience without reaching for the fire extinguisher.

- **Internet Mailing Lists:** The most difficult audience to reach online, and yet one of the most responsive. I'll show how to visit these virtual communities.

- **America Online:** Many internauts look down their noses at America Online. When you see how responsive their members are, though, you'll make this a regular campaign stop.

- **CompuServe:** CompuServe's forum structure rewards certain announcements and discourages others. We'll show you how to give them what they want.

- **Prodigy:** Most publicists have written off Prodigy. With more than a million members, that write-off could cost you.

- **Other Services:** There are many smaller services and regional boards that cater to niche audiences, and large web sites are adding user forums.

- **Defending Your Postings:** Know your rights, and know when you're wrong. We'll talk about both the *theory* and everyday *practice* of discussion group postings.

- **Top Tips:** Simple instructions for walking on coals without scorching your feet.

The Announcement Campaign

Imagine a politician at a rally being told she or he can't shake anyone's hand and you'll understand the agony the Internet publicist goes through. As a publicist, you hear stories about 30 million people online (or 50 million, or even 100 million), then you're told you can't talk to them about your products or services. That's so frustrating! If you ignore the warnings and try to post messages to all these people, there are self-appointed "judges" on the Internet who will make your life miserable in a nanosecond.

The goal of the announcement campaign is to reach your target audience through messages in discussion groups that are appropriate and where they will be welcomed. Most discussion groups prohibit outright commercial advertisements, so you have to be very careful with both the content and style of your message. The best way to understand what you're hoping to achieve is to look at the result of an announcement campaign: the Distribution Report. Figure 7.1 shows the Distribution Report for an announcement campaign my firm did for John Wiley & Sons. We were promoting the book *World Wide Web Marketing* by Jim Sterne.

Figure 7.1 The Distribution Report shows where messages were posted during an announcement campaign.

Distribution Report

Discussion Groups Where Messages Were Posted

Client: John Wiley & Sons
Book: World Wide Web Marketing

Usenet Newsgroups:

alt.business.misc

misc.entrepreneurs

misc.entrepreneurs.moderated

rec.arts.books.marketplace

alt.books.technical

misc.books.technical

comp.internet.library

alt.internet.services

alt.online-service

alt.cyberspace

alt.wired

(continues)

Figure 7.1 (*Continued*)

comp.infosystems.www.misc

comp.infosystems.www.authoring.misc

comp.infosystems.www.authoring.html

comp.infosystems.www.announce

comp.internet.net-happenings

Internet Mailing Lists:

htmarcom@rmii.com

adforum@listserv.unc.edu

biz-marketing-consulting@world.std.com

buscom-l@utepvm.ep.utexas.edu

inet-marketing@popco.com

market-l@mailer.fsu.edu

mt-l@uhccvm.uhcc.hawaii.edu

newprod@world.std.com

prforum@indycms.iupui.edu

product_dev@msoe.edu

America Online:

Excerpt Stored in Business Strategies Forum in the Advertising/Demos Library

AD SIG - Advertising/Internet & WWW

INTERNET - Internet Center Message Board/Internet books

INTERNET - Internet Center Message Board/World Wide Web

INTERNET - Web Diner/Diner Chat/Marketing Gumbo

EPUB- Resource Center/Web Publishing

SIMBA - Cowles Media Daily/New Media

SIMBA - Message Board/Advertising

BW - Business Week/Marketing/Web Information for Business

INBIZ - Internet Bus. Forum/Marketing/ Safe & Effective Advertising

EZONE - Business Strategies/Marketing/Marketing Tools

CompuServe:

Excerpt Stored in PR & Marketing Forum/Products & Services Library

Book Preview Forum +   PREVIEW/Previews & Overviews

Internet New Users Forum +   INETNE/Business on the Net

Internet Publishing Forum +   INETPU/Internet Marketing

Internet Resources Forum +	INETRE / Books & Magazines
Computer Consult. Forum +	CONSULT / Business Issues
PR and Marketing Forum +	PRSIG / Using Internet
PR and Marketing Forum +	PRSIG / Products & Services
The Entrepreneur's Forum +	SMALLBIZ / CyberBusiness
Industry Week Forum +	IWFOR / Sales & Marketing
Fortune Forum +	FFORUM / Entrepreneurs
PC World Online +	PPCWFORUM / Cyberspace

Prodigy:

Books & Writing BB / NonFiction
Internet Support BB / Internet Information
Internet Support BB / WWW
Computer BB / News & Announcements
Money Talk BB / Internet / Biz on the Internet
Your Business BB / Computer Industry / Marketing
Your Business BB / Great Ideas / WWW Marketing

In each section of the Distribution Report is a list of discussion groups where messages were posted. Some of the names of the discussion groups are cryptic. Usenet uses a hierarchical classification system for newsgroups, which we discuss shortly. The commercial services have *topics* inside *forums*. The groups listed in the Distribution Report begin with the forum name (and/or its Go word or Keyword), the topic name, the subtopic, and so on, until you get to where the messages were actually posted.

Now let's take a look at the message we posted in these groups. Figure 7.2 shows the generic version; the actual wording had to be adjusted for each group.

Figure 7.2 Discussion group posting for the book *World Wide Web Marketing*.

Discussion Group Posting

Client: John Wiley & Sons
Book: World Wide Web Marketing
Subject Line: Sample Chapter: WWW Marketing

(continues)

Figure 7.2 (*Continued*)

Would you like to see a sample chapter from a plain-English guide to Internet marketing? If so, just send me e-mail with the subject line: "Send Sterne."

I'll send you back a chapter from World Wide Web Marketing, a new book by Jim Sterne, author of the popular "Marketing on the Internet" seminar series. The book is a nontechnical guide to Web marketing offering tips on managing your company's image, finding customers, selling products, monitoring your success online, and much more.

You can also find information about the book at two Web sites (of course): Jim Sterne's Target Marketing site <http://www.targeting.com> and John Wiley & Sons, Publishers <http://www.wiley.com>

The goal of the announcement campaign is to get your message in front of people who potentially have an interest in it. The Internet and commercial online services have thousands of discussion groups where people exchange ideas on specified topics. Your audience, therefore, is conveniently segmented into special-interest groups. If you can identify the discussion groups where people will be interested in your message, you can post to them.

Here are the basic steps in conducting an announcement campaign.

1. Write an announcement.
2. Locate appropriate discussion groups.
3. Post your message.
4. Follow up.

Whether it's Usenet newsgroups or Prodigy forums, the pattern is the same: find the groups, post your message, and follow up. Figure 7.3 shows the Announcement Campaign Checklist we use to organize our efforts at Internet Publicity Services.

Figure 7.3 Announcement Campaign Checklist.

Announcement Campaign Checklist

Digital Flyer:

❑ Write Copy _____

❑ Spell-check/Print/Proofread _____

❑ Save as Text _____

❑ Upload to Libraries on AOL, CIS _____

Announcement:

❑ Write Announcement _____
❑ Spell-check/Print/Proofread _____
❑ Save as Text _____
❑ Create Usenet List _____
❑ Create Mailing List List _____
❑ Create Forum Lists for AOL, CIS, PDY _____

❑ Get Approval for Announcement _____

Posting:

❑ Post to Usenet _____
❑ Subscribe to Mailing Lists _____
❑ Send to Mailing Lists _____
❑ Post to AOL, CIS, PDY _____

Follow-Up:

❑ Check Usenet Every Day for Three Days _____
❑ Check Mailing Lists and Note When Message Hits _____
❑ Check AOL, CIS, PDY, Once or Twice _____

Inquiries:

❑ Print All Feedback _____
❑ Send Digital Flyers _____
❑ Notify Client of Important Responses _____

❑ Unsubscribe from Mailing Lists _____
❑ Prepare Distribution Report _____

We will look at the kinds of announcement campaigns you are likely to run. Then we will examine how to prepare a good announcement. We'll deal right away with the subject of netiquette: spammers, flamers, and appropriate postings. Then I'll show you how to find discussion groups and post to them on the Internet and the commercial online services.

Spammers vs. Flamers

I want to deal with this issue immediately, because there are many misconceptions about posting announcements in discussion groups. You may have heard that you can't advertise on the Internet without being flamed. This is simply not true. People advertise all the time; sometimes they get flamed and sometimes they don't. If you follow my advice in this chapter, you are likely to get very few flames, and you'll know how to handle any you receive.

To repeat, spamming is the indiscriminate posting of messages, either in discussion groups or through e-mail. The key word here is indiscriminate; that is, posting messages without attempting to determine whether they're of interest to the audience. A classic example of spam is the low-cost long-distance telephone ads you see plastered around the Net every few days. Spam is not always commercial, though, you sometimes see humorous or innocuous spams.

If you post inappropriate messages, you might get flamed. Again, flaming is done by people who object to your message and tell you about it, usually in unkind e-mail. Most discussion groups are unrestricted forums and flames are an attempt to get you to reconsider your behavior. There are other consequences for violating netiquette, the Internet's unwritten code of behavior. People who know how to use the new technology can make your life miserable. You could be blacklisted, your messages may be canceled, you might receive e-mail bombs that clog your mailbox, your outgoing mail could be blocked, your Internet service might be cut off. The list of possible repercussions goes on and on, up to and including death threats.

Rampant hostility on the Internet is a subject worthy of sociological dissertations. It seems to stem from a combination of an unrestricted environment and the absence of the calming effect of actual human contact. Spammers and flamers have a difficult time regarding each other as human beings. In the detached world of cyberspace, tempers don't just flare, they spontaneously combust. As more discussion groups move to moderated vehicles, however, the hostility online is starting to ease. Still, you need to monitor what you say if you don't want to be targeted by Internet vigilantes.

Acceptable Use Policies

There are two basic types of discussion groups: *moderated* and *unmoderated*. Moderated means that someone is in charge and has the authority to block or remove posts he or she doesn't approve of. All discussion groups on commercial online services are moderated. They usually have two levels of control over postings. First, there are the terms of service you consented to when you opened your account. These describe acceptable and unacceptable behavior. Here is an excerpt from America Online's terms of service concerning commercial activity:

> Advertising and Solicitation. You may not use AOL to send unsolicited advertising, promotional material, or other forms of solicitation to other Members except in those specified areas that are designated for such a purpose (e.g., the classified area).

The second level of discussion group control is exercised by forum administrators or *sysops*. They may have their own sets of guidelines for the kinds of messages they will allow in their forums. There's really no point in trying to fight with these sysops about whether you can post your message. They have the authority to remove any posting they want for any reason. You might be able to negotiate with them, but they have the final say.

Many Internet discussion groups are also moderated. Your postings must be approved by a moderator before they are distributed to the group. If the moderator approves, your posting is acceptable. If the moderator doesn't approve, your posting doesn't go up. Moderated groups really cut down on spam and flame wars, which is why more people are forsaking unrestricted groups in favor of these moderated forums.

Unmoderated discussion groups are wide-open forums. There may be *guidelines* for postings, but no *rules*. You are free to post whatever you want. Some people act like they own these groups, and may flame you or retaliate against you if they don't like your postings. But they aren't owners, and they have no legal right to restrict your contributions. The only law that governs unmoderated discussion groups is the authority claimed by various governments (prohibiting distribution of obscene material, for example) and the rules set by your Internet service provider.

Here is a relevant passage from the acceptable use policy (AUP) my Internet service provider uses:

> Advertising may not be "broadcast" or otherwise sent on an intrusive basis to any user of the network or any directly or

```
indirectly attached network.  However, when requeste
user of the networks, product information and other co
messages are permitted to be transmitted over the networ
```

I suggest you check the boilerplate of your online services agreeme to see what they say about commercial messages. If you end up with legal dispute on your hands, these documents will probably determine the outcome. But if you provide information only to those who are likely to want it, then you won't run into any disagreements you can't solve quickly and calmly.

At the end of this chapter, I have some suggestions for defending your postings. At this point, I don't want the discussion of flames to take away from the positive information about how to distribute your message in an appropriate way. For now, let's just say you shouldn't post messages indiscriminately. Now let's take a look at the kind of message you *can* post, and how.

Writing Good Announcements

You can tell what works and what doesn't just by spending a few hours reading discussion groups. When presented with a menu of subject lines to choose from, which ones attract you and why? Have you ever opened a message, then immediately closed it because it was too long or poorly formatted? When you're spending your valuable time online, what do you like to see and what do you hate? If you write the kind of message you'd want to read, chances are other people will also find it valuable.

All discussion group postings, whether on commercial online services, Usenet newsgroups, or Internet mailing lists, have the same basic structure: a header, a subject line, and the body of the message. These parts are illustrated in Figure 7.4, a sample message from a Usenet newsgroup viewed with NewsWatcher software. We'll look at each part and see how to make them work for you.

The Header

The header identifies the sender of the message. It usually includes the date and the subject line as well, but we'll deal with the subject line separately. You can control the information in the header by setting your

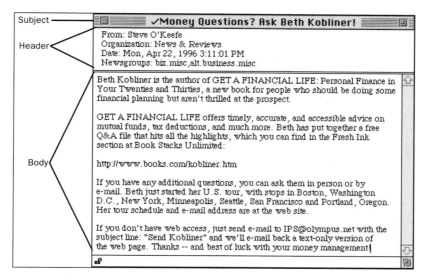

Figure 7.4 A Usenet newsgroup posting, showing the structure of most discussion group announcements.

preferences in whatever software you're using. For example, you may choose to use your name, a company name, or some other name. Your e-mail address is embedded within your message. Even though it's not shown in the header in Figure 7.4, people can reply to your message via e-mail from Usenet, and they can trace your message if they need to. You can get around this with anonymous remailers, but that's beyond the scope of this book.

Some e-mail and news reader software programs allow you to include an organization name as well as your personal name and e-mail address. You can leave this field blank or use it convey extra information. For example, you might want to put your toll-free phone number in the organization field so that it's automatically included in the header of every post. The more material you include in the header, the less you have to include in the body of your message.

Subject Line

When people are following discussion groups, they often decide whether to read your message based on its subject line. Figure 7.5 shows a list of subject lines from the Usenet newsgroup alt.business.

		alt.business.misc

395 articles, 395 unread

-		Ron in Seattle	Police/Security Guard stuff F S/trade
-		Peggy Hendricks	-->BEST Opportunity for "AVERAGE" Networker<--
-		Info	*** Webspace Rental $10 - No Setup Fee.
-		onering@tribeca....	!!DON'T READ THIS!!
-		ComPlex Plastics...	PLASTICS ? we are looking for agents , R U interested ?
▷	2	Greg Mathews	**** Main Agents wanted ****,
-		J.F. Simms & Co.	*** Advertise FREE ***
▷	5	Rob Harford	It's Tax Time Again! Have You Had Enough?
-		Larry Burnett	+++++ UPGRADE YOUR LIFE +++++
-		Larry Burnett	^^^^^ EASY TURNKEY BUSINESS ^^^^^
▷	2	hmjobs1051@aol...	EARN $500+ WEEKLY !............PT FROM HOME
▷	2	jjeirles@csrlink.net	***A GREAT OPPORTUNITY TO MAKE MONEY***
-		FREE Report !!!	HOW TO Receive a WebSite for LESS than $2.00 a Day...
-		S. Reidy	===> Honest PC Business (for a change) <===
-		NEW WebSite !!!	"NEW" Opportunities Site !!!!
▷	2	Hypersex	EXCITING BUSINESS OPPORTUNITIES
-		Jay H Williams	BROCHURES-**-BROCHURES-**-BROCHURES-*...
-		Bill Chapman	REDUCE INVENTORY
-		Nike_M@ltec.net	Re: Affordable Southwest Living- Buyer BEWARE
-		mario carta	MUST SELL 8 CONDOS MIAMI EXCELLENT INCO...
-		Sidney Lieberman	Pay your home mortgage at a discount
-		homer.s@lds.co.uk	CD-ROMS.
-		Tom Mearis	Re: WINNING BLACKJACK
-		Kenneth Kwong	Make $$$ Using Internet

Figure 7.5 Subject lines from a Usenet newsgroup.

misc. The first column shows the number of messages in each thread. The second column shows the sender's name. As you can see, some people use the name field to deliver an extra message, such as "FREE Report!!!" The third column shows the subject lines of the messages. People use a lot of formatting gimmicks to get their messages to stand out. Which messages would you read first?

The best subject line is one that is irresistible to members of your target audience. But that's an elusive goal. Usually, you'll have to modify your subject line to appeal to the audience of the particular group you're posting to. For example, people in the newsgroup sci.life-extension are going to be more focused than those reading alt.misc.

The most overworked subject line in all of cyberspace is "Check Out My New Web Site!" I've found the best results come from subject lines that pose questions, such as "Confused about Chat?" If you are giving away a help file as part of your campaign, then you can ask a question in the subject line and offer a solution in your message.

Also try to incorporate so-called power words in your subject line. You can find a list of these words in any direct marketing manual. They include tried-and-true manipulators like "new," "fast," "hot," "save," "sex," and "free"—you get the idea. Keep your subject lines shorter than 55 characters so they aren't truncated. And DON'T USE ALL CAP-ITAL LETTERS. As I said before, this makes your subject line harder to read and is considered shouting online and bad netiquette.

I did an announcement campaign for my brother's advertising agency that was unusual and very successful. I noticed that the second most popular page on my own Web site was the one called dud.html where I displayed a campaign that failed. People love looking at fail-ures—it's like driving by an accident, but on the info highway. That gave me the idea for my brother's campaign.

"Kelly," I said, "We're going to build your announcement campaign around the theme 'World's Worst Web Site.' What do you think?" There was a long pause at the other end of the line. Kelly eventually went along, though; his ad agency is unconventional, and he doesn't mind taking risks. I figured that people love to bash Web sites, and advertis-ing agencies are kind of notorious on the Net for building pretentious sites. We decided to poke fun at ad agencies while calling attention to the strengths of my brother's site: great graphics that are quick to load. Here's the posting:

```
Subject: World's Worst Web Site?

Advertising agencies. Bandwidth busting graphics. Idiotic
image maps. All style, no substance. Don't use complete
sentences.

O'Keefe World. Full-service advertising agency. E-Z load
graphics. Best banners in the business. Exploding thumbnail
portfolio. Some complete sentences.

http://www.okeefe.com

Ideas worth stealing.
```

We built a lot of traffic with this message—and a lot of goodwill on the Net for our sense of humor. No one could resist the subject line, "World's Worst Web Site?" It gave us the opportunity to talk about our client's strengths without the hyperbole associated with most Web site announcements. The tag line "ideas worth stealing" also plays into the Internet's fondness for larceny. If the ideas are really worth stealing, many people will find them worth paying for.

In many cases, just getting people to open your message is more important than getting them to respond. If you're promoting a product or business, much of the benefit of an announcement campaign comes through the name recognition you get from your postings. A good subject line will prompt your target audience to open the message. After that, a message that's brief and to the point will help them remember your name.

For some people, the subject line *is* the message. I like to work the name of the client or product into the subject line if I can, because more people see the subject line than open the message. Here's a fictitious announcement that needs no body, only a subject line:

```
Subject: Got Books? http://www.books.com
```

Books.com is the URL for Book Stacks Unlimited, a fantastic online bookstore. The proprietors could use the message body to talk about their store, but most of the work is done by the subject line alone. You might consider using this approach to promote your Web site.

The Body of the Message

As I've said, you can use your posting for almost any type of announcement: a new Web site, an event, a contest, an online appearance (chat), a new product or service—you name it. And, if you follow three simple guidelines, you'll reduce the number of flames you get and improve your standing online: give something away, keep it short, and be creative.

Give Away Something of Value

On the Net, it has become standard practice for promoters to give away something of value. When my firm promotes books, we always offer a sample chapter, an excerpt, or a help file of some sort. Most contests have no entrance fee, and you can offer to send the rules or an entry blank. If you're announcing a chat, offer to send transcripts for those who can't attend. In the case of a news release, we usually don't post the actual release; rather, we post an offer to *send* the release upon request.

Keep It Short!

People don't read online, they scan. They open messages, read a few lines, close them, and move on. You have to come to the point immediately, then provide a way of getting more information, either by e-mail or at a Web site, Gopher site, or FTP site. This strategy is known as layering: giving people a way to find ever deeper levels of information. Instead of trying to present everything at once, you give them a little piece along with a button to press for more.

More than a screenful is wasteful is my motto for writing announcements. You want to make an impression quickly. Three paragraphs is usually enough: the hook, the message, the contact information. The hook grabs the people you're trying to target. The message tells them what you have to offer. The contact information tells them how to get all the details. Add a URL for your Web site or a telephone number and you're done.

Many messaging systems enable users to see how large messages are without opening them, either in number of pages or the size of the message in kilobytes. It doesn't take long for people to learn to avoid huge messages. When I open messages on America Online and my cursor spins from the upload, I bale out and move along. If you have a lot of information to share, you're better off enticing people into requesting it than packing it into a single message.

Be Creative

Here's a posting my firm did to promote a party. This campaign was run before America Online, CompuServe, and Prodigy had access to the Web, so we had to provide a little more information than you would need today:

```
Subject: microserfs PARTY PAGE

Douglas Coupland is throwing a party and YOU'RE INVITED!

Coupland is the author of "Generation X" and "Shampoo Planet."
The party is a coming-out bash for his new book, "microserfs,"
which documents the lives of fictional Microsoft employees.

The party will be held in a simulated clean room at The Tech
Museum of Innovation in San Jose, California, Wednesday, June
21 at 6:30 p.m. You'll be presented with a complimentary clean
room jumpsuit at the door so that you can mingle on a no-
status basis with Silicon Valley luminaries and temp slaves.

Other party favors are included. There will be a rare showing
of "Close Personal Friend," Jennifer Cowan's short documentary
```

```
about Douglas Coupland. A six dollar cover charge goes to The
Tech Museum to support their efforts.

For more information, see the microserfs PARTY PAGE on
HotWired at the following URL:
<http://www.hotwired.com/Coin/WS/microserfs/microserf.html>
```

When I placed the *microserfs* announcement, one person wrote to me, "You're obviously new to the Internet. Don't you know that humor is not allowed in Usenet postings?" His sarcasm is a sorry comment on the parched quality of most Usenet postings. Like a lot of people, I don't mind commercial announcements in "my" newsgroups; what bothers me is how unimaginative folks are.

You want to have a successful announcement campaign? Sharpen your cursor! Make the words dance! Pare down your prose, spike up the humor level, enlarge your vocabulary. Just because you're using a computer to distribute your message doesn't mean it has to sound like a computer wrote it. I know it's not easy to be creative on command. I recommend you let your announcement simmer for a day before sending it, so you can read it with fresh eyes. Printing your announcement sometimes helps you see how stiff it is. And reading your announcement aloud will alert you to poor phrasing. Ask a friend or co-worker to look at your announcement before you send it out. Spend a little more time creating a clever posting, and people will spend more time reading it and less time flaming you.

Signature

A signature is a short piece of information automatically appended to your announcements. It usually contains the same information as your letterhead: name, address, phone numbers, URL, and so on. Here is my signature file:

```
~~~~~~~~~~~~~~~~~~~~~~~~~~~~~~~~~~~~~~~~~~~~~~~~~~~~~~~~~~~~~~
STEVE O'KEEFE       Internet Publicity Services
(360) 385-5967      871 "H" St, Port Townsend, WA 98368 U.S.A.
(fax) 385-9502      E-mail: okeefe@olympus.Net
Web Site:           http://www.bookport.com/welcome/okeefe/IPS
~~~~~~~~~~~~~~~~~~~~~~~~~~~~~~~~~~~~~~~~~~~~~~~~~~~~~~~~~~~~~~
```

You don't need a signature in your announcements as your header should contain all the basic information people need to know: your name, company name, e-mail address. People will almost always respond by e-mail rather than phoning. However, if you want to include a phone number, you can either try to embed it in the header or put it at the end of the body of the message.

When people go to the second level of your message, then you can give them your snail mail address and anything else you want to throw in your signature. By second level, I mean the point at which people respond to your message, either by e-mail or by going to your Web site, Gopher site, or FTP site. At that point, they're seeking more information and it's appropriate to send them all your contact info.

Usenet Newsgroups

Usenet distributes discussion groups throughout the Internet. At this writing, there are more than 14,000 newsgroups available covering an astonishing range of topics. In communications history, there's never been anything like Usenet. Comparisons to party lines or APAs (alternative press associations) don't capture either the depth or vitality of Usenet newsgroups.

Imagine getting a daily newspaper with an article written by one person on every block of your city. What is that like? Well, if there were a big event (like a fire or accident), you might get 20 or 50, or 1,000 similar reports on it, some keenly written and others barely literate. You would also get articles describing the most personal feelings, which you wouldn't find in a professionally edited newspaper. You would also have neighbors bringing their private wars online, sniping at each other through their columns. That's what Usenet feels like to me.

People speak much more freely online than they do on the telephone, in person, or through the mail. The smallest annoyance is cause for reams of bombast online. As more people crowd onto the Net, the temperature in Usenet newsgroups is steadily rising. The same folks who brought us telemarketing scams now jam newsgroups with a steady diet of "Make Money Fast" spam. Net vigilantes retaliate, and suddenly there's a flame war.

As Usenet degenerates into a battlefield of spammers versus flamers, intelligent discourse is gravitating to moderated discussion groups. Usenet, "the world's newspaper," is hiring editors, and that's a shame, because the moderated groups just don't have the vitality of free-range newsgroups. When historians write about Usenet, will they tell us that for a brief moment communication was free, instantaneous, completely unregulated, and humans took the opportunity to blow-torch each other?

For the time being, newsgroups are still an important part of a publicity campaign. Announcements are welcome in newsgroups if they're on-topic, fit the tenor of discussion, and bring something of value to the group. Let's look at how you can find appropriate newsgroups to post to.

Finding Appropriate Groups

You can only post messages to newsgroups available from your Internet service provider. Most providers offer only a fraction of the thousands of newsgroups available. If your provider does not offer a complete "news feed," you can use some of the many services listed in Chapter 12 for discovering newsgroups, then ask your service provider to add these groups to the feed.

My favorite service for finding newsgroups is part of the Sunsite project at the University of North Carolina, http://sunsite.unc.edu/usenet-i/search.html. You can easily craft a custom search to look for newsgroups on specific subjects. Figure 7.6 shows the Sunsite search page. By checking the Short Description box, you'll get a one-line description for each matching group. More in-depth information is available for some groups.

The best way to determine whether your posting will be appropriate is to read the newsgroup and use common sense. Are there commercial messages in the group? Do they result in flames? If your message seems like it would fit in, post it. You can't decide by the name of the group alone; you have to get in there to see what people are talking about.

Most newsgroups also have "charters," a statement of purpose drafted when the newsgroup was first proposed. UUNET houses them in an FTP directory, but unless you're an historian, they're pretty useless, which is why none of the other major Usenet resource sites archives charters. If you were trying to decide which political party to join, would you base your decision on party platforms written in the

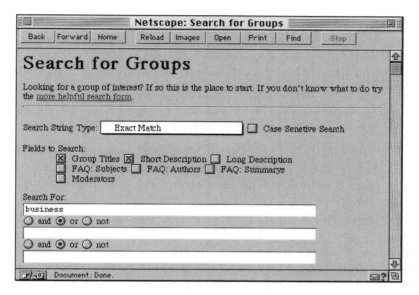

Figure 7.6 Sunsite's Search for Groups is a fantastic resource for finding appropriate discussion groups for your announcements.

1800s? Charters have a similar relevance to deciding what is appropriate discussion for a newsgroup.

Another tool for determining whether the group is appropriate is the FAQ (Frequently Asked Questions) file that some newsgroups maintain. You can find FAQs using the Usenet sites listed in the Resources chapter. Sunsite has some FAQs (see Figure 7.6), and Oxford University has an easy-to-use interface for finding FAQs at http://www.lib.ox.ac.uk/internet/news/. But you shouldn't judge a newsgroup by its FAQ either.

Some of these FAQ files are longer than this book. I've waded through 20-page FAQs only to find they never address the purpose of the newsgroup or provide guidelines for appropriate messages. Some FAQs are entertaining documents; but they're lousy resources for determining what sorts of messages are welcome in the group. Many of the FAQs were written by one member of the group a long time ago and don't come close to reflecting current standards.

Common sense again is your best guide, but some people lack it. A while back, a fellow posted an inquiry on one of the mailing lists I read.

He wondered why he was getting flamed for a posting he thought was appropriate. He posted an announcement for his financial services in alt.cancer.support, reasoning that people dying of cancer would need financial planning. I don't have to tell you his message was not appreciated. He should have been sensitive to the purpose of the discussion group. If cancer victims are looking for information on estate planning they'll go to discussion groups dealing with financial services.

When a group is moderated, all postings must be approved by a moderator before being released to the group. If the moderator approves your posting, it is *de facto* appropriate. In unmoderated groups, anyone can post any message they want. There are no restrictions. If your message is inappropriate, you'll hear about it, though, either through flames or retaliation. If you were wrong (and I've been wrong many times), admit it, and cancel out your posting. If you were right, defend your posting. I close this chapter with some suggestions on when, why, and how you should defend your postings.

Posting to Usenet

The mechanics of posting to Usenet newsgroups are fairly simple. With whatever news reader software you're using, compile a set of newsgroups where you think your message will be appropriate. Visit the groups to see if your message will fit with the current level of discussion and cull your list. Figure 7.7 shows a list of newsgroups my firm compiled to promote a financial planning book.

You can post to all the newsgroups at once, but you risk waking up the "Cancel Moose." The Moose automatically detects identical postings to large numbers of newsgroups and issues forged cancellation notices to wipe the postings out. The Moose will then visit your mailbox to tell you about it. What the Cancel Moose does is illegal, but since it operates through anonymous re-mailers, the people behind the Moose have never been identified. You don't want to wake up the Moose or any of his pyromaniac friends, so you should cross-post to no more than five groups.

Cross-posting means posting to multiple groups at the same time. The idea is that people don't want to run into the same message in every group they read. When you cross-post, people will only see your message the first time they open it, and not in the other groups it was

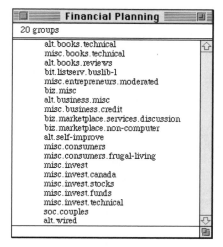

Figure 7.7 Usenet newsgroups for a personal finance announcement.

cross-posted to. Cross-posting is welcome to a degree. But every time someone responds to your message in one group, the response is sent to *all* the groups in the cross-post. You have to strike a balance, cross-posting to similar discussion groups, avoiding cross-posts to very different groups.

Consider sorting your newsgroups by the way you intend to cross-post. The newsgroups in Figure 7.7 are sorted by topic, starting with book groups first, then business groups, and so on. When you create your messages, address them to small batches of similar groups. Figure 7.8 shows a posting to the first three newsgroups on the list.

You can write your message ahead of time in a word processor where it's easier to spell-check. As I've said, spelling is atrocious on Usenet, but flamers nonetheless enjoy roasting people for any minor errors. When you're happy with the way the message reads, copy it into your news program and send it off. Make sure that you've eliminated any non-ASCII characters: tabs, curly quotes, bold, italics, large point sizes, and so on. Usenet is ASCII-only at the moment, and sometimes these non-ASCII characters convert to undesirable alphanumerics upon posting.

You may need to vary the subject line and content of your message depending on the newsgroups you're posting to. Sometimes it helps to

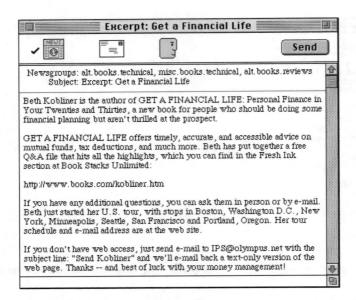

Figure 7.8 A sample newsgroup posting ready to send off.

tailor the message more closely to the readership to avoid flames and improve results. Varying the subject line and content also helps you stay out of the clutches of the Cancel Moose and its friends, who may be looking for identical postings.

You should not cross-post to moderated newsgroups. If the posting is not approved by the moderator of one group, it won't show up in any of the groups. Also, post individually to groups such as comp.infosystems.www.announce, a popular newsgroup for announcing new Web sites, which have very strict formats they want you to adhere to. They might want your subject line to begin with WWW>, or whatever, or they might want your e-mail address in the body of the message.

If your Internet service provider is stingy with the news feed, you might want to visit Zippo. Zippo is a commercial news service that allows public access to more than 14,000 newsgroups for a fee of $12 per year. On the Web, it's located at www.zippo.com. Once you're a member, you can get to Zippo using your favorite news reader by changing the server setting to news.zippo.com. At Zippo, you can browse newsgroups by category, search for certain topics, or peruse the whole list.

Zippo is not a great resource for posting to newsgroups, however. It gets so much traffic that it's incredibly slow. You can subscribe to SuperZippo for greater speed and versatility, but you'll pay for the privilege. And Zippo does not tolerate anything that looks or smells like spam. If you post a message to 15 or more newsgroups, you may have your access revoked, even if your messages were completely on-target. Zippo has an automated "Hippo" that detects multiple postings and sits on them, then revokes your access; no questions asked, no appeals, no refunds.

When you're done posting your messages, save the list of newsgroups you posted to. In NewsWatcher and other news reader programs, you can save the list as a newsgroup file. Every time you open the file, it will automatically check those groups for new messages. This helps you track responses.

Following Up on Usenet

Depending on your Internet service provider, your postings may appear in a matter of seconds. I've done postings from America Online, however, that took more than three days to appear. America Online used to have terrible delivery problems with anything going to, or coming from, the Internet. It has improved a lot since, but you can still wait a long time for your Usenet postings to appear.

If your postings don't appear within a day or two, you've got a problem. They may have been canceled by a vigilante. If you suspect you've been canceled out, you might want to visit the newsgroup alt.current-events.net-abuse and see if someone is bragging about shutting you down. If you followed netiquette, you shouldn't have a problem. But you never know when some clever vigilante is going to find a message offensive and have it removed. If this happens, you can carefully repost different versions of your message.

On the other hand you might just have a technical problem. Contact your service provider to see if there's some reason Usenet postings are not getting through. You may have to find another news server to post from. If you have multiple Internet accounts, try using a different service. If my Usenet pipe is broken, I post from America Online, and if AOL is slow, I go to CompuServe.

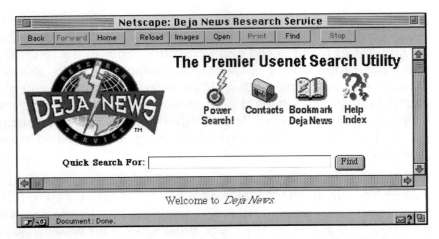

Figure 7.9 Deja News is a free service for searching Usenet newsgroups.

Once your message appears, follow the newsgroups for a few days and respond to any feedback. People often ask me how long messages stay up. The answer is, forever. Each service provider decides how far back they want the news feed to go. At some point, old messages are removed from the feed and archived somewhere. Realistically, you'll get any responses within three days. After that, it's old news. (Note: As I was writing these words, I received a response to a message posted two months ago!)

My NewsWatcher software has the ability to search multiple newsgroups for responses to my postings. I can search for subject lines containing words I used in my posting and NewsWatcher delivers a set of messages that meet that criteria. This search feature makes follow-up a snap. You can also use a news services such as Deja News (http:// www.dejanews.com/), which enables you to search newsgroups for your name, company name, or any other keyword. At this writing, there's no charge to use Deja News (Figure 7.9).

As I said, at the end of this chapter is information on defending your postings. You'll also find more suggestions in Chapter 11, Firefighting and Follow-Up. I want to add here that flames are not always a bad thing. They can generate additional interest in your messages and give you an opportunity to talk more about whatever it is you're promoting. Before you add more fuel to the fires, though, calm down, read the relevant passages in this book, and learn to respond strategically.

Internet Mailing Lists

Newsgroups live on the Net where anyone may come and read them. Mailing lists are delivered via e-mail to subscribers, and thus tend to have much smaller audiences than newsgroups. However, subscribers are more dedicated to participation than their newsgroup counterparts who may make one posting and never come back. In general, I have found mailing lists to be much more responsive to announcements than newsgroups, but also much more sensitive about commercial postings.

There are many places to find information on mailing lists. One of the best is Liszt, a Web site devoted to mailing lists at http://www.liszt.com (Figure 7.10). In mid-1996, Liszt's catalog of mailing lists numbered over 34,000—an amazing quantity. You can search through the list using words or phrases, and Liszt will return a menu of mailing lists that meet your criteria. Liszt provides the address for subscribing to the list and some information about the content of the list when available.

There are many other good sites for finding mailing lists and you can use the Resources chapter (Chapter 12) to locate them. The Interna-

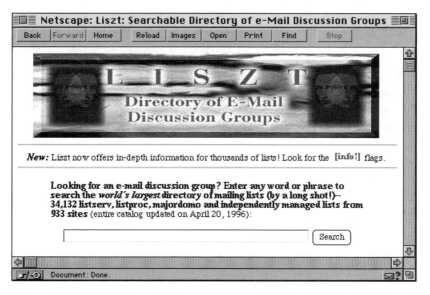

Figure 7.10 Liszt is an awesome resource for finding mailing lists.

tional Federation of Library Associations and Institutions (IFLA) maintains a Web site with basic information on how list servers work and hotlinks to other mailing list resources available on the Net. This is probably the best place to start your search: http://www.nlc-bnc.ca/ifla/I/training/listserv/lists.htm.

Mailing lists range from completely private affairs to wide-open discussion groups. I've tried to classify the types of mailing lists you'll find here. These aren't official terms or categories, just the way the lists seem to be structured to me:

- **Private/Read Only:** Many companies use mailing lists to distribute news about their products. These lists aren't discussion groups and are not open to contributions from the public.

- **Private/Read and Write:** You must apply for membership before being granted rights to participate in these discussions. For example, an accounting list might limit membership to those who can prove they passed the CPA exam.

- **Moderated:** Membership is open to anyone, but postings must be approved before being released to the group.

- **Subscription Required:** Not moderated, but you must be a subscriber before you can send messages to the list.

- **Completely Open:** Unmoderated, and no subscription required. You can post messages without even subscribing to the list.

Using Liszt and the other resources described here, you should be able to get the addresses for mailing lists where your messages will be appropriate. You can then send an "info" message to the list server to get more detailed information about each list. It's difficult to tell from the name of the list alone whether your message will be welcome. You'll usually be sent guidelines when you subscribe to the list. Subscribing is covered next.

Posting to Mailing Lists

Mailing lists are a little more tricky to post to than newsgroups. When my firm does announcement campaigns, we like to make a list of groups we think are appropriate, then subscribe to all of them. We read the information that is sent upon joining and unsubscribe from lists that seem inappropriate. We post messages to the remaining lists, follow the discussion for a few days, then unsubscribe. Here's a group of mailing lists we used to promote a Web site for kids that was based on a fiction book series:

BOOKTALK—Children's literature and classroom use
KIDLIT-L—Children and Youth Literature List
ffk—Families for kids & Kellogg Foundation Project
KIDS-PT—PreTeen discussion list
KIDS-TE—Teen discussion list
KidsPeak—Announcements
KIDZMAIL—Kids Exploring Issues and Interests Electronically
FICTIONCHAT-L—Fiction Chat List
world-design Forum on Designing Fictional Settings/Worlds
YAFICT-L—Young Adult Fiction Writers List
HSJOURN—High School Scholastic Journalism

For every mailing list, there are two important addresses: the address of the *server* and the address of the *list*. Membership commands such as Subscribe and Unsubscribe are sent to the server. Announcements and other postings are sent to the list. For example, here are the addresses for the mailing list Market-L, a popular marketing discussion group:

The Server: listproc@mailer.fsu.edu
The List: market-l@mailer.fsu.edu

To subscribe to a list, you send e-mail to the server with the word *subscribe* in the body of your message and the name of the list you're subscribing to. You may also need to include your name, depending on the type of software used to manage the list. There are three major types of mailing list software: *listserv*, *majordomo*, and *listproc*. They each use slightly different commands, but the following format should allow you to subscribe or unsubscribe from any of them. Just substitute the name of the list for "listname" and your own name for "yourname":

To Subscribe, send e-mail to the server address with the following text in the body of the message: subscribe listname yourname

To Unsubscribe, send e-mail to the server address with the following text in the body of the message: unsubscribe listname yourname

When you subscribe to a mailing list, you'll receive an e-mail acknowledgment and a set of instructions for communicating with the list. *Save these instructions!* Mailing lists can generate an enormous about of e-mail, and it's very frustrating trying to staunch the flow if you have lost the instructions for getting off the list. A good suggestion is to set up a separate e-mail folder for mailing list instructions.

After you've subscribed and you're confident that your message will be appropriate, send your announcement to the list. Adjust the wording of your announcement to match the preferences of each group. I repeat many mailing lists are moderated, and your announcement won't be distributed unless the moderator approves. Several times, moderators have asked me to adjust my phrasing slightly before they'll release my message. The most common request is to include an e-mail address in the body of the message, since asking people to "reply via e-mail" might result in people replying to the *list* rather than to the *sender*.

Following Up in Mailing Lists

Once you've sent your message, keep an eye on the mailing list for a few days to gauge reaction to it. If your message never appears, write to the moderator and ask why. The address for the moderator should be in the instructions you saved when you first subscribed. Some lists are not very active or the moderator is on vacation, and it could be weeks before your message goes up.

If you're getting heat for a posting, be prepared to defend yourself. If the list is moderated, then your critics should be flaming the moderator, not you. If it's an unmoderated group, then you're free to post what you like. If you think the message conformed to the guidelines for the group, then say that. People are entitled to have different opinions about what messages are appropriate. If you blew it and posted a message totally out of character with the list, apologize.

Some readers will be horrified at these hit-and-run tactics. Let me give you an example of how appropriate such postings can be. We had a client who wanted to tell people about a news conference in New York City. The conference dealt with the subject of genetics and criminal behavior. We subscribed to a dozen or so mailing lists dealing with genetics, criminal justice, and so on and invited people to attend the press conference. For those who could not attend, we offered to send a complete packet of information. We didn't receive any flames—just many letters thanking us for the invitation.

After you have followed up on any resulting discussion, you can unsubscribe from all the mailing lists. You can usually do this by sending e-mail to the server with the word unsubscribe in the body of your message. If that doesn't work, refer to the instructions you received when you joined the list.

America Online

Posting on commercial online services has a different feel to it than posting on the Net. There are several layers of restrictions governing your activity, from the company's terms of service to the forum hosts' guidelines to standards of acceptable behavior set by the membership. But beyond the rules, there is the simple matter of economics: how does this service make money? Find the revenue stream, and you find opportunities built into the system.

America Online is a private, commercial online service. It makes its revenue two basic ways: through fees charged to subscribers and through fees charged to "advertisers" or sponsors. If you want to advertise on America Online (AOL), management would prefer that you paid for the privilege rather than posting free ads in discussion groups. Therefore, they want to remove any postings that smell like ads.

On the other hand, the forum hosts at America Online get paid, in part, by the amount of traffic generated in their forums. The longer people stay online, the more money America Online makes, and the more it kicks back to forum hosts. Forum hosts want to build traffic to their sites and will be supportive of activities that help them achieve this goal. If the subscribers don't find information of value, they won't spend their time or money online.

When you post messages referring people to a Web site or a giveaway file, you are encouraging them to spend more time on America Online, either in the Web browser or downloading your file. When you provide valuable material in your giveaway files, you are adding to what America Online offers to its members. You are providing "content," as they call it, at no cost to America Online other than storage space.

America Online is probably the most relaxed of the commercial on-line services. Management is too busy trying to grow the company to spend time monitoring the discussion groups. You can post anything you want on America Online as long as the forum hosts go along. They're a pretty cooperative bunch; if you can show them you're increasing the value of their forums through your postings, they will let you say whatever you like. The membership on America online is fairly young and freewheeling; they're open to new ideas and willing to explore the Web if something piques their curiosity.

Finding Forums

There are three good ways to find forums for your messages on America Online. The cheapest and most comprehensive is to download the complete list of forums and their keywords. A *keyword* is a shortcut to the forum. For example, to get the Internet Business Forum, you can type the keyword "INBIZ." To find the list of AOL keywords, type the keyword "keyword list" and you'll be taken right to it.

America Online is a marvelously fluid service: forums are always consolidating and breaking free, changing names and merging. But this means you can't rely on an old keyword list to find the active forums. Use the pull-down menus to search the Directory of Services. Figure 7.11 shows a search for the words "business and management." AOL returned 13 suggested forums. I don't know who cross-references the forums, but I have to point out that searches like this will often miss the best places for postings. We once did a search for "humor" and failed to turn up The Comedy Club!

An even simpler way to search on America Online is to type in a keyword, but instead of hitting the Go button, hit Search (see Figure 7.12). You will get a list of services that match the word you typed in. But again, America Online doesn't do the best job of indexing its forums, so if you're searching for humor forums, for instance, you should try several searches using words like "comedy," "laughter," "fun," and so on.

Once you find an appropriate forum, you need to find the right message board for your announcement. Figure 7.13 shows the main window for the Business Strategies forum on America Online. Most forums have a similar look. By clicking on the Messages icon, you are taken into the public discussion area.

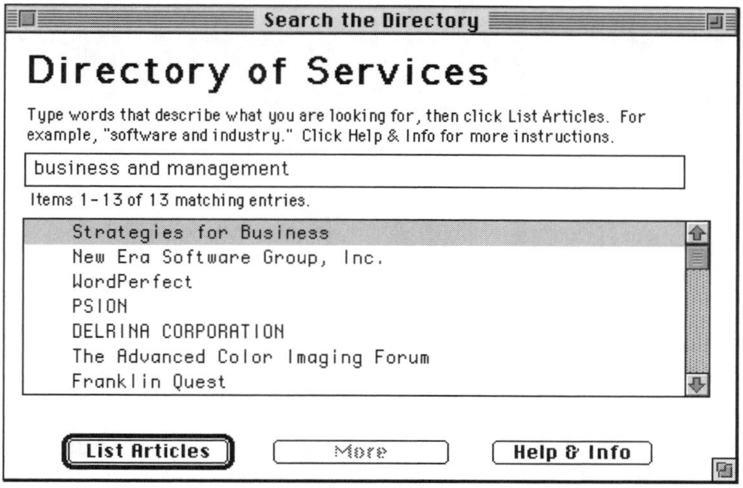

Figure 7.11 Searching America Online's Directory of Services.

Once you're into the message boards, you next have to drill down through the layers of topics until you find the thread where your message belongs. Figure 7.14 shows the categories list for the Business Strategies Messages board. There are 11 discussion categories. The Marketing & Public Relations category contains 35 topics with 2,906 messages. You can find hot discussion groups by looking for high-traffic areas. Business Strategies is a busy forum; many AOL forums don't generate enough messages to have categories as well as topics.

If you keep drilling through the categories and the topics, you'll eventually get to a thread where you can post a message or announce-

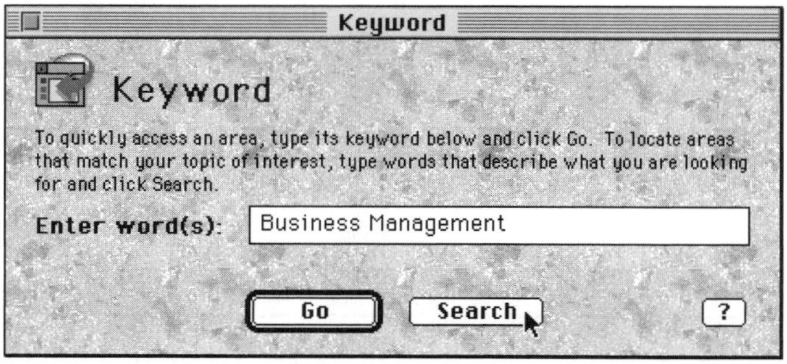

Figure 7.12 Searching America Online using its keyword capability.

Figure 7.13 The main window for the Business Strategies forum resembles most other forums on America Online.

ment. Figure 7.15 shows the thread for the Promotional Ideas topic. At the top of the window is the general description for this topic. Some de-

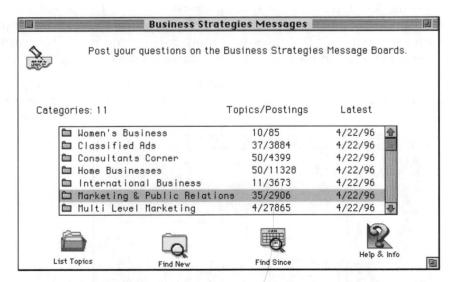

Figure 7.14 A list of discussion areas in America Online's Business Strategies forum.

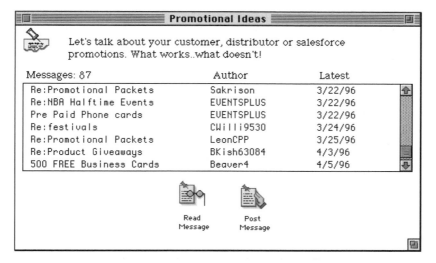

Figure 7.15 The topic for this America Online discussion thread is Promotional Ideas.

scriptions are provided by the forum hosts, but many forums allow members to start topics and write the descriptive text. In the list of messages, you can see the subject line of each posting, the screen name of the author, and the date posted. In general, I recommend you post in active threads, although it is possible to revive a dead thread.

You can see how your choice of a subject line is critical to getting your message opened. All the Re: subject lines are responses to previous postings. I'm guessing that the subject line "500 FREE Business Cards" in Figure 7.15 is an ad. On Prodigy, that message would never make it past the forum host, but because America Online doesn't heavily regulate its message boards, it has a vitality that the people at Prodigy never experience.

If your announcement campaign includes a free giveaway file, you can upload it in a forum library then tell people how to find it in your announcement. Figure 7.16 shows what a fictitious posting for this book might look like. This brief message tells people exactly where to find the giveaway file. We cover the procedures for uploading files in the Document Transfers chapter.

There are many places to announce a Web site on America Online. AOL has several forums dedicated to helping people use the Internet.

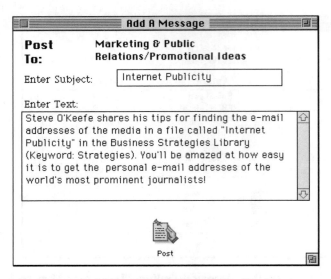

Figure 7.16 A fictitious posting for this book.

You can get to them through the Internet Connection (keyword: "Internet"). But you don't have to limit yourself to Internet forums. Almost every special interest forum has a discussion thread for recommended Web sites where your announcement would be appropriate.

Following Up on America Online

It's a good idea to check your messages for the first few days to see if there are any responses. People aren't bashful about expressing themselves on America Online. If they like your post, they'll respond; if they object to it, they'll flame you right there in public. I have some suggestions for putting out those flames at the end of this chapter and in the Firefighting chapter (Chapter 11).

America Online is home to a fast-moving crowd; after three days, you won't hear much, although your message will stay up indefinitely. Last week, someone asked me for the giveaway file for a promotion I did a year ago! That person had to dig deep to find that message.

Sometimes the forum host will remove a posting if it's too commercial. As America Online's membership has grown, being a forum host has gone from a hobby to big business. Some hosts make a comfortable living running their forums, and they like to keep the place clean and inviting. If this happens to you, you can reword your announcement and ask the host if it's acceptable. A little commercial activity is tolerated on America Online, as long as you are contributing something to the discussion, not just plastering ads.

If you plan on regularly contributing to America Online, get to know the forum hosts. There are human beings behind those screens, though they often seem anonymous. The forum hosts can really help you out, setting up a chat, suggesting places to post your messages, even defending your announcements. Many of the forum hosts on America Online now solicit material from me for their forums.

CompuServe

CompuServe is another popular commercial online service. Like America Online, CompuServe (CIS) has several layers of authority governing your behavior, from the terms of service to the forum sysops to peer pressure. Here's the official line concerning commercial announcements from CompuServe's Operating Rules:

```
CONTENT & USES OF THE SERVICE

Member agrees not to publish on or over the Service any
information, software or other content which violates or
infringes upon the rights of any others or which would be
abusive, profane or offensive to an average person, or which,
without the approval of CompuServe, contains any advertising,
promotion or solicitation of goods or services for commercial
purposes. This paragraph, however, shall not be interpreted to
restrict member from utilizing CompuServe mail in the conduct
of a legitimate business except that member may not, without
the approval of CompuServe, send unsolicited advertising or
promotional material.
```

It's one thing to *say* you don't allow commercial postings, and quite another to *enforce it*. You only have to read a few forum messages to know that CompuServe does not strictly enforce its rules. In fact, many of the most commercial messages on CIS come from the forum sysops themselves, promoting their books or consulting services, or whatever. Yet CompuServe is stricter than America Online when it comes to commercial traffic.

I mentioned that you need to understand the flow of revenue to understand the prejudices built in to an online service. As on AOL, CompuServe's sysops are compensated according to the amount of traffic in their forums. If you help them generate traffic, your material will be welcome. If you post messages that turn people off, you will be shown the door.

It took awhile for me to learn the lesson of the revenue flow. I use giveaway files a lot in my promotions. America Online has some sort of housekeeping utility that searches the service for duplicate uploads and removes them, so on AOL, you upload to one library, then post messages telling people where to find the file. But on CompuServe, if you tell people the file is in another forum, the sysops get mad and remove your postings—you're sending their customers to another store, and the sysops don't like that.

One CIS sysop finally put it in black and white for me. He told me that my message announcing a giveaway file had been removed because it violated CompuServe's prohibition on commercial postings. However, if I uploaded the giveaway file in *his* library, my message would be acceptable. You can't have it spelled out for you more clearly than that. Now when I do a promotion on CompuServe, I might upload the same file in 20 different forums. It's more work, but it keeps the sysops happy.

In general, CompuServe caters to a more professional audience than America Online or Prodigy. The membership seems a little older and more business-oriented, and the sysops are more diligent in their roles as censors. CompuServe has started to loosen up as it tries to compete with AOL's popular chat rooms, but it's still a little stiff when it comes to promotional announcements.

Finding Forums on CIS

Like America Online, CompuServe has a comprehensive index of services and corresponding Go words. You can find the list by typing Go Index, then download it to your computer where you can work with it offline. You can also use the Find command under the pull-down menu for Services (see Figure 7.17).

Figure 7.18 shows the results of a search for services related to "business management." CompuServe returned 38 matches along with

Figure 7.17 CompuServe's Find command is a quick way to get a forum list.

Go words. Compare this to 13 matches on America Online. Part of the difference is due to CompuServe's business-minded membership, but most of the difference is due to better indexing at CompuServe. On AOL, you have to perform several similar searches to catch all the forums. On CIS, one search usually brings more than enough matches.

The first time you visit a forum on CompuServe, you will be asked whether you want to join. I think this practice dates back to when CompuServe charged extra fees to use the forums. It doesn't seem to have any purpose now, but if there's no charge to join the forum, there's no harm

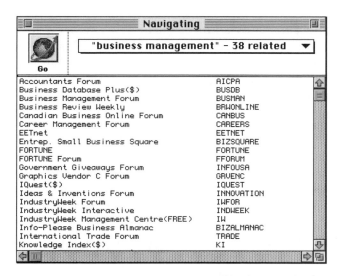

Figure 7.18 The results of a CompuServe search for business management forums.

Figure 7.19 The Forum Status window is the first thing you see when visiting a forum.

in clicking that Join button. You can't post messages until you join, and you can't create forum messages offline until you join.

Most CIS forums present the same window when you visit, shown in Figure 7.19, although CompuServe is moving to more individualized graphics for its forums the way America Online has. However, even when a CIS forum has a graphical front, the message boards are usually behind a Forum Status window like the one shown in Figure 7.19.

When you select the browse messages icon, you are shown a list of discussion areas for that forum (see Figure 7.20). This is where you'll look for appropriate topics to include your message. After visiting the topics to gauge the level of discussion, post your message. In Figure 7.20, there are 11 message sections. You can see where all the action is by looking at the number of topics and messages for each section.

CompuServe has a lot of vendor forums where companies purchase space for private forums. Businesses use these forums for customer support, user groups, product announcements, and more. They're usually identified as a vendor forum in the index, but not always; nevertheless you can tell when you get to the message boards whether it's a private forum. Be very careful when posting to vendor forums; say something that supports the sponsor or is in line with the goals of the forum.

Posting Announcements on CompuServe

CompuServe has one of the best interfaces for posting messages to discussion groups. Once you've joined a forum, you can create your mes-

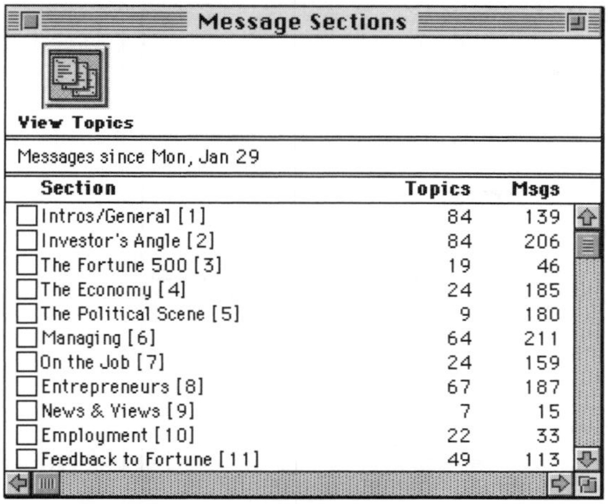

Figure 7.20 A list of discussion groups in the *Fortune* Magazine forum on CompuServe.

sages offline and store them in your Out Basket. On other services, you must create messages online. You can't use *flash sessions* to automatically post all your forum messages, though. You have to visit each forum, at which point CompuServe will prompt you to send anything in your Out Basket for that forum.

To create a forum message on CompuServe, use the Mail pull-down menu and go to Create Forum Message. You'll get a window for creating your message like the one shown in Figure 7.21. Give the message a subject line short enough to fit in the limited space provided. You have your choice of addressing the message to an individual, or you can put the word ALL in the To: field for a public message.

To select the forum on which to post your message, click on the Forum button in the Creating Forum Message window. You'll get a new window showing a list of the forums that you're a member of. Only the forums you joined will appear in this window (see Figure 7.22). After you select a forum, you can choose the section where you want your message to go. These sections correspond to the discussion sections that were available last time you visited the forum. By clicking on the Section bar in the Creating Forum Message window, you will be shown a list of the available sections.

Put the text of your message into the area at the bottom of the Creating Forum Message window, then store the finished message in your

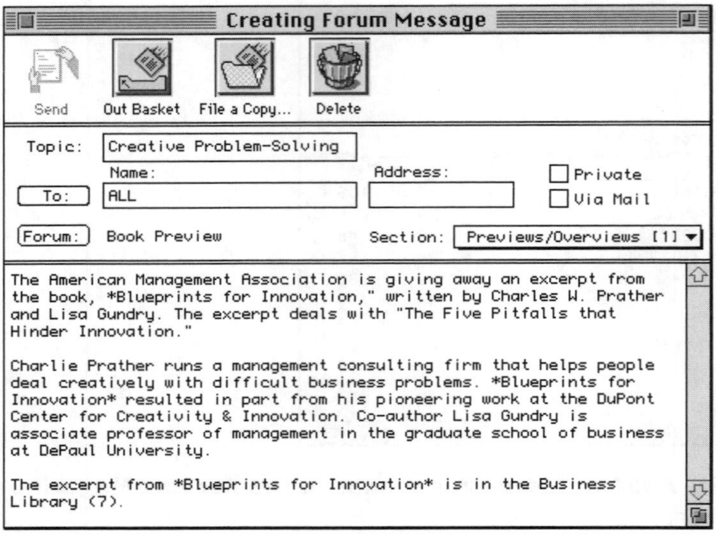

Figure 7.21 You can create messages offline for uploading to CompuServe forums.

Out Basket for delivery next time you're online. You might want to write your message in your word processor, where you can spell-check it and edit it until you're satisfied, then copy it into CompuServe.

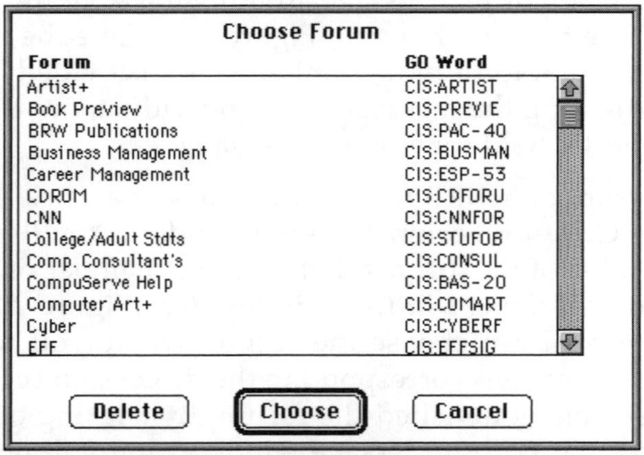

Figure 7.22 Your CompuServe software keeps a list of the forums you've joined.

When you're finished creating messages for all the different forums, you'll have an Out Basket full of messages waiting to be delivered. Log on to CompuServe and go from forum to forum on your list. If you try to leave the forum without sending your messages, CompuServe will prompt you to send them. Just click on the Send Them Now button and your messages will be dispatched.

Following Up on CompuServe

While CompuServe's mechanism for creating messages offline is better than its competitors, the process for following up is much worse. If someone reacts to your posting with a comment, question, or flame, instead of being sent to your mailbox, the message waits for you inside the forum. If you look at Figure 7.19 again, you'll see that the Forum Status window has an icon for Waiting Messages. Unfortunately, there's no way to collect these waiting messages without visiting each forum.

For the first few days after your posting, therefore, you'll need to visit each of the forums looking for waiting messages. You can download the waiting messages and write your responses offline if you want. I often find it faster to reply to them immediately. There also might be messages in the discussion threads that aren't in your Waiting Messages area because they weren't directed to you. In addition, you might get e-mail in your CompuServe in-box.

I get a lot of positive feedback from CompuServe members and sysops because of the giveaway files I use. If they're genuinely informative, people are happy to have them. Most of the complaints I get are from sysops who don't appreciate it when I send people to other forums looking for a file. When that happens, I ask if I can upload the file to their forums and the answer is almost always yes. Sometimes, though, I have to reword my postings to better fit the current level of discussion in the forum.

I once promoted a book of light verse on the Internet. Let's just say the online community isn't rushing to download all the light verse they can find. It was a tough book to promote, but it had some lovely illustrations by a fairly well-known artist, so I put a message in a forum for illustrators on CompuServe. The response I got was something I'll call "heavy verse"; forum members started a thread on how to deal with "people like me." I explained why I posted the message, and admitted I should have uploaded some illustrations. I had never uploaded graphics to a library and I was somewhat intimidated. The sysop helped me through it, the illustrations were released, then everyone welcomed me to the forum. All that talk of a virtual lynching disappeared.

A reminder: There's more advice on handling flames at the end of this chapter and in the Firefighting chapter (Chapter 11). You need to follow up to see how people are responding to your postings. If you made a mistake—such as posting to a private vendor forum—admit it, apologize, and try to make the situation right. These forums are like clubs; if you can't bring something of value to the discussion, they don't want to hear from you.

Prodigy

Prodigy is probably the least satisfying of the Big Three commercial online services. They have fewer than 100 public forums, or *bulletin boards* as they're called. Reading and writing messages on this service is frustratingly slow. Prodigy also painted itself into a corner by regulating the content of even private messages. Now it has to police its service very closely to maintain the "family" standards it set for itself.

Like the other commercial online services, Prodigy has its own terms of service and its bulletin board hosts have their own sets of guidelines. If your posting is removed for being too commercial, the host will probably send you a form letter quoting Prodigy's guidelines. Here are the relevant passages:

```
6. Please, No Advertising or Soliciting
Members use the boards to communicate with other members.
You've told us that you don't want the boards cluttered with
commercial messages—it's like having an unwelcome salesperson
show up at your door. For this reason, please do not post
commercial or classified ads on the public boards.

This includes solicitations or offers to buy, sell, or trade
goods and services of significant value.
```

Notice that the guidelines say nothing about news or announcements. The standards within Prodigy's bulletin boards are fairly liberal; that is, the membership seldom complains, although the forum hosts often do. And none of the bulletin boards has libraries where members can exchange files, making giveaways much harder to use on Prodigy.

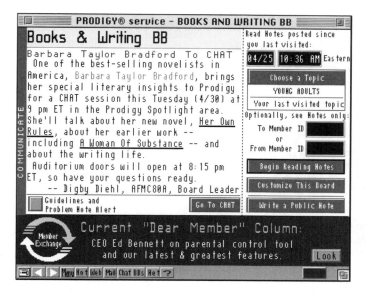

Figure 7.23 All Prodigy bulletin boards have a similar main window.

You can find a list of Prodigy bulletin boards in the free Member Services area. Look under Basic Features: Bulletin Boards A-Z. From there you can print the bulletin board list so that you can work with it offline.

All the bulletin boards have a similar structure. Figure 7.23 shows the opening window for the Books & Writing bulletin board. When you visit a bulletin board, you can read messages or write them. If you click on Write a Public Note, you'll be asked to select a topic. Figure 7.24 shows part of the topic list for the Books & Writing bulletin board. You can pick an existing topic from the list or add a new one if you like.

The create message window in Prodigy looks like the one shown in Figure 7.25. You can't create messages offline, though you can write the message in your word processor and copy it into Prodigy's message window. Prodigy's editing features are clumsy to use, accounting for the poor formatting and spelling you find on their bulletin boards. You can address your note to an individual, or leave the NOTE TO field blank to reach the general public.

You'll notice a big difference between Prodigy and the other services when you're done writing your message and you click the OK button. Your message isn't posted—it's "submitted for approval" (see

Figure 7.24 A partial list of discussion topics from Prodigy's Books & Writing bulletin board.

Figure 7.26). On most services, messages are posted until the sysop takes them down. On Prodigy, forum hosts must approve postings before they go up, but because of volume, many Prodigy hosts automati-

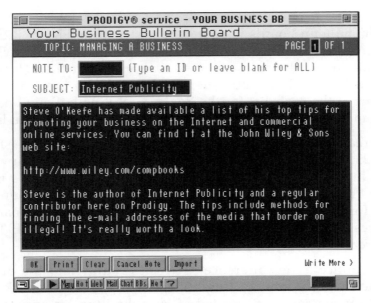

Figure 7.25 Creating a bulletin board message using Prodigy.

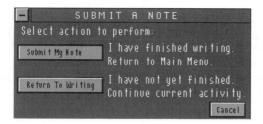

Figure 7.26 On other services, you post a message; on Prodigy, you submit it for approval.

cally approve postings and only take them down when someone complains. Between Prodigy's clumsy interface and bureaucratic approval process, dialogue on Prodigy is about as stilted as it gets.

Follow-up is routine on Prodigy. Because it's so difficult to upload giveaway files, I usually offer to e-mail them upon request. Most of my feedback comes from people wanting giveaway files. Occasionally, bulletin board hosts will complain about a posting. I try to reword the announcement to meet their standards.

Other Commercial Online Services

There are many smaller commercial online services where your announcements would be welcome. I've done postings on Delphi, GEnie, and eWorld, to name a few. Each of these services has a niche audience that may fit perfectly with your work. For example, GEnie has very active programmer and gaming forums. eWorld appeals to Apple and Macintosh computer enthusiasts. If the demographics of the service match your target audience, it can be an important outlet for your messages.

There are many regional online services and bulletin boards, as well. For example, the WELL is a popular Internet provider in the San Francisco Bay area. If your target audience is geographically defined, you can achieve your most rewarding results using regional discussion groups. As you have no doubt discovered from the material we've covered so far, the process is pretty similar for every online service:

1. Find an index of discussion groups.
2. Visit the forums to see if your message is appropriate.
3. Post your messages.
4. Follow up.

In the future, you'll find more discussion groups attached to popular Web sites. HotWired has a Threads section where people discuss current events and comment on HotWired stories and articles. iGuide, the joint venture between Mecklermedia and NewsCorp, has a bulletin board section that they hope will mimic the success of America Online or CompuServe forums. These discussion groups don't get a lot of traffic yet, but as the interface improves, more people will participate, and they'll become important outlets for your messages.

Defending Your Postings

At the beginning of this chapter, we discussed spam and flames and acceptable use policies (AUPs). Legally, there are only two restrictions on your online activities: the terms you agreed to when you opened your account, and the legal statutes of the geographical area you live in. When you are challenged about your activities, you may want to consult these authorities.

In practice, the AUPs have little meaning; what matters is the standards set by participants and moderators. Internet vigilantes can make your life miserable, whether you are right or not. Therefore, it's wise to try to peacefully resolve conflicts with other members of the online community. Set an example by treating other people with respect even if they do not treat you that way. Try to disarm conflicts, rather than escalate them, because you don't know what your anonymous antagonist is capable of.

You will find that many AUPs prohibit commercial activity and yet commercial activity goes on all the time and is encouraged. One Internet provider I know attaches a slug line promoting his service to the header of all his customers' outgoing e-mail, who can't remove the slug line themselves. This is tantamount to America Online members having to include an ad for America Online in all their outgoing e-mail. Yet this same Internet provider makes his customers agree to not broadcast commercial messages!

On America Online, CompuServe, Prodigy, and the other online services, you will see forum hosts hawking their books or plugging speaking engagements, even as they remove your announcements for being "too commercial." On Usenet and Internet mailing lists, people use their signatures as ads and it's considered acceptable. An entire post might consist of one or two words—"ditto" or "I agree"—followed by a 20-line signature packed with commercial information.

In theory, you may be within your bounds to post a message, but restrain yourself if you suspect someone might attack you. In theory, commercial announcements may be prohibited, but you should look at the current standards set in the discussion group. As long as you are contributing something of value to the discussion, your postings will be welcomed by most people in the group and most forum hosts.

Usenet Flames

There are always those who think they own the newsgroup. They will flame anyone for posting anything they don't like. These pyromaniacs actually ruin newsgroups by chasing away intelligent discussions. I used to be intimidated by these folks, until I realized that most of them are just bullies. If you get flamed for posting to a newsgroup, follow these steps:

1. Double-check the newsgroup. Did your posting fit with the current level of discussion in the group? Are there similar messages in the group?
2. Read the charter or FAQ. Does your posting seem appropriate?
3. If you posted inappropriately, apologize to the flamer and cancel your posting.
4. If you feel your posting was appropriate, defend it. Don't let bullies drive you out of a discussion group. They have no more right to determine appropriateness than you do.

If you are using a giveaway file, and your posting simply tells people how to get the free file, it is not a commercial announcement. Nevertheless, here's a flame I got for a posting about the book *Everyday Cooking with Dr. Dean Ornish*.

```
This posting is blatantly commercial, and is totally off-
topic. The sci.life-extension group is for discussions about
vitamins, life extension, etc; not for services or commercial
businesses.
```

Here's an abbreviated version of my reply:

```
Perhaps you don't care for my posting to sci.life-extension,
but it is neither off-topic nor commercial. As a reader of
```

```
life extension literature, I'm sure you're aware of how
important proper diet is to life extension, particularly a
diet low in animal fats. Dr. Ornish has done pioneering work
in this area. Secondly, my posting was not commercial. I am
not selling anything, nor asking people to buy anything. I'm
simply informing them of the availability of an excellent
article about Dr. Ornish and his new book. I would have posted
the article in its entirety, but such long posts are
considered bad netiquette. This is an open discussion group
and the information I provided was clearly within the bounds
of the charter.
```

The flamer sent me an apology, admitting that my posting was appropriate and that he didn't examine it carefully before turning on his torch. He then confessed to spending many hours each week scanning his favorite newsgroups and flaming anyone who made "inappropriate" posts. After a few encounters like this, I've become a little hardened. If my post is inappropriate, I apologize and remove it. But if it is appropriate, I vigorously defend it.

Commercial Service Encounters

When your postings are challenged on a commercial service (or a moderated newsgroup), the approach is a little different. My first reaction is to ask the forum host if there is any way I can change the message to make it acceptable. These people are used to dealing with hotheads and crass commercial spammers. If your posting is a legitimate contribution to the group, there should be a way for you to rework it to satisfy the host.

Sometimes it's hard to remember that *people* run these forums and make these decisions. If your posting is taken down, it's a little disconcerting to ask 102473,923 for an explanation, or appeal your case to JP4793Z. But, remember, there's always a *name* behind the number, and it's a lot easier to connect with Host Janet or Sysop Paul. When you let these folks know you want to make a contribution to their forums, and you just want to know how to adjust something to make it work, they'll start to treat you with respect, too. Once you've won over a forum host, you'll seldom have trouble in the future; when you do, it will be easy to talk it over.

There are two things forum hosts frequently object to. The first is a blatant commercial advertisement. If you post a message that says, "I'm selling widgets for $15.00 each. Please send e-mail for a product description," hosts are not going to like it. It's not that they want to spare the members commercial announcements—on Prodigy, there are commercials on almost every screen—it's that they prefer you *pay* for the privilege of commercial announcements, like other advertisers.

Forum hosts also hate when you aren't contributing to the discussion. If you're promoting a product, you should be ready to engage in discussion about it. You don't have to post ads—let your signature do the selling. When you contribute to the discussion, you're joining a dialogue with equals, not marketing to sheep. There's always a way to phrase your announcement so that it sounds like a news item rather than an ad.

You can satisfy some forum hosts simply by moving your announcements or giveaway files. Some forums have special places for commercial announcements. Rather than remove your posting, they'll ask you to put it in the commercial area. Other forums have special threads for announcing Web sites so that the message boards don't get cluttered with these kinds of announcements. If you have a posting removed, it might just be a matter of finding a more appropriate thread to put it in.

The most successful online marketing is done by people who get involved in the discussion groups. They respond to other people's messages. They answer questions and offer advice. They don't push their business but let their signatures do the selling. Their participation is not only tolerated but welcomed by forum hosts and members alike. It's known as the "soft sell" and it's very effective. If you plan to market online, then you should get close to the forums that are important to your success and become an active participant. People always welcome someone who makes valuable contributions to the group.

Top Tips

- **Don't Spam:** Don't post messages indiscriminately. Make an effort to determine whether your message is appropriate for each discussion group you post to.

- **Let Current Standards Be Your Guide:** Forget about FAQs, AUPs, terms of service and the like. Common sense and current activity are your best guides to appropriate behavior.

- **Get to Know Your Hosts:** Forum hosts are people, not machines. They can help you reach your target audience with minimum resistance.

- **Provide Value:** Back up your announcements with free help files or other giveaways that members of the discussion group will find of value.

- **Use a Good Subject Line:** A good subject line inspires your target audience to open the message. Sometimes the subject line *is* the message.

- **More Than a Screenful Is Wasteful:** Keep your messages short and offer to provide more information on request.

- **Participate:** Follow up your announcements and contribute to discussions. Being helpful is the best kind of ad.

- **Don't Overheat:** Try to diffuse conflicts before they escalate into flame wars. Even if you're right, you never know what the other person is capable of.

CHAPTER 8

Document Transfers

One of the unique characteristics of Internet communication is the concept of *layering*. On the information superhighway, the audience is in the driver's seat. If they see a message you posted, they might finger the throttle and visit your Web site. If they like what they see, they might hit the gas a little harder, perhaps requesting further information via e-mail. On the other hand, if your message bores them, they can turn on a dime and travel elsewhere.

Throughout this book, I've stressed the importance of layering information for your target audience. When you post publicly, either through e-mail or in discussion groups, your messages must be brutally short. You should write only enough to catch the attention of your target audience and tell them how to reach the next layer. It took me years to learn this strategy; hopefully, it won't take you as long. When I look at the messages I posted when I first came online, I'm shocked at how long they are. Today, I try to make my public messages one screenful or less—and I have a small screen. I would never think of posting something that would be more than one printed page. Years ago, I posted book reviews that went on for several pages. Now, I just post a note that I have a book review and tell people how to get it.

If one marketing mistake is overloading your public messages, another is not providing enough information when asked for it. Once people cross the line and ask for more, provide them with everything they could possibly need to make a decision. This chapter is all about that second layer: providing detailed information to those who request it.

Some of the topics covered include:

- **Kinds of Documents to Use:** Some files travel better than others. I'll help you decide when to use the Net and when to send your documents the old-fashioned way.

- **Copyright Issues:** How to protect the information you're delivering, and how to make sure you're not violating someone else's copyright.

- **Formatting Documents for Electronic Delivery:** Sure it looks good on your screen, but what about on mine? How to dress up files so that they look pretty on multiple platforms.

- **File Transfers via E-Mail:** One of the simplest ways of responding to inquiries. We'll look at how to attach files, how to embed them, and how to manage an address book.

- **Using Autoresponders or Mailbots:** Repetitive requests can be handled by a machine—your computer. I'll show you how to set up a bot and warn you about the pitfalls of autoresponders.

- **Using List Servers:** The company newsletter is a tried-and-true PR vehicle. I'll show you how to set up a list server and how to use three electronic butlers: listserv, majordomo, and listproc.

- **Online Document Storage:** In addition to sending your files, you might want to put them online where people can grab them. We'll look at three popular storage units: FTP, Gopher, and the Web.

- **Commercial Online Services:** A crash course on document transfers on America Online, CompuServe, and other private online services.

- **Top Tips:** Sound bites on sending megabytes over the phone lines.

Kinds of Documents to Use

The Internet provides an inexpensive means for delivering information, but not every document is suited to electronic delivery. There are two common errors in the ways people use the Net for document delivery—one is not providing enough information. A little later in this section, I'll give you some ideas for the kinds of things you could be delivering over the Net. The other problem is trying to do too much with this technology. Let's look at some examples.

Files That Don't Travel Well

You may be tempted to attach news releases or announcements to e-mail because it's convenient to do so. Resist that urge. Whenever you attach documents to e-mail, they are sent as separate files and some people can't receive them or read them. At this writing, people on America Online can't get more than one attachment per message. Other people automatically filter off attached files to a corner of their hard drive (which is like being sent to cyberia). Some people get e-mail for free but have to pay extra to download files. It's better to embed small documents in the body of your e-mail message or post them publicly.

Some documents are too beautiful to send online. If the information looks a lot better in print, you might not want to give people the option of electronic delivery. The way a document looks has a huge impact on how effective it is. When you transfer files online, you often have little control over how the receiver sees your material. The look of your Web site is determined by the browser's software: browser's can choose the typeface, background color, even the relative sizes of the display type. On text-only browsers such as Lynx, the information on your Website might look drab or, worse, messy.

Even text files delivered via e-mail may look different on the receiver's screen from yours. The typeface, type size, and line endings could all display differently and be ill-suited to the file you sent. If you transfer Web pages to a prospect, and those pages have graphics, the graphics might not load properly in the receiver's Web browser. The look of the materials you send online could turn off the person at the other end, even if the printed version looks terrific.

For all these reasons, you should consider carefully the amount of graphic content and formatting you implement in your documents when you plan to transfer them electronically. If the piece relies on formatting to convey meaning, for example, you should avoid electronic delivery. One of my clients wanted to offer a sample chapter of a computer programming book as a giveaway file, but the chapter relied on two different typefaces: one for the code, one for the commentary. As a text-only file, we would have been limited to one font, and the document would have been unintelligible. We had to use something else.

If you're putting information on your Web site, consider the physical dimensions of the piece. Have you noticed how difficult it has been for newspapers to make the transition to the Web? On paper, newspapers usually are made up of large pages you can quickly scan. On a computer, any image larger than the screen can't be scanned without scrolling. Likewise, maybe your brochure looks fantastic on a 21-inch monitor, but what about the person trying to read it on a portable?

I had a client who built a Web site to promote a trade show. People interested in renting exhibit space could examine the floor plan at the site. What a mistake. If prospects hung in there, waiting for the 150K graphic to load, they were rewarded with a giant schematic that was impossible to use online. The map was 17 inches by 22 inches—you could see only a tiny piece of it in the screen at one time. When you consider that the smallest booth cost several thousand dollars to rent, it wasn't a good idea to have the potential buyer make a decision based on what they saw online. A better strategy is to entice people into requesting information, then send a quality sales package and have a professional representative make a sales call.

When you have a product that costs hundreds or thousands of dollars, make it easy for your prospects to give you their addresses and/or phone numbers. You might not want to make all your information available online. Think about holding something back as an incentive to request further information. Then you can follow up with a professionally produced sales piece or have a trained sales rep call on the prospect. Some people ask too much from their Web sites and lose valuable prospects as a result.

Files That Work Well Online

Many documents do work well online, particularly news items. You can tell people about breaking news in short public announcements, then offer the full details in an electronic press kit or news release. When someone requests a press kit, you know that person is seriously considering covering the story. You can often increase the amount of coverage you get by providing graphics electronically, for example, a promotional photo or artwork that accompanies the story. It's convenient to send this artwork over the Net—the journalist can pass the file along to their art department where it can be embedded in a story and sent to the printer. If the artwork is used in a television news segment, it may never be printed at all—just passed along from computer to computer.

Anything that demands immediate action is well-suited to the Net. Announcements about events or appearances are perfect when sent just before the big day. My firm has found that we can double the turnout at book signings by posting announcements within one week of the event. And book tours, which don't get much coverage on TV, radio, or in print, in part because the times and locations are often not finalized until a few days before the tour, are great items for the Net. The Net is a great way to get an audience for political rallies, concerts, or any typically underpublicized gathering.

The Net is also ideal for delivery of newsletters—if they aren't too long and don't rely on graphics. Newsletters are too long and too focused to post in full in public discussion groups, but it is perfectly acceptable to post messages telling people how to get a newsletter. Events calendars are good candidates for online delivery, too. Bands make their tour schedules available, festivals offer a rundown on the top talent, conferences and trade shows provide daily schedules—all these are good candidates for online delivery.

Customer service files are very popular online. FAQ files (Frequently Asked Questions) are one of the more vital artforms of the Net. A good set of FAQs cuts down on expensive customer service inquiries while bolstering your image online. Anything you can do to help people will be appreciated. Be careful, however, not to overwhelm people with 100-page FAQs. And always give them the alternative of calling, e-mailing, or writing for help.

Sometimes, very colorful pieces are better delivered through your Web site than in print. It costs nothing extra to use four-color art online, whereas the expense might be prohibitive if printed. Unfortunately, you will have little control over the quality of the image—that will depend on the viewer's computer configuration. But if image quality isn't critical and you can't afford to print four-color, you can achieve better marketing results using color images online.

Copyright Issues

Copyright is one of the most controversial issues surrounding the new media. On almost every mailing list I subscribe to, the subject of copyright is broached frequently. Discussions about copyright flare up every couple of months and threaten to dominate dialogue. The Net is littered with FAQs about electronic rights, with one attorney after another adding some nuance missed by the others. Beneath it all, the basics are very simple:

1. If you own it, you own it online.
2. If you don't own it, you need permission to use it online.

That said, realize that those two simple statements mask a whole slew of subtleties that could become important to you. If copyright is a major concern, I suggest you review the electronic rights situation with an attorney who specializes in this area. You also can study the current status of electronic rights at some of the copyright sites on the Internet. Two excellent sources of information are the CyberSpace Law Center, http://www.cybersquirrel.com/clc/index.html, and the Electronic Frontier Foundation, http://www.eff.org/. Here, though, we'll look at some of the major copyright considerations that could impact your on-line promotions.

You Own Your Work

When you write something, paint something, assemble something, say something, *create* anything original, you own it. You own all the rights to it. You don't have to put a copyright notice on it and you don't have to register your copyright. You own it from the moment of creation, and anyone who uses it without your permission is violating your copyright. That's the law.

In practice, people can swipe whatever they want and use it, then it's up to you to defend your rights. If you registered your copyright and used the copyright notice, you may have greater legal standing than if you didn't. By registering your copyright, you have a verifiable date on which you claimed ownership. By putting a copyright notice on your work, you're alerting people that you claim the rights to this work; hopefully, they'll think twice about using it without permission. Your work may be more vulnerable on the Net, but your rights online are the same.

Ownership of Correspondence

Correspondence follows a slightly different set of rules than other creative works. When you write something, you own the rights to it. When you send a letter to someone, though, that person acquires the rights to the document. You still own the ideas in your letter, but the recipient owns the physical letter and can sell it or trade it or publish it.

Similarly, when you e-mail someone, the receiver gains rights to use your e-mail (though not the ideas in it). And if you attach files to your e-mail, you still own the copyright to those files. When you subscribe to a newspaper, the journalists don't lose their copyright the minute the paper is delivered; they own the rights although you own the physical newspaper. Likewise, people don't have the legal right to take ideas or phrasing from your letters or e-mail and claim them as their own.

Even when you participate in an online discussion group, you own the rights to your words. One of the mailing lists I'm on sends a boilerplate informing newcomers that a condition of subscription is that the moderator has the right to store contributions online as part of the list. Most list servers aren't so formal. Once attorneys are involved, a boilerplate can stretch on *ad infinitum*. Simply, you own your words, but when you utter them in a public forum, other people may acquire the rights to display those words.

Look at the transcripts for chat sessions on America Online, and you'll see that America Online claims copyright. I've been a chat guest on America Online. I still own my words—the ideas I expressed that day. But America Online owns the transcripts, and I'm not legally entitled to distribute them without their permission. When I write articles for magazines, I specify exactly what rights I'm selling. In many cases, I can't reproduce articles I've sold to magazines on my own Web site without getting permission. On the other hand, *Internet World* magazine reprints my articles on its Web site, even though they clearly do not have the right to do so.

Legality vs. Practicality

There's a big difference between what you're allowed to do by law and what you can get away with. There are so many gradations to copyright law that you probably violate it frequently without knowing it. Many people use pithy quotations in their signature files (the bits of text automatically appended to outgoing messages). Unless the copyright has expired, using quotations this way is a violation of the law. I always get a kick out of electronic rights vigilantes who quote song lyrics in their sigs—a well-established violation of copyright.

Realistically, it's probably impossible for anyone communicating regularly online to avoid copyright violation. It's not important to understand all the nuances (unless, of course, you get sued); you should, however, be aware of some of the major copyright violations related to typical marketing and publicity activities online.

First, you can't reprint entire product reviews without permission. You can say your software was awarded five stars from *Byte* magazine, which said it was "fantastic," for example, but you can't reprint the complete review or substantial portions of it without permission. In practice, as we all know, people photocopy such reviews and mail them to customers all the time and it's tolerated (though illegal). But, if you put the review on your Web site or archive it somewhere online, you're asking for trouble.

Artwork has similar restrictions. You can find all sorts of copyright-free artwork on the Net: bullets and buttons and banners that you're free to use as you see fit. But most artwork is copyrighted and you need permission to include it at your Web site or in files you distribute over the Net. Even the design of Web sites is copyrighted. If you download someone else's Web site and replace its text with yours, you're violating that person's right to the look and feel of his or her Web site.

Unfortunately, getting permission to use material online can be a Herculean task. In many cases, no one is sure who owns the electronic rights; if you ask for permission, you might never get a response. Sometimes the publisher owns the rights; sometimes the writer or artist. Most often, no one really cares. I'm not a big fan of copyright law. Legally, I must tell you to get permission to use anything you don't own. Practically, as long as your use of copyrighted materials is benign, you're not likely to upset anyone. If you're not trying to profit by ripping off the work of someone else, you don't have a lot to worry about. If you make a good faith attempt to get permission when you believe it's required, that will go in your favor if you end up in a legal dispute. If you agree to stop using something when informed it belongs to someone else, few people will haul you into court.

Copyright law is complicated. If you work for a large company or have assets you need to protect, you will want to investigate the electronic rights issue thoroughly before putting any material of questionable ownership online.

Formatting Documents for Electronic Delivery

Formatting documents for electronic delivery is always a little tricky because, as I've said, the way they look is determined by the *viewer's* computer configuration, not yours. As far as I can tell, you can transfer *any* kind of file over the Net: word processor, database, spreadsheet, graphic, program, or anything else. I could probably send you everything on my hard drive attached to an e-mail message. If you lacked certain software, however, you might not be able to open any of the files.

Text Transfers

Most of your promotional materials will be text documents, and these are the easiest files to transfer. You should transfer word processor documents only if you know the people on the receiving end will be able to read them. A lot of people upload files on America Online believing any member can download them and read them. But if you upload Microsoft Word files, people using WordPerfect won't be able to read them unless they have translation software. Even if they can translate the document, it won't necessarily look as nice on the readers' screen as it does on yours, especially if you used fonts that the reader doesn't have.

To avoid problems of incompatibility, you should attempt to convert your documents to text-only files before you transfer them. All word processing programs have the option of saving files as text or as ASCII. When you save files as text, you lose some of the formatting, such as:

Type Styles: You can't control the font used.

Type Sizes: All the text will be the same size.

Emphasis: All bold, italics, underlining, and so on will be lost.

Tabs and Indents: These are usually converted to space bands.

Margins: Your margins will not be the same as the reader's.

Non-ASCII Characters: No bullets, dingbats, or curly quotes.

Most of us have become so used to formatting documents in word processors that it's often hard to make the transition to text. I recommend double-spacing between paragraphs rather than indenting them. White space is one of your only formatting tools; use it to set off headings and subheads. Add emphasis by using ALL CAPS or setting off phrases in *asterisks* or _underscores_. Probably the hardest rule to remember is "no curly quotes." Even the most professional online marketers frequently forget to turn off the curly quotes, which are translated into ugly ASCII characters when converted to text.

Controlling the length is particularly difficult. Most word processors automatically wrap each line at the margin. But when you send a text file over the Net attached to Eudora e-mail, it automatically inserts hard returns every 76 characters. When someone with margins narrower than 76 characters opens the document, the line endings break horribly, making the document very difficult to read. Here's a portion of a news release I received, showing the jagged line-ending effect.

```
HAVE LIABILITY EXPOSURE ON THE WEB?  GET FREE
INFORMATION ON
HOW TO MINIMIZE
THE LEGAL AND FINANCIAL RISKS OF HAVING A WORLD-
WIDE WEB
PRESENCE

         Any business that communicates on the
internet,
creates or disseminates
information (such as on the Web), or who does
similar work
for others, needs
to address the liability risks. Risks include the
legal and
financial
liability of any error or misstatement which causes
damages,
loss of
revenue, damaged reputation, or copyright
infringement.
```

To circumvent this, set your word processor for narrower margins and add a hard return at the end of each line. That sounds like a lot of work, but you should be able to do it automatically. First, set your margins to no longer than 55 characters. (You may have to change your font from a proportional font to a monospaced font in order to calculate your margins.) When you save your document as text, you should have the option of converting soft returns to hard returns (your word processor might default to this). Below is a portion of Netsurfer Digest, one of the most popular electronic zines covering the Internet. It truncates lines for a nice, readable presentation:

```
APPLIANCE HEAVEN

Continuing the trend of customizeable sites, Hamilton Beach, of
blender fame, creates a page for you based on a few "lifestyle
```

```
questions". Enter your virtual kitchen and design your perfect
appliance, or submit an entry to win one already built.
<URL:http://www.hambeach.com/>
```

If you're used to Apple computers, you might not be familiar with the dreaded "Rule of Eight and Three." That's the format for DOS or Windows file names: no more than eight characters for the file name and three for the extension. When you're planning on transferring files over the Net, follow the Rule of Eight and Three when naming your files. It will make your files more universally useful.

Graphics Transfers

There seem to be many more graphic formats than text formats. Computer graphics may be GIF or JPEG or PICT or TIFF or any number of other formats. The point is, people won't be able to view your graphics if they don't have the right software. And even if they *do* have the right software, the graphic may look a lot better on your high-resolution, 21-inch color monitor than it does on their 12-inch black-and-white, low-resolution screen.

The two most popular graphic formats on the World Wide Web are GIF and JPEG. If you are making your promotional materials available on the Web, I recommend that you use GIF or JPEG for your graphics. If you're sending your promotional materials as HTML files, the graphics should be GIFs or JPEGs. If you want to use other graphics formats, try to determine whether the receiver will be able to view your files. You might want to make your graphics available in several different formats and let your audience choose the ones they prefer.

Other File Transfers

One file format gaining popularity on the Internet is PDF, often called Acrobat files. Acrobat is the name of both a viewing program that allows you to read these files, and a program that allows you to create them. At this time, the Acrobat reader is distributed free of charge, although you must pay to use the Acrobat file creator. Acrobat works a little like an online fax machine: the file looks the same on the viewer's screen as it does on the sender's.

Acrobat is part of the next wave in online document delivery. People want to control the way their documents look: the fonts, the placement of graphics, everything about the viewing experience. These new document formats allow that to happen. One hurdle Acrobat must clear before gaining widespread acceptance is the resistance to its large file sizes; conveying all that additional information requires much larger files. As these issues are resolved, you will be able to design better-looking documents and transfer them more quickly and easily.

You're not limited to text and graphics on the Internet; you can transfer video, audio, and software, too. But with any file transfer, remember, your audience must have the proper software and hardware to make use of the files. As you get into more exotic file types and formats, you reduce the number of people that can use your files. But when your audience is a select group that will benefit from these files, it can be worth going through the trouble of preparing these files for electronic delivery. For example, if you're trying to make television news, you may want to explore transferring video clips over the Net.

The technical details of these sophisticated file transfers are beyond the scope of this book. Just be aware of the potential for using them. As the technology improves, you'll see more video transfers. I have yet to see a publicist offering to e-mail audio or video, though I have started to see clips on Web sites. In the future, Internet news releases will include audio and video clips that broadcast journalists can upload right into the news feed. For now, those files are just too big to transfer on anything but a prearranged basis.

Compression

That brings up our next subject: compression. Large files are often compressed before being transferred across the Net. Compression makes file transfers quicker and saves storage space. Both GIF and JPEG incorporate compression. When you view a graphic on a Web page, the files actually uncompress in your browser. Whenever you transfer large files online, you get into the compression issue. For example, America Online and CompuServe require that file uploads exceeding a certain size be compressed. Now your audience not only has to have the right software to view the file, they need the right software just to uncompress it. You might want to avoid sending large files until the mechanism improves considerably. In the meantime, you can invite people to get files from your Web site or FTP site, where you can make them available in a variety of formats and compressions.

Two popular file compressors are StuffIt/StuffIt Expander and Zip/Unzip. There are many variations of Zip, and there are also many other compression programs out there. You can find freeware or shareware compression programs online at the software sites list in the Resources chapter (Chapter 12).

Your audience can only use a compressed file if they have the software to uncompress it. Unless a decompression program is widely available, you limit your audience when you compress your files. At many FTP sites, you'll notice people offering multiple versions of compressed files: Zipped, Stuffed, MacBinaryII, or whatever.

File Transfers via E-Mail

Probably the easiest and most common way of distributing files on the Net is through e-mail. Even if you have a Web site and/or an FTP site, you'll find a lot of people prefer to get their information via e-mail. There are two ways to send files through e-mail: you can *attach* them or *embed* them.

Attaching Files

Figure 8.1 shows a Eudora e-mail message with several files attached. You can bunch different file types together in one e-mail. In this example, there is one HTML file and three GIFs attached to the mail. This

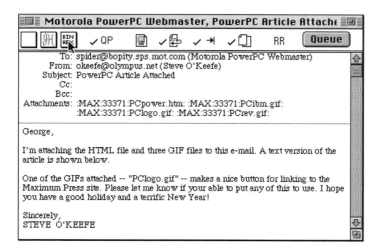

Figure 8.1 Transferring files as attachments to Eudora e-mail. The cursor points to the encoding pull-down menu.

was a prearranged transfer, so I was pretty certain the recipient would be able to read the files.

There are several different transfer protocols or encoding schemes for sending files over the phone lines. Eudora defaults to BinHex encoding, but you can choose from many other formats. The cursor in Figure 8.1 points to the encoding pull-down menu. If people have trouble using the files you transferred, you might have to change the encoding. I've had good luck sending graphics using UUencode when BinHex has failed.

One problem with attaching files is that they're often dumped on the recipient's computer in some remote location where they might never be found. My e-mail program has a setting that lets me direct where I want file attachments stored. Sometimes I forget to look at the files I downloaded when I'm done reading my e-mail, and days might pass before I notice those mysterious files on my hard drive. That's one reason I like to avoid sending attached files to other people: they might get set aside and never opened.

The other reason for not sending files attached to e-mail is that it's considered rude unless the files were requested. The other day I received a news release that had an unsolicited file attached. I immediately deleted the file unopened. I expose my computer to all kinds of viruses, and even though I have software to protect myself, I don't trust unsolicited file transfers. I consider them intrusive and I delete them. I expect many people feel the same way. It's good netiquette *not* to transfer files unless someone asks for them.

Embedding Files

For news releases and other documents that are too large to put in a public message but not so large that they can't be sent via mail, embedding them in your e-mail is better than attaching them. If you followed the instructions for preparing the document as a text file, you can just open the file, copy it, and paste it into the body of an e-mail message.

Every day, I send many different messages embedded into e-mail. I have a file with basic information about my business, another file referring people to other Internet publicists, several files with sample chapters from books I'm promoting, and so on. I find it convenient to keep a separate folder that contains only files prepared for electronic delivery. That way, I reduce the chances of sending someone a file he or she won't be able to read. You might want to set up a similar attachments folder.

Most people receiving documents embedded in e-mail will be able to read them right from their e-mail software. However, some commercial online services convert long e-mail messages into files that the reader must download before viewing. This puts you in a file-transfer situation whether you like it or not. As long as the person requested the information, you shouldn't have a netiquette problem.

Address Book Management

You can use e-mail to distribute newsletters, news releases, and other promotional announcements without having to buy special software. We'll look at setting up *bots* and *list servers* later in this chapter. Much of the work done by these specialized programs can be done manually through e-mail. This may be the best way to handle the company newsletter or other regular announcements, if the group you're sending to is small.

As I explained in a previous chapter, Eudora allows you to set up nicknames that contain multiple e-mail addresses. You can use these nicknames to store contact lists. I have a customer list, a prospect list, and several different medialists I use. Figure 8.2 shows a portion of my Internet journalists list.

You can set up similar nicknames for your customers, prospects, suppliers, investors, key media contacts, and more. You can also set up nicknames like this for special events; say, for example, to send daily updates to people attending a conference. E-mail nicknames are a low-cost, low-maintenance way of handling such needs. And you can set up address books like these on most commercial online services as well as on the Net.

The subject of address book management was covered in more detail in Chapter 6, E-Mail News Releases. There you will find guidelines for formatting your lists and suggestions for using each of the major commercial online services. When transferring information this way, be sure to use the blind carbon copy field of your e-mail message for the distribution list. This, too, was covered thoroughly in Chapter 6.

Using Autoresponders, or Mailbots

An autoresponder is an e-mail address that sends a canned message to anyone who sends e-mail. For a remarkably simple idea, it goes by many

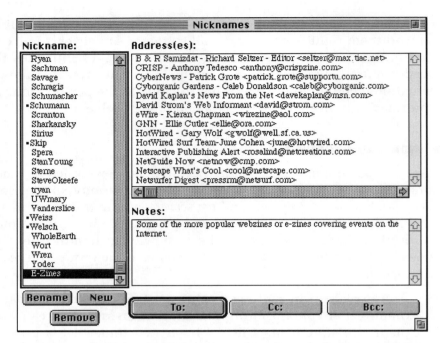

Figure 8.2 The Eudora nickname "e-zines" contains the e-mail addresses of popular webzines and electronic journals.

different names: mailbot, e-mailbot, autoreply, autobot, mail reflector. You'll call it a blessing if you get a lot of similar inquiries that can be handled automatically.

The prototypical autoresponder is the *infobot*. You'll see messages online that read: "For details, send e-mail to info@mysite.com." Anytime someone sends e-mail to the infobot, it instantly replies with a preprogrammed message. The message sent to the infobot doesn't need a subject line or any special words in the body—*any* mail sent to the infobot address will generate the same reply, even stray mail.

Mailbots have many good uses. A lot of businesspeople use them to distribute basic information about their products or services. Other good uses include sending contest rules, tour schedules, store locations, street directions, product support files, help files, electronic coupons, order forms, inventory lists, giveaway files used in promotions, and more. Most autoresponders keep a log of every e-mail address that requested information, which can then be used as a prospect list or mailing list.

Anyone familiar with Fax-On-Demand services will be comfortable using autoresponders. You'll save money on your faxback charges if you can shift people from your fax machine to your mailbot. For many good examples of the innovative ways people are using autoresponders, visit Info@, a Web site with e-mail links to hundreds of autoresponders where you can get free information. The address is http://www.autoresponders.com/newlist.htm.

I've had mixed results using autoresponders. They're great time-savers when you know you're going to generate a lot of similar e-mail requests. I had my best results using them for contest rules. But I don't think they're a great way to send basic info about your company. Why? Because people often send e-mail when they have a specific question or problem they want help with.

The problem with autoresponders is that they send the same packet of information for every request. When I offer sample chapters of books I'm promoting, I could easily set up an autoresponder to deal with the requests, but I don't. Every now and then, I get a request for a sample chapter from someone working for, say, *People Magazine*, or a motion picture studio or a foreign literary agency. These are major hits for my clients. Their requests would get buried by a mailbot, because when an autoresponder tells you who requested information, it only gives you the e-mail address, not the entire message. If the person is asking for help or for something special, you'll never know it. That person will be sent your canned reply, and a major sale could be lost to the cold embrace of your form letter. To guard against this, at my firm, we open every request for information and take a quick peek at the message before we paste in the giveaway file and send it back. About one out of every 25 messages requires special handling. If you're selling products or services with a high sticker price, you don't want your mailbot acting as your sales rep.

The most popular way to give out your mailbot address is in your signature file: the text automatically appended to outgoing messages. I've even seen some mailbots registered in directories like Yahoo! You can link to a mailbot off your Web page using a mailto link or a form. Some browsers are not forms-compatible, though, and enough people fall into this category to warrant providing alternative methods for getting the information. You can use multiple mailbots on your Web page and set them as in this example:

```
Please check off the information you desire and
I'll send you the reports via e-mail. If your
browser is not forms-compatible, just drop me a
line at webmaster@mysite.com.

Special Reports available by E-Mail:
[ ] How to set-up an autoresponder.
[ ] How to set-up a list server.
[ ] How to set-up an FTP site.

E-Mail address where you want the reports sent:
[_____]


[Click here when finished.]
```

Setting Up Mailbots

To set up an autoresponder, first contact your Internet service provider to see if it offers this service. If you are on America Online, Compu-Serve, or another commercial online service, you may not be able to use autoresponders through your main account. However, you won't be locked out of the market for these wonderful tools—you can rent autoresponder service from firms on the Internet. Even those with direct Internet accounts may want to shop around for these services rather than using their access provider, since prices vary greatly. A good place to begin comparison shopping is Yahoo's "Internet Services" category. Here are the names of two mailbot providers I found:

Success Marketing
http://kwicsys.com/success/respond.html

Visions by Hand
http://www.wbm.ca/visions/auto/

An autoresponder is just a dedicated e-mail account, so the charges are similar to the cost of maintaining an e-mail address, but you need a separate account for each autoresponder. You also must provide the file that the mailbot will send out. It's best to prepare this file as ASCII text using the formatting suggestions given earlier in this chapter.

There are companies that will set you up with an autoresponder for as little as $5 per month, so don't let your Internet service provider gouge you. Ask for a daily activity report or address log; if you are paying a small fee for each hit the mailbot registers, you'll want to be sure someone's not padding the account. Ask about any hidden charges, such as:

- per message sent
- if volume exceeds x number of messages per day, per month, and so on
- per byte transmitted, or based on message size
- for changing the text of your message
- for reports showing who requested info

Your Internet service provider might let you set up and manage your own mailbot once you learn how to do it. Marcia Yudkin, author of *Marketing Online* and a well-known Internet publicist, offers a free file telling how to set up a mailbot on a Unix server. You can contact Ms. Yudkin by e-mail, yudkin@world.std.com, or you can get information from her autoresponder, yudkinfo@world.std.com.

One disadvantage with autoresponders is that you need to tie up an e-mail account for each mailbot. If you have your own domain and/or a direct connection to the Internet, you can use a list server program to do the work of a mailbot. That way, people always send e-mail to the same address (the list server address), varying the body of their message to get different files. That's just one of the wonderful things a list server can do for you. Let's see what else they're capable of.

Using List Servers

A list server is a software program that distributes information to members of a list. Most Internet mailing lists are run on list server software. List servers are popular for distributing discussions, newsletters, and product information. If you have a direct connection to the Internet, you can set up your own list server. If you have a dial-up account, you can ask your Internet service provider to set one up for you, or you can find companies on the Internet that sell list management services.

Most list servers have the same basic structure. People join the list by sending a subscribe e-mail message to the server address. They usually receive an acknowledgment and instructions for getting off the list. Once they've joined, they'll receive every document sent to the members of the list. They can unsubscribe at any time by sending a properly worded message to the server. As an example, here are the instructions for getting *Netsurfer Digest*, one of the best e-zines covering the Internet:

```
You can subscribe via e-mail. Send all e-mail
subscription requests to:

    nsdigest-request@netsurf.com

To subscribe to the HTML version send the following
command in the BODY of the message:

    subscribe nsdigest-html

To subscribe to the TEXT version send the following
command in the BODY of the message:

    subscribe nsdigest-text

To unsubscribe send one of the following commands
in the BODY of the message:

    unsubscribe nsdigest-html
    unsubscribe nsdigest-text
```

As you can see, you aren't limited to sending only text files through a list server. Depending on the software, you should be able to send almost any sort of file: graphics, programs, audio or video clips, and so on. List servers are most often used to communicate short bits of information, though. They're perfect for keeping in touch with your customers or prospects. And you can configure list servers to work like autoresponders, sending a file back to anyone who sends e-mail to the proper server address.

Most list server software enables you to have a moderated discussion group via e-mail. Many shrewd marketers have used these discussion groups as a subtle way to promote their businesses and keep their names in front of the public. My friend Glenn Fleishman ran the popular Internet Marketing list for many years. He also builds Web sites and provides other online marketing services for clients of his Point of Presence Company. As moderator of a popular list, his name was always in front of his potential market. You didn't have to be on the list very long to realize that Glenn has one of the sharpest minds in the business, combined with a strong sense of integrity. In the course of moderating the list, he got more customers than he could handle.

Running a moderated discussion group has become a road to online marketing success, but there's a catch (isn't there always?). In order for the discussion group to be successful, the moderator has to stay active, encourage discussion, remove spam, provide answers, maintain archives, and troubleshoot technical problems. You may find that moderating the list actually costs more in time than the value of the business it brings in. The best moderators are seldom in it for the money, although they seldom lack for it, either.

There are three major types of list server software in use on the Net: listserv, listproc, and majordomo. Listserv is considered the Cadillac of list servers. It's made by L-Soft Corporation and runs on Unix, Windows, VM, and VMS. The pricing structure is complicated and starts at around $500 per year. For more information, contact:

L-Soft International
sales@lsoft.com
1-800-399-5449
1-301-731-0440

Listproc is made by CREN, the Corporation for Research & Educational Networking. For nonmembers of CREN, the program sells for as low as $2,000 per year. There is a free version of listproc available on the Net, though it's no longer supported by CREN. You can get the free version via FTP from ftp://cs-ftp.bu.edu/pub/listserv/. For more information about listproc, e-mail listprocinfo@listproc.net (an example of using list server software for an autoresponder) or contact:

CREN
cren@cren.net
1-202-331-5360

Majordomo is a popular list server because the price is right: it's available free on the Net. You can get it via anonymous FTP from ftp://ftp.greatcircle.com/pub/majordomo/. Majordomo was developed for Unix-based systems but it can be fussed with to run on other systems. You can find gateways to majordomo on the Web at the following two addresses:

Mailserv: http://iquest.com/~fitz/www/mailserv

LWGate: http://www.netspace.org/users/dwb/lwgate.html

Not all list servers have the same capabilities and capacities. If you are interested in setting one up, contact your Internet service provider for more information. An excellent place to find answers to all your list server questions is Bob and Varda Novick's Web page devoted to e-mail discussion groups, mailing lists, and related resources. They have links to the three major list servers and many others. You'll find them on the Web at http://www.wbcom.com/impulse/list.html.

Online Document Storage

We've covered most of the *active* transfer systems, where you send the information to people who ask for it. Now we'll examine some of the more popular *passive* systems, where you store your documents online where people who want them must come and get them. These include the World Wide Web, FTP, and Gopher.

The Web

The Web needs no introduction. If you haven't already seen the Web, you've no doubt heard so many stories about it—and you've seen so many URLs—that you're probably sick of hearing about it. The World Wide Web is the Internet's multimedia matrix, where even stale, boring information comes to life with colors, sounds, animation, in an easy-to-use, point-and-click, multilayered structure. The dramatic growth of the World Wide Web is probably the biggest business story of the decade.

Whether or not you have direct access to the Internet, you can setup your own Web site. The lure is the ability to cheaply store gigabytes of information where people who want it or need it can retrieve it at very low cost. You can use the Web to deliver product information, news, and entertainment. Because the Web is interactive, you can also use it for conferences, customer service, and sales. The vast capabilities of a Web site are beyond the scope of this work, but there are many fine publications available that can help you use the Web to its full potential. Here, I'll stick to some of the important publicity aspects.

A publicist has many audiences, and a Web site is a good way to keep in touch with them. They include investors, customers, suppliers, employees, and governmental authorities. Anyone you are communicating with *offline* is potentially interested in communicating with you *online*, and you should take them into consideration when building your Web site. I've watched many corporations go after the online consumer market (which is thin, in my opinion) and turn their backs on their best customers—the wholesale market (which is strong online). I've seen manufacturers trying to compete in online entertainment when they should be using their Web sites to assist their sales reps.

You can use your Web site to distribute free help or giveaway files. You can distribute news releases and press kits from the Web site, and use it to relay artwork to journalists who are covering your announcements. You can use the Web site to collect addresses for newsletters, mailing lists, and bulk e-mail. But don't forget that investors and government regulators are cruising the Web, too, so be careful about the kinds of content you put on the Web. What looks like entertainment now could be evidence later.

For information on setting up a Web site, contact your Internet service provider or look around the Web. Most commercial online services allow you to set up a small personal Web page at no extra charge. If you shop around on the Web, you'll find some incredible bargains on Web space—probably cheaper than what your Internet service provider charges. Make sure you check references, though, before committing to a Web site; it's a drag to launch a site, only to have to change your Web address later.

File Transfer Protocol (FTP)

According to the latest MIDS survey (see Chapter 2, Who's Online), File Transfer Protocol, or FTP, is still more popular than the Web; that is, people spend more of their online time at FTP sites than they do at Web sites. This is amazing when you consider how old-fashioned FTP looks next to the wonders of the World Wide Web.

File Transfer Protocol is a way of distributing large files over the Net. When you visit an FTP site, you'll see a directory like the one

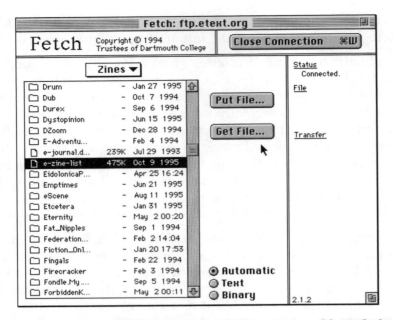

Figure 8.3 An FTP directory, from the etext archive of electronic zines at ftp://ftp.etext.org/pub/zines. The highlighted entry is a file; most of the remaining entries are folders containing files.

shown in Figure 8.3. Each line in the directory is hyperlinked to a either a file or a folder. Click on the hyperlink to a file and your computer begins downloading it.

You can use FTP to distribute any kind of file: software, graphics, text, audio, video, and so on. Files are often stored and transferred in a compressed format, so that they take up less space on the FTP server and transfer more quickly. As stated earlier in this chapter, you need special software to compress and expand these files. You can get such compression software for free on the Net from several different FTP sites. See the Resources chapter for the location nearest you.

Most Internet service providers maintain an FTP directory and will allow you to store files there. You can then give people the FTP address—including the directory your file is in and the file name—and they can fetch the file for themselves. You can also link to FTP files from a Web site. People who activate the link will begin downloading the file through their Web browser.

FTP servers are often used to distribute software, which accounts for the high levels of usage they see. Free software is one of the Internet's major drawing cards. Because the files tend to be very large, it's economical for software manufacturers to distribute updates via FTP. It saves on the cost of diskettes and postage.

FTP is not the best way to deliver most publicity documents, however, because there are too many steps involved in reading the file. The person has to visit your FTP site, download the file, possibly uncompress it, then open it. Do you really want to send journalists a message that you have a news release and they can get it from your FTP site? It's much better to offer to send the information via e-mail than to make them retrieve it. FTP is more useful if your promotion includes a very large file (say, a free software program) that people are likely to want badly enough to come and get.

Gopher Servers

Gopher servers are yet another way to distribute information online. Named for the University of Minnesota mascot where Gopher software was first developed, a Gopher server is a nongraphical information system. You can download files from a Gopher site, just as you can with FTP, but you can also view them at the site.

Just when Gopher servers started getting popular, they were pretty much made obsolete by the Web, although they're still frequented by people using nongraphical browsers such as Lynx. But as more content has become available only on the Web, there are very few people online using text browsers. At one time, the Gopher was an efficient storage mechanism; now everything a Gopher does can be handled better through a Web site.

Figure 8.4 shows a Gopher directory from the WELL, a virtual community headquartered in the San Francisco Bay area (gopher://gopher.well.com). The entries are either files or folders containing files. Note the dates in the illustration; most of the files are dated 1993 or 1994—the heyday of the Gopher site.

You can still use Gopher to distribute documents. Your Internet service provider may run a Gopher server, and you should be able to store documents there at little or no cost. Or you can find companies on the Internet that will sell you space on their Gopher servers. Another alter-

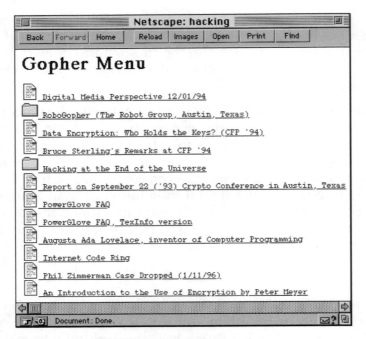

Figure 8.4 A Gopher menu from the WELL.

native is to approach administrators at your favorite Gopher sites and ask if you can store files for free—I wouldn't be surprised if many of them said yes.

Commercial Online Services

Most commercial online services have a variety of ways for transferring files to other members. You can attach files to e-mail, although sometimes only to other service members (you can't always send them to outside addresses). On America Online and CompuServe, you can upload files into libraries, where, if they are approved, they'll be made available to the public. You can also set up mailing lists, FTP files, and even Web pages on most commercial online services. We'll look at the simplest ways for transferring information on each online service: *file attachments* and *uploads*.

CompuServe

CompuServe doesn't enable you to attach files to e-mail, but you can send files separately to other members. At the time of this writing, you

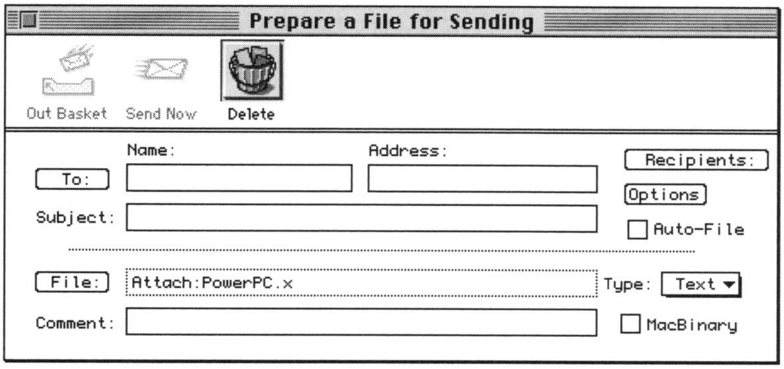

Figure 8.5 CompuServe's File Send window.

can't send files outside of CompuServe—you can send only to other members. To send a file, use CompuServe's pull-down menu and you'll get a window like the one shown in Figure 8.5.

Clicking on the To button brings up your address book; or you can keyboard the recipient's address. Clicking on the File button allows you to roam your hard drive looking for the file you want to send. Because the file is not attached to a message, you need to address the file transfer, add a subject line, and, optionally, include a comment. You can send the file immediately or put it in your out basket to send later.

CompuServe has a library in virtually every forum. Members are welcome to contribute or download files. These libraries are one of CompuServe's best ideas and strongest assets. They're also a good way of distributing information to interested parties. You simply prepare the file as described earlier in this chapter, upload it in a library, then post messages telling people about the file and how to get it. Most forum hosts are happy to take any file that is more than just a commercial announcement, and some forums even have a library set aside for ads.

Most CompuServe forums have multiple libraries—one for each category in their message boards. Figure 8.6 shows the contents of the Business library in the Book Preview Forum. There's a list of file names all following the Rule of Eight and Three (no more than eight characters for the file name, and three characters for the extension). You can see how important the choice of a file name is. Which files would you open?

From the Library window, you can also tell the type of each file (text, graphic, etc.), the date it was uploaded, its size and, most impor-

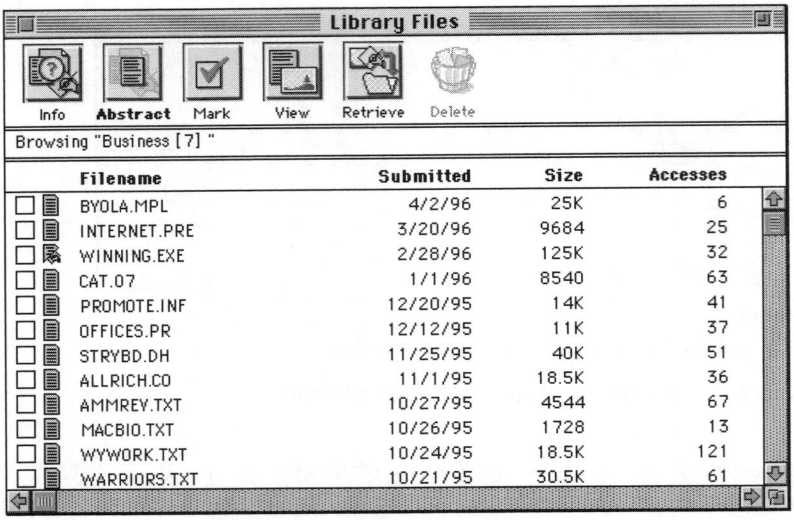

Figure 8.6 Partial contents of a CompuServe library.

tantly, how many times people have downloaded it. I call this last item the "heat index." I suggest you examine the files that get the most heat to see what all the fuss is about. You can also use the heat index to track the success of your own promotions. The file Warriors.txt in Figure 8.6 was one of my giveaway files. It didn't get the most downloads in the library, but it's up there with the leaders.

When people are deciding whether to grab a file, they usually look at the abstract. An abstract for one of my promotions is shown in Figure 8.7. It contains basic information about the file and a one-paragraph description of the contents. If people like what they read, they can download the file or view it online.

Before you upload a file, you should quickly look for instructions, which you'll usually find in the library. The procedure is the same in all forums, but some sysops have certain preferences on how you name your file or what content is acceptable. Sometimes uploads must go into a holding tank library for new files. You can use CompuServe's pull-down menus to get a short description for each library, as shown in Figure 8.8.

Once you know where you want to put your file, use CompuServe's pull-down menu to Contribute File. You'll get a form like the one shown

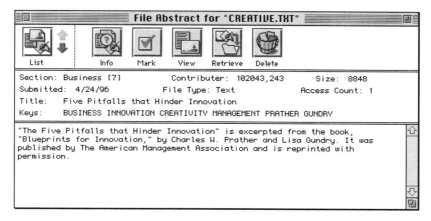

Figure 8.7 The abstract for a library file on CompuServe.

in Figure 8.9. Click on the File button to roam your hard disk looking for the proper file. Then you can name the file using the Host Filename section and give it a longer title, too. The Keys field is used to index your file in CompuServe's file search mechanism. It's easy to forget to choose which Section (or library) you want your file to go into; CompuServe defaults to the first library and you have to change it if you want a different one. Add a one-paragraph file description and you're ready to contribute. CompuServe actively solicits member contributions, and credits your account for the time it takes to upload your file.

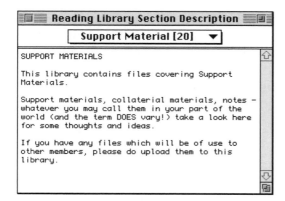

Figure 8.8 Look for the Library Descriptions before uploading files on CompuServe.

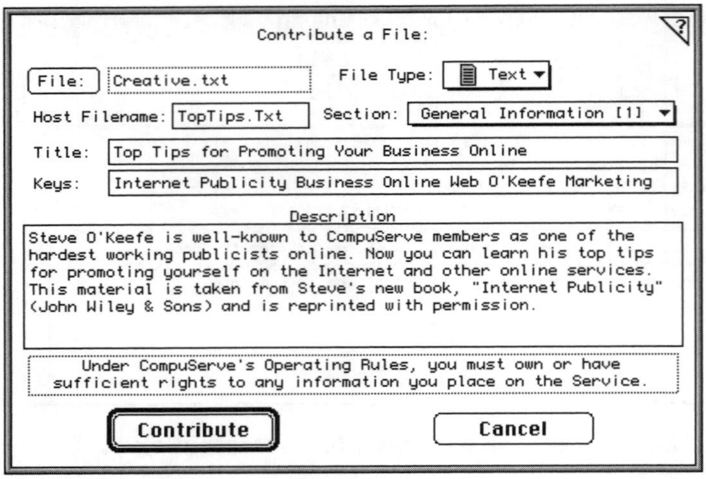

```
┌─────────────────────────────────────────────────────────────┐
│                    Contribute a File:                    ◥?  │
│                                                               │
│  ┌───────┐ ┌─────────────────────┐  File Type: ┌──┐          │
│  │ File: │ │Creative.txt         │             │▤ │ Text ▾    │
│  └───────┘ └─────────────────────┘             └──┘          │
│  Host Filename: ┌────────────┐  Section: ┌──────────────────┐│
│                 │TopTips.Txt │           │General Information [1] ▾││
│                 └────────────┘           └──────────────────┘│
│  Title:  ┌──────────────────────────────────────────────┐   │
│          │Top Tips for Promoting Your Business Online     │   │
│          └──────────────────────────────────────────────┘   │
│  Keys:   ┌──────────────────────────────────────────────┐   │
│          │Internet Publicity Business Online Web O'Keefe Marketing││
│          └──────────────────────────────────────────────┘   │
│                          Description                          │
│  ┌──────────────────────────────────────────────────────┐   │
│  │Steve O'Keefe is well-known to CompuServe members as one of the│   │
│  │hardest working publicists online. Now you can learn his top tips│   │
│  │for promoting yourself on the Internet and other online services.│   │
│  │This material is taken from Steve's new book, "Internet Publicity"│   │
│  │(John Wiley & Sons) and is reprinted with permission.     │   │
│  └──────────────────────────────────────────────────────┘   │
│  ┌ ─ ─ ─ ─ ─ ─ ─ ─ ─ ─ ─ ─ ─ ─ ─ ─ ─ ─ ─ ─ ─ ─ ─ ─ ─ ┐   │
│     Under CompuServe's Operating Rules, you must own or have   │
│     sufficient rights to any information you place on the Service.│
│  └ ─ ─ ─ ─ ─ ─ ─ ─ ─ ─ ─ ─ ─ ─ ─ ─ ─ ─ ─ ─ ─ ─ ─ ─ ─ ┘   │
│                                                               │
│     ┌──────────────┐              ┌──────────────┐           │
│     │  Contribute  │              │    Cancel    │           │
│     └──────────────┘              └──────────────┘           │
└─────────────────────────────────────────────────────────────┘
```

Figure 8.9 Contributing a file on CompuServe.

After your file is uploaded, you'll have to wait for it to be released by the sysop or library administrator for the forum. CompuServe's forum hosts are usually quick about this, but forums have a life of their own, and the life has gone out of some of them. If the forum isn't getting much traffic, and you can tell from the libraries that it has been months since the last file was uploaded, you are probably better off looking for a more active forum.

If you see files released with upload dates later than yours, there's definitely a problem, and you should send an inquiry to the library administrator. Some sysops can be as tough as nails about any commercial content in your files. Ask how you can adjust the file to meet their standards. If you are contributing anything of value to the forum, there should be a way to fix the file to please the host.

Once your file has been released, *check it for errors*. A lot of problems can happen during a file upload, especially if you didn't prepare the file as described earlier in this chapter. If you open the file and it looks unreadable, immediately e-mail the library administrator or forum host and ask that the file be removed. Fix the file and try again. When you're confident the file looks good, you can post messages telling people how to find it.

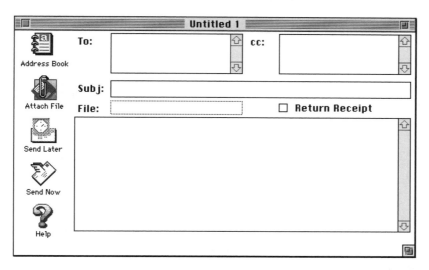

Figure 8.10 Attaching files to e-mail is simple on America Online.

America Online

On America Online, you can attach files to any outbound e-mail, whether it's going to another AOL member or someone on another service. Figure 8.10 shows AOL's Create Mail window. You simply click on the Attach File button and search your hard drive until you find the file you want to send.

Uploading files on America Online is similar to CompuServe. First find an appropriate library for the file. Not all forums have libraries on AOL, and the forum hosts may have restrictions on what goes into them. When you find a library, look for instructions on uploading files—they should be easy to spot. Figure 8.11 shows the library listings for America Online's Business Strategies libraries. Like CompuServe, you can see the date uploaded and the heat index—the number of times each file has been downloaded. Unlike CompuServe, the file names are long enough to give you a clue about the file's contents.

You can't view a file online in AOL the way you can on Compu-Serve—you must download it before opening it—but you can get a short description of the file. You write the description when you upload a file.

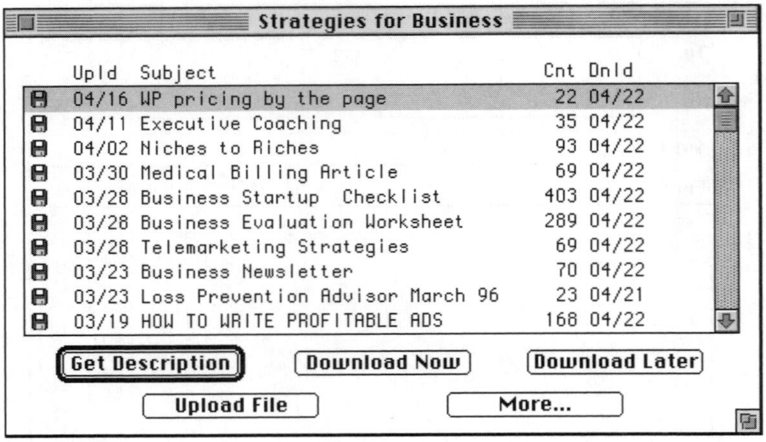

Figure 8.11 A partial list of files in America Online's Business Strategies library.

To upload a file on America Online, just go to the library where you want to place it and hit the Upload File button. You'll get a form to fill out, as shown in Figure 8.12. The Subject line will become your listing in the library. Since you can upload any kind of file on America Online—software, text, graphics, audio, and video—there are two fields

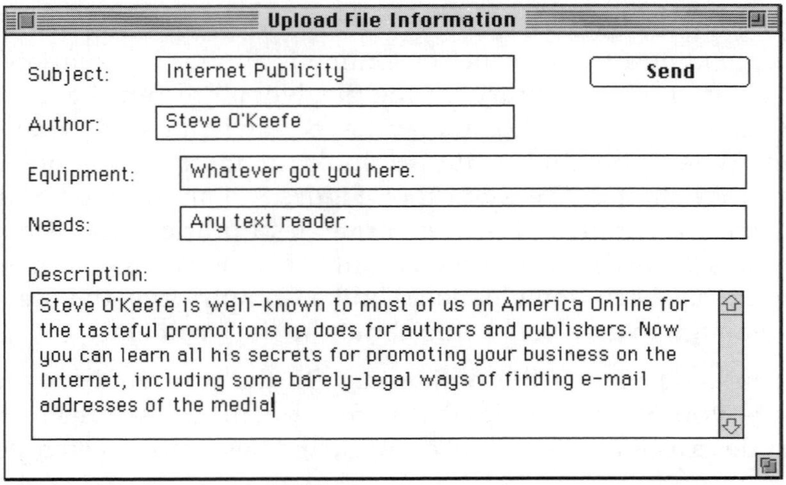

Figure 8.12 Uploading files on America Online is simple.

in the File Upload form to tell people what equipment or software they'll need to access the file. For maximum audience reach, text files should be prepared using the instructions given earlier in this chapter. Since people have to download the file before they view it, your file description could be the determining factor on whether they grab your file.

After you upload your file, it has to be checked for viruses and approved for release by the library administrator or forum host. This usually takes a couple of days. Check back often, and if you see files in the library with an upload date later than yours, send an inquiry to the forum host. Again, you might have to adjust the content of your file to meet their standards.

One forum host on America Online asked me to put all the commercial information at the end of my file so it wasn't the first thing people saw when they downloaded the file. But in general, forum hosts are busy people; they don't have time to closely examine every file. If your file is formatted properly and looks straightforward from the opening screen, they might not venture into the document. Also, if you've worked with the forum hosts and contributed files in the past, your future uploads might be approved sight unseen.

Once your file has been released, *download it yourself and make sure it looks good!* There have been many times when I've tried to download files on America Online, only to find that I don't have the right word processor, or they've been formatted so poorly they're unreadable. If there's a problem with your file, wouldn't you want to be the first to know? If this happens to you, ask the forum hosts to remove any problem files and try again.

Prodigy

Prodigy's file-attach procedure is pretty straightforward: just hit the Attach button while you're creating an e-mail message and choose the file you want to upload. Figure 8.13 shows my reply to someone on Prodigy who requested a giveaway file. You have to write something in the message area—you can't just reply by attaching a file.

When Prodigy users receive a file attached to e-mail, they must download it before they can open it. If they choose to download it, they get an ominous warning, as shown in Figure 8.14. It begins, "File trans-

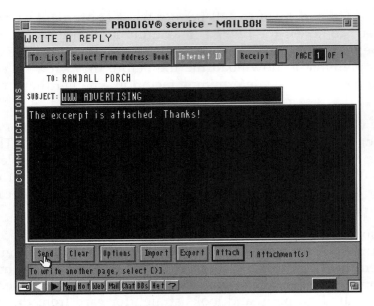

Figure 8.13 Attaching files to Prodigy e-mail is e-z.

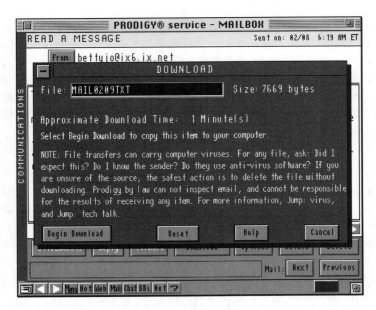

Figure 8.14 Prodigy's virus warning is a deterrent to downloads.

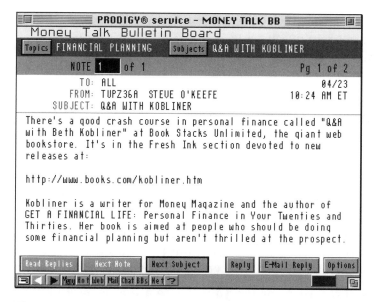

Figure 8.15 A typical Prodigy bulletin board message offering free information.

fers can carry computer viruses" and goes on to say that the safest course may be to delete the file without downloading it. How many people will download your file after seeing a message like that?

I haven't found a satisfactory method for uploading files onto Prodigy. The bulletin boards don't have libraries, and with Prodigy's strict supervision and scary messages, people are not that comfortable downloading files. When I post messages to Prodigy, I prefer to tell people how to find my files on the Web or get them by e-mail. Figure 8.15 shows a sample Prodigy bulletin board message offering a giveaway file.

Other Services

As I've mentioned previously, there are many smaller online services that may be important outlets for your promotional materials. File transfers are very popular online, and most commercial services will have some mechanism for swapping files with other members. Look for instructions online or ask for help from a host. Whatever service you use, put yourself in the reader's seat and try to format your documents so that anyone can enjoy them.

Top Tips

- **Be Selective:** Just because you *can* transfer files over the Net doesn't mean you *should*. Some promotional pieces work much better in print.

- **A Mailbot Is Not a Sales Rep:** Don't ask too much from your automated information systems. A personal call from a knowledgeable sales representative is still the best way to close a deal.

- **Format for Readability:** Take care to make your files universally readable so your customers aren't thwarted when trying to open them or read them. Once you get the hang of it, it's routine.

- **The Right Tool for the Job:** There are at least a half-dozen ways of transferring documents online. For large files, use FTP. For small files, use e-mail, or post them on your Web site.

- **Empathize:** Download a file from your own FTP site. Visit your Web site through a 14.4 modem. Examine your America Online or CompuServe uploads before telling everyone about them. Be your own worst critic before someone else gets a crack at it.

- **Ask for Help:** Your Internet provider can perform programming miracles. Ask about using autoresponders, list servers, FTP sites, and other online power tools. Comparison shop on the Web for better pricing and service.

CHAPTER 9

Online Appearances

Cyberspace is alive with talk. In the Spotlight at Prodigy, a soap opera star is telling his fans how he landed his part. In the Piazza at HotWired, a cybersleuth is snorting with the digeratti in telnet. In some dimly lit chat room at America Online, a journalist is pretending she's a man for a story, and she's coming on to a man who's pretending he's a woman. On Internet Relay Chat, teenage boys strike the pose as hardened hackers.

Welcome to chat. People online love to talk, maybe because it's one of the activities the system handles best. The Internet is not passive entertainment. You can ask questions and get answers. Some of the chat is so juvenile it's hard to believe people pay money to do this. At other times, it can save lives; medical schools use chat to teach new procedures to doctors all over the world. On the Internet, the banal and the profound are on channels right next to each other.

This chapter doesn't deal with chat room style chat, where members of online services look for company on a lonely night. I'll be describing *auditorium chat*, where guests are scheduled in advance for entertaining or educational conversation. I describe the many different kinds of conferencing software in use on the Internet, and tell you exactly how to book a *cybertour*, a series of online appearances.

You'll learn how to get the most mileage out of your time online by doing advance work for the chat and hawking the transcripts when it's over. I'll tell you what to expect during a chat, and teach how to deal with the unexpected: the bad connection, the heckler. If you follow the instructions in this chapter, you'll probably have a rewarding chat, and news of your appearance will reach millions of people, online and off.

Subjects covered include:

- **Can We Talk?:** If you've been anywhere online, you know what chat is. But does it work? Is anyone having fun doing this? Do chats move the merchandise?

- **Booking Chats:** Everything you need to know to find chat venues and schedule appearances. I cover America Online, CompuServe, Prodigy, WebChat, Global Chat, and other gigs.

- **Advance Materials:** You'll improve the quality of your online appearances and the quantity of people you reach by assembling a few materials in advance.

- **Promoting Online Appearances:** While only a few dozen people may attend your chat, millions might see the announcement. I'll show you how to make the most of the opportunity.

- **Live and In Person:** It's chat day—are you a little nervous? Relax and enjoy. What could possibly go wrong (except your computer crashing)?

- **After the Chat:** And you thought it was over. Now you have to move those transcripts to double, triple, quadruple the impact of your appearance.

- **Fifty-Dollar World Tour:** An alternative to live chats is to stop in at discussion forums and say hello. I'll show you how to build a tour bus and get directions.

- **Top Tips:** Without preparation, chats are a waste of good electricity. If you're going to do them, you might as well do them right.

Can We Talk?

I don't know if you've visited many online chats, but I've always found them kind of lame. You park your cursor in this auditorium and wait for the main guest to show. Maybe you kill time conversing with other members on your "channel" or in your "row." This small talk is often more fun than the main event. Finally, the moderator shows up. The guest is introduced and you get a plug for his or her new book or CD or movie or whatever, and then the chat begins. You've always wanted to know what the guest thought about working with So-and-So. You write your question and send it to the moderator. Now you're just waiting for your question to be asked. You see all the other questions go by, and they all sound the same:

CyberDude22: I've been a fan of yours since the very beginning. What is your favorite [book, record, movie, movie star, color, song, hairstyle, scene, character, outfit, instrument, pet, lipstick, etc.]?

Isn't someone going to ask an intelligent question? In the long pause between question and answer, as the guest is furiously typing a reply, the moderator slips in another ad for Chevrolet or some online event or another plug for the guest's latest release. Finally, *your* question gets asked. The moment you've been waiting for. All these years, you've wondered what it was like working with So-and-So, and now the answer:

Guest: Interesting.
Moderator: Our next question comes from...

Huh? That's it? "Interesting." No detail? No follow-up? I'm outta here! And so you log off, and once again the lure of the Net fails to live up to its promise. You swear to never come to an online chat again. But a month later you see an ad for a chat with Tweak, the drummer from Zappa's Ghost, and you just gotta find out what it was like working with So-and-So. And so you go . . . .

Does Anyone Like These Events?

No.

Last year, I did an informal poll on a couple of popular mailing lists. I asked people what they thought about online chats. If they had been a chat guest, did they like it? Did they find it a good way to promote their products or services? If they sat in the audience, was it an interesting or rewarding experience? I was a little surprised at how overwhelmingly negative the responses were.

In fact, the responses from audience members were 100 percent negative. The main complaint was the stilted nature of online chat. It's not like talk radio where you can ask a question and follow it up or clarify or interrupt, or the guest can ask you to rephrase the question or get into a little dialogue with you. In online chat, you have to write a good question, send it to the moderator, and wait for it to be asked. There's no way to engage *discussion*. Answers to questions are often brief, partly due to the interface and also to the lack of true dialogue. There's seldom an opportunity for follow-up questions. And so chats seem shallow.

Then there are the technical problems. If the guest is well-known, you may never get into the auditorium. Many online auditoriums tap out at 300 visitors. If you put a TV star on Prodigy, thousands of people will want to attend. More people will be shut out than be admitted into the chat. For the lucky few who make it inside, chances are their questions will never get asked. That's assuming you can figure out how to ask a question. An online chat is very confusing the first time you join one.

Chat guests are not thrilled about the results either. The number one complaint in my poll was technical difficulties. They couldn't connect to the service. They logged on, but then the connection was dropped. They couldn't get into the auditorium. Their computers crashed. They spent hours setting up software for a lame, half-hour chat. They couldn't figure out how to reply to questions. Chats are just as confusing for first-time guests as they are for first-time audience members. They're getting messages from the moderator that no one else sees, and people in the audience are making comments they can't see. What a mess!

But does it move the product? Once again, chat guests were not pleased. Very few sales or inquiries resulted from their appearances. In many cases, the moderator or host failed to mention that the guest had something to sell: no plugs for their new book or CD or whatever. In some cases, no moderator was provided, and rude people dominated the discussion.

Even some moderators hate online chats. They know from experience that both the guest and the audience are likely to be disappointed, and the hosts take the flak when someone's question doesn't get asked. They have to hype the guest's latest release or post other plugs. Often the guests don't show or are late and hosts have to improvise. They get to deal with all the lovely technical problems. What a headache!

So Why Are Chats So Popular?

Chats are popular because we live in a celebrity culture. People simply can't resist the opportunity to "meet" their favorite performers, whether they be movie stars, CEOs, authors, recording artists—anyone who is known beyond their immediate family. Why do people attend concerts or sporting events in giant stadiums where they can't see or hear the performers? Because it's a scene—there's just something about being there.

People will attend chats even if they hate chats. Even if they know they won't be able to ask a question. Even if they can swing by and pick up the transcript the next day and read it for free offline. There's always the chance that lightning will strike, that the guest will say something interesting and intelligent and original, and that *your* question will result in some startling, shocking, headline-grabbing utterance from the guest.

Chats are popular because they're interactive, even if it is the most lame sort of interaction. They take advantage of the most powerful lure of the Internet—the potential that the user might have some impact on the event. We've all seen Mary Hart on *Entertainment Tonight* or Barbara Walters on *20/20*; now *we* want to ask the questions, *we* want to interview the guests. Chats hold out that promise, even though they seldom deliver.

Despite the technical difficulties, chats *are* popular with guests. For an author, a terrible chat session is still usually better than a typical bookstore signing. They don't have to be publicly humiliated by low turnout, and it costs almost nothing to do an entire tour online. Actors and other celebrities like chats because they don't have to get made up or worry about loonies the way they do at in-person appearances. Chats are safe.

Publicists like chat because they actually *do* move the product. Even if the chat is a disaster, so what? Millions of people may have seen the announcement for the chat on their log-in screens, building name recognition for the guest and his or her latest release. That recognition will help all the other PR work better: TV ads, interviews, newspaper ads, point-of-purchase displays. The Internet is a fantastic way to get a "buzz" going about something. If the product is any good at all, the buzz will help it sell.

More than anyone else, online services *love* chat. It gets people to log in and spend their time online, racking up big fat bills. A lot of stuff can be done quickly online: logging on, grabbing mail, downloading software, logging off. But if you visit a chat, you may be there for hours. It's no secret that chat is the big moneymaker on America Online. I used to have to beg to get authors on AOL chats. Now they beg me for guests. The same goes for Web chat sites: chat brings people to the site. No chat, no hits. No hits, no sponsors. No sponsors, no money.

Finally, some really positive results can come from chats. For authors and others, it's a chance to hear from fans when they can't do a real tour. A chat can be a big boost to their self-esteem. Educational chats are often rewarding. For example, the Mayo Clinic hosted a series of chats with some of its best-known doctors. Employers can use chats to coordinate big projects. In the poll I conducted, the only people who had positive chat experiences were those involved in small, educational chat sessions where there was an opportunity for follow-up questions and deeper discussions.

For all these reasons, online chats are here to stay. And chats will likely improve with the technology. In fact, as online video and audio become commonplace, online chats will look more like TV talk shows (sorry about that). But those days are still long off, and no matter what technology is currently available, you can dramatically improve your chat results with careful preparation. That's what this chapter is all about.

Booking Chats

Even though online services want to have lots of chats, it's becoming more difficult to book them. Chats are so easy for guests that there seems to be an endless supply of actors, athletes, authors, experts, and musicians willing to do online appearances. Public relations firms and talent agencies are the biggest providers of chat guests. So it's getting harder to break into chat without the assistance of a professional.

You can still get into chat rooms without the assistance of a pro, but don't be surprised if your e-mail to the host of a major auditorium goes unanswered. The Internet has grown so much that there are now major chat venues, which I collectively call *auditoriums*, and minor chat venues, which I refer to as *forums*. Major auditoriums include such places as America Online's Center Stage, Prodigy's Spotlight, HotWired's Club Wired, and Sony's NetSpace, among others.

Auditorium Chat

Auditoriums have enough room to accommodate a large audience. They usually have a good interface, allowing audience members to chat with each other or ask questions of the guest. Auditorium hosts prevent annoying technical messages from cluttering up the screen (there's nothing worse than a chat session consisting mostly of log-on and log-off messages as in Figure 9.1). They provide a host and a moderator. They know how to do an introduction and how to plug a guest's new release. They offer links to Web sites, help files, purchasing opportunities, and more. They clean the transcripts and make them available quickly.

Figure 9.1 A sample of HotWired's telnet chat, showing how much "noise" creeps into a chat.

```
— Logged on channel 01: tenofdiamonds/dreamer
sven asks: do you think Netscape stock is a good long term
investment?
guestspeaker/Mary: Netscape is in many ways the next Microsoft,
the only difference here is that Bill Gates sees Netscape coming.
I'd buy it up when the
— Logged off channel 01: kwarwick/lagslayer
guestspeaker/Mary: More Netscape stock: when Netscape has a final
beta and sell when Microsoft adds those features.
— Logged off channel 03: lward/ByteMe
— Logged on channel **: ohia/all's fair in foreplay
— Disconnected! channel 03: jessicat/bubblicious
— Logged on channel 03: stephanec/steph
guestspeaker/Mary: Tip #1 was the META tag to load better pages
for the Netscape crowd.
guestspeaker/Mary: Tip #2: Use a 1 pixel by 1 pixel transparent
image to do spacing for the times when
— Logged off channel 02: shayl/shayl
guestspeaker/Mary: Tip #2-cont:you want to force a specific margin
```

A good chat stage is run a lot like a TV talk show. There are usually several people on the staff. The main contact is often a "producer." You might also work with an art director, a traffic coordinator, a moderator, a publicist, and other people who can help you put on a successful show. You can usually find the staff's real names or screen names in the credits (if it's a Web site), in the help files, or in member services (if it's a commercial online service).

To book a guest in one of the major auditoriums, I suggest you first approach the producer via e-mail. Make the guest sound as irresistible as possible. Your e-mail pitch should include the following items:

- the name of the guest
- a suggested topic or title for the chat
- the guest's credentials
- your offer to provide a moderator
- your plans for promoting the appearance
- your complete contact information (address, phone, etc.)

Producers like to work with people who understand how a chat goes down. Supply a title for the chat that will grab an audience. If you offer to provide a moderator, you reduce the amount of work the host has to do. If you tell them you're going to promote the appearance, they'll be more likely to take a "no-name" guest. A professional-sounding e-mail will give the producer confidence that you'll show up on time and the chat will run smoothly.

If you receive a reply—or if you don't hear back within a couple days—the next step is to phone. People in this business get so hooked on e-mail they forget what a powerful tool the telephone is. It's harder to say no to someone on the phone than it is in e-mail. I like to send e-mail first so they know I'm coming, but after that I use the phone. It's the fastest, easiest way to book chat appearances.

Forum Chat

Forum chats are held in smaller rooms attached to bulletin boards or online forums. For example, all of CompuServe's forums have chat areas, and very few of them attract large audiences. An appearance in a forum is more relaxed than an auditorium event. Only 10 to 50 people

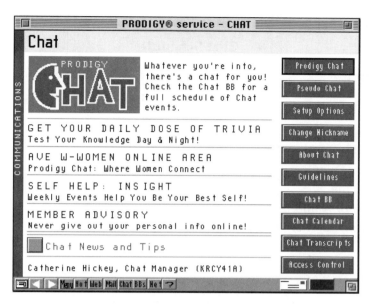

Figure 9.2 Prodigy's Chat center is the gateway to dozens of chat opportunities.

might attend, but as I said earlier, that's better than a bad bookstore signing. There usually will be a host but no other moderator. The interface is rougher, with a lot of extraneous messages visible; and sometimes transcripts are made available, but they're not always cleaned up.

Figure 9.2 shows the main page for Prodigy's Chat center. It advertises three ongoing chats—one for trivia, one for women only, one for self-help. These are just the tip of the iceberg, though. Beneath the surface, Prodigy offers dozens of forum chat opportunities.

You can book forum appearances by contacting the sysops or hosts. Many forums have regularly scheduled programs and they'll take any guest they can get. The Your Business forum on America Online has Your Business Lunch every day during the lunch hour. It's not hard to find these gigs. The tricky part is increasing the impact of your appearance through careful preparation.

Figure 9.3 is a form you can use when booking a cybertour. It will help you keep track of where you're supposed to be and when.

Figure 9.3 A Chat Schedule used to keep track of a cybertour.

Chat Schedule

Guest Name: **Phone Number:**

Book Title: **Publisher:**

Venue #1:

❑ Date and Time _____

❑ Location/Keyword _____

❑ Host Name _____

❑ Moderator Name_____

❑ Hyperlink to Client Web Site Available? _____

❑ Log-In Account _____

❑ Modem Phone _____

❑ Voice Phone _____

❑ In Case of Emergency _____

Venue #2:

❑ Date and Time _____

❑ Location/Keyword _____

❑ Host Name _____

❑ Moderator Name_____

❑ Hyperlink to Client Web Site Available? _____

❑ Log-In Account _____

❑ Modem Phone _____

❑ Voice Phone _____

❑ In Case of Emergency _____

Venue #3:

❑ Date and Time _____

❑ Location/Keyword _____

❑ Host Name _____

❑ Moderator Name_____

❑ Hyperlink to Client Web Site Available? _____

❑ Log-In Account _____

❑ Modem Phone _____

❑ Voice Phone _____

❑ In Case of Emergency _____

Coordinating time zones can be tricky, and many guests have shown up early or late due to confusion over the start time. Get a back-up modem number in case the main number is busy. CompuServe, America Online, and Prodigy all have 800-modem numbers, but they're not free—your account is billed for the long-distance charges. *Be sure to get an emergency voice phone number* in case *everything* goes wrong.

Booking a Chat on the Internet

Internet chat is not nearly as high-profile as appearances on the commercial online services. The software just isn't that good and few Web sites generate enough revenue to make it worth investing in better interfaces. HotWired recently upped the stakes with a new Java-based chat system with capabilities similar to America Online's. In the coming years, more Web sites will add improved chat software and the number of venues will explode.

Nevertheless, there are several different kinds of Internet chat available: Internet Relay Chat (IRC), Web chat, telnet chat, and dead chat, to name a few. Infoseek has a good directory of chat resources and venues (http://www.infoseek.com/). Let's take a look at some of the more popular services.

Internet Relay Chat

Internet Relay Chat (IRC) is not part of the Web—it runs independently. To participate in IRC, you must have IRC client software, and the chat host must have IRC server software. The best software I've seen for IRC is called Global Chat (see Figure 9.4). Originally produced by Prospero Systems, it was purchased by Quarterdeck, which is wheeling and dealing with other software makers to bundle Global Chat with Web browsers. Global Chat client software is available for free online from http://www.quarterdeck.com/globalchat/.

I don't mind going out on a limb and telling you that Global Chat is a fantastic product. Internet Relay Chat has been around for a long

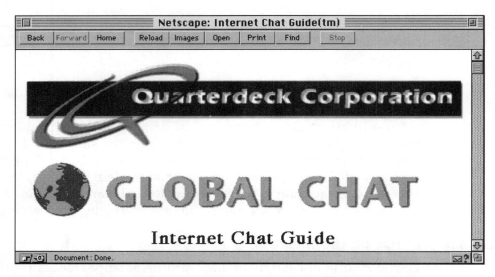

Figure 9.4 Global Chat is a popular interface for Internet Relay Chat.

time and has always been popular with the Internet underground of hackers and high-tech thrillseekers. Until Global Chat came along, though, to enjoy IRC, you had to master sophisticated and arcane commands. Global Chat works in conjunction with your Web browser. First, you visit a global chat server site and look for a chat room or event. Global Chat software is used at Pathfinder (http://www.pathfinder.com)—Figure 9.5—and at Sony's NetSpace (http://www.sony.com)—shown in Figure 9.6.

When you find a chat that interests you, click on the hyperlink to launch your Global Chat software. You'll have two windows open on your computer screen: your Web browser and your Global Chat window. The Global Chat window (Figure 9.7) organizes the information; live chat scrolls on the left side, a list of participants appears on the right side, and a banner spans the top.

The banner is one of the reasons I like global chat so much. It carries advertisements or other messages. The server can rotate several messages or ads, and they can be hotlinked to Web sites. If you see an ad for Amnesty International, for example, you just click on the banner and your Web browser will go to the site. All the while your chat window continues to follow the conversation. It's a fantastic way to integrate IRC and the Web. For advertisers, the good news is, there's no way to

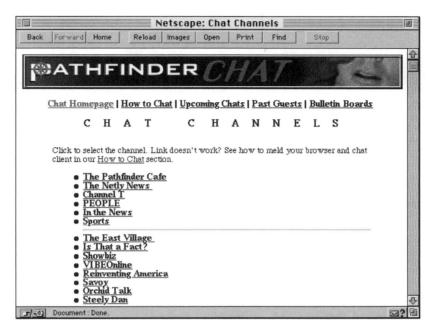

Figure 9.5 Pathfinder offers ongoing chat rooms and serves up chat for some of the world's most well-known magazines.

Figure 9.6 Sony Online's NetSpace is a major server for celebrity chats.

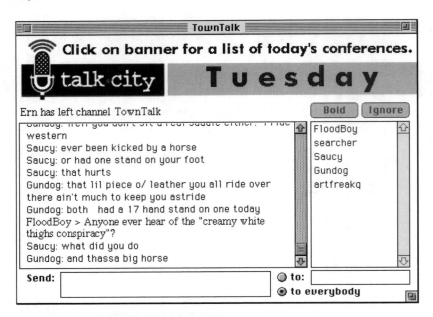

Figure 9.7 A Global Chat session in progress.

turn off the ads (unlike Netscape, where you can browse the with graphics turned off).

If a site such as Pathfinder is using IRC server software, it can hold more than one chat at a time because the chats are each carried on different "channels." Global Chat allows you to display a list of the channels at any time (see Figure 9.8) and switch from one to another. Global Chat includes many other features that make it easy to enjoy the chat, such as being able to boldface a person's comments so they stand out, or "squelching" annoying people so you never have to see anything they write.

Global Chat is not the only IRC client around, it's just the best I've seen so far. You can expect to see competitors and significant software improvements in the near future. There are several other excellent IRC server sites dishing up chat around the clock. A good place to look for chats is the Internet Chat Guide sponsored by Quarterdeck (http://www.qdeck.com/chat/schedule.html). Another good source is Talk City, which has a calendar for every day of the week, plus a list of ongoing chats (Figure 9.9). You can find Talk City on the Web at http://www.talkcity.com/.

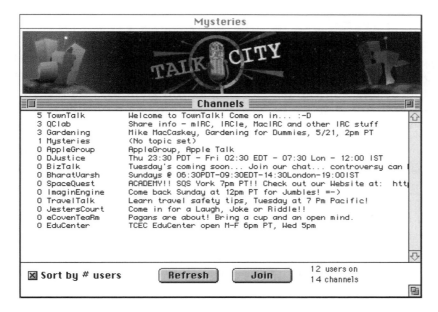

Figure 9.8 A list of channels available on the Talk City server, showing the number of people currently in each channel, the name of the channel, and a brief description.

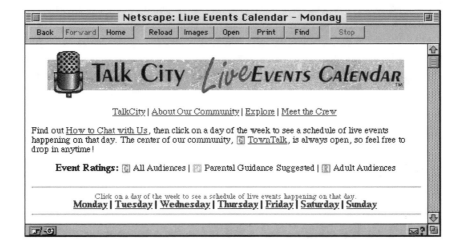

Figure 9.9 Talk City is one of the busiest IRC servers on the Internet.

Web-Based Chat

Some Web servers have been programmed to enable you to run chats on your Web browser. There are many advantages to chatting this way. One is that you can include graphics and hotlinks in your messages; another is that you can take as long as you want to compose your answer before sending it. Figure 9.10 shows a portion of a chat with Senator Arlen Specter held at the Internet Roundtable Society's Web site.

One of the disadvantages of Web-based chat is that you have to refresh the screen manually (although new Java-based chat software may eliminate this problem). Also, chat on the Web feels slow once you're used to the wild ways of IRC or commercial chat on America Online, CompuServe, and Prodigy.

The best interface I've seen for chatting from a Web site is made by WebChat, which is the software illustrated in Figure 9.10. I flipped when I first saw WebChat in action: you can use logos, photos, or other

Figure 9.10 Chatting on the Web allows you to include graphics in your responses.

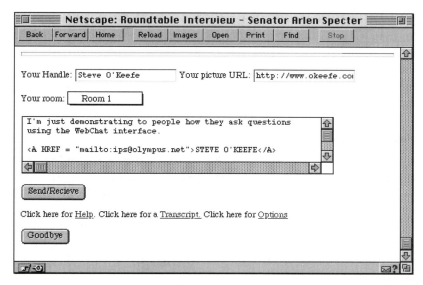

Figure 9.11 The portion of a WebChat page used to create messages.

graphics in your messages, and WebChat automatically sizes them; you can also put hotlinks—including e-mail links—in your messages. Figure 9.11 shows the form you use to compose your messages at the bottom of every WebChat page.

In Figure 9.11, you can see that WebChat allows you to choose a "handle" and the chat room you want to contribute to, and gives you the option to include your picture. Your picture must already be on the Net somewhere in order to include the URL in your message. Your message can be as long as you like (unlike many chat mechanisms that limit you to a couple of hastily composed lines). When you send your message, the Web page is automatically refreshed, displaying all the new conversation since the last time you refreshed the screen.

You can hire the makers of WebChat to host a chat for you or your clients. As of this writing, it costs $2,500 an hour for a professionally produced chat, including chat venue, moderator, and transcripts. The chats accommodate 50 people or less. For a surcharge of $3,000, you can hold the chat in an auditorium that will hold up to 600 people. You can expect these prices to fall as competing software becomes available, however.

You can find more information at WebChat Communications' Web site, http://wbs.net/wcc.html. For a list of WebChat events, visit WBS, the WebChat Broadcast Network at http://wbs.net/. WBS claims over 50 million hits a month, but when you consider that each screen refresh could be counted as a hit, that number is not a useful measure of how many people use the service.

Other Forms of Chat

IRC and Web-based chat are the most popular forms of Internet chat, but there are a couple others that might prove valuable to you. Some services use telnet-based chat. HotWired's Club Wired is probably the best example (http://www.hotwired.com/Piazza/Club/), but you need telnet software to participate, and it's not pretty. In fact it's almost impossible to follow a line of conversation. Take a look at some of the transcripts and you'll see what I mean (see Figure 9.1, earlier in this chapter).

Another variation is *dead chat*, which is not really chat at all. Dead chat is similar to a Usenet-style discussion group. People leave messages for a guest who hopefully checks them daily and responds. Figure 9.12 shows the dead chat forum at Prodigy, which they call Guest Spotlight.

Dead chat is useful when live chat would completely overwhelm a host's resources. There are dead chat areas on most commercial online services and many Web sites, and the software is a lot cheaper to buy than live chat programs. It's also appropriate when you want thoughtful discussions, not just chitchat. Professional people often prefer dead chat to live appearances for getting real information from an expert or authority.

Booking Chat on Commercial Services

America Online has a series of auditoriums, the largest of which can now hold up to 50,000 people. Since a typical one-hour chat allows for about 10 audience questions, however, there's very little chance anyone will actually get to participate. The largest auditorium is called AOL Live. To book an appearance there, contact Amy Arnold, special events producer (AmyA@aol.com)—but don't bother her unless the guest is a household name.

Figure 9.12 Prodigy's Guest Spotlight, where members leave questions for visiting guests.

Other auditoriums on AOL include Coliseum, Odeon, The Globe, The Bowl, Hollywood Live. You should be able to book these by contacting individual forum hosts. For example, to book authors, contact the Writer's Club host; for businesspeople, work through Hoover's Online, and so on. You can also try the following two people who were part of the old Center Stage staff and still book guests:

RJScottV@aol.com
Jennifer05@aol.com

CompuServe has two main chat venues: the Convention Center and the Auditorium. To book chats there, work through the forum hosts. All the forums have chat areas where they hold special events or where people just shoot the breeze when no events are taking place. Figure 9.13 shows the main window for the Book Preview Forum. You get to the chat area by clicking on the Enter Room icon.

You can use CompuServe's pull-down menu, labeled Conference, to get a description of each one of the chat rooms in the forum. Some may be used for regularly scheduled shows or meetings. For a list of all

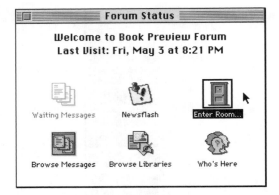

Figure 9.13 Each of CompuServe's forums has chat rooms for holding special events.

CompuServe's forums, go to the index (GO Index). You can download it and search it offline, looking for the best venues for booking a chat.

Prodigy hosts celebrity chats in its Spotlight auditoriums. These can accommodate about 500 visitors, although they can ramp it up for special occasions. Figure 9.14 shows the gateway window into Prodigy's auditoriums. To book a chat, contact Catherine Hickey, chat manager, KRCY41A@prodigy.com. You can also arrange for appearances with

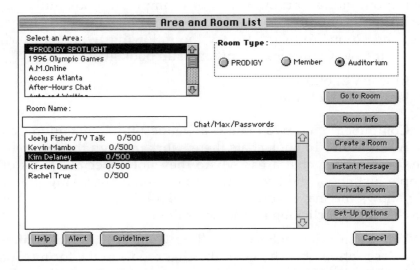

Figure 9.14 Prodigy hosts special guests in its Spotlight auditoriums. You can also book chats through the bulletin board hosts.

bulletin board hosts, who each have chat rooms they can book you into. For more information about Prodigy chat, JUMP CHAT.

Advance Materials

Once you have the tour set up, you need to start putting together your advance materials. Figure 9.15 shows the checklist we use at Internet Publicity Services when designing a cybertour. We'll go through each of the steps in the checklist to show you how to maximize the impact of your online appearances.

Figure 9.15 Chat Checklist for use in compiling advance materials.

Chat Checklist

Guest Name: **Phone Number:**

Book Title: **Publisher:**

Advance Materials:
- ❑ Get Photo _____
- ❑ Embed Text in Photo_____
- ❑ Save as JPEG or GIF _____
- ❑ Prepare Other Artwork_____

- ❑ Write Introduction_____
- ❑ Write Sample Questions _____
- ❑ Spell-Check/Print/Proofread _____
- ❑ Save as Text Files _____

Promotion:
- ❑ Prepare Any Giveaway Files _____
- ❑ Spell-Check/Print/Proofread _____
- ❑ Save as Text Files _____
- ❑ Upload on Service_____

- ❑ Write Announcement _____
- ❑ Spell-Check/Print/Proofread _____
- ❑ Get Author/Publisher Approval _____
- ❑ Post Announcements _____

(continues)

Figure 9.15 (*Continued*)

Follow-Up:
- ❏ Download Transcripts and Check for Formatting _____
- ❏ Request Permission to Use Transcripts _____
- ❏ Send Transcripts as Requested _____
- ❏ Install Transcripts on Web Site _____

- ❏ Prepare Report for Publisher _____

Preparing Artwork

One of the great advantages of electronic communications over print is how cheap it is to use four-color artwork. Don't let this opportunity pass you by. You can take a color photo to just about any printshop and have it scanned for less than $10. Then you can transfer the file over the Net to your host and have it installed at the chat venue.

An even better way to prepare the file is to embed text below the photo, identifying who the person is and the name of his or her book/CD/show and how to contact the person (an 800-number or a URL). Figure 9.16 shows a photo I had prepared for an appearance on America Online. You can hire a graphic designer to scan the photo, re-touch it, and embed the text, all for about $30.

Save the image in the preferred JPEG file format or, second best, as a GIF. JPEGs take up less space than GIFs and produce a better result for large color images. Contact the host ahead of time and ask which format he or she prefers. To deliver the artwork, attach it to e-mail addressed to the host.

For those who think this is a lot of work for a little chat, consider this: on America Online, a typical Center Stage appearance may draw 300 visitors. Celebrity photos, on the other hand, can be downloaded 50,000 times or more! Even if you don't look like Brad Pitt or Sharon Stone, provide a publicity photo and make sure it includes contact information. The photo may reach a lot more people than the chat.

If you can include other artwork, go for it. I always provide a book jacket scan when my authors do a chat. In some cases, you can get the site to install a graphical hot button that links to your site. Chapter 5, The Linkage Campaign, has information on creating these buttons and deploying them online.

STEVE O'KEEFE
Internet Publicity Services
E-Mail: okeefe@olympus.net

Figure 9.16 A photo of your humble narrator, showing embedded text.

Even if you don't have a hot button graphic, ask the host to provide a link to your Web site. As I said at the beginning of this chapter, chats are remarkably shallow, and they often feel like they're over before anything has been said. It's nice to be able to refer people to more detailed information at your Web site. Now that all the commercial online services have Web access, it's become a standard courtesy to provide a hotlink to the guest's Web site. The link usually goes up well before the chat and may stay up for months.

Introduction and Sample Questions

Write a brief biography the host can use to introduce the guest. Just a paragraph or two will do, clearly stating the name of the guest, his or her most important credentials, the address of his or her Web site, and the name of his or her latest release. I've seen transcripts for chats where there was no information provided about a guest beyond a name; for some authors, it was impossible to know they had written a book, or what it was about.

Sample questions are a lot of help for a moderator. Do you think David Letterman reads a book every time he has an author on his show? Some chat stages have a different author every night. There's simply no way for the hosts to be completely prepared for each guest. If they are, so much the better, but if they aren't, you want to provide a few questions that will spark some discussion.

Providing sample questions also lets you guide the chat into more productive areas. Stay away from questions that require long, elaborate answers—there's simply not enough time to go very deep. Provide questions that the guest can answer in a couple of sentences and that leave time for the audience to ask follow-up questions. For example, instead of asking a writer, "How did you get started writing," ask "When did you get your first piece published as a professional writer?" Steer clear of vague questions and go for questions that can be answered with specific, helpful responses.

Send your sample questions, introduction, Web address and artwork to the host well ahead of time. He or she will use these materials to create promos for your appearance. On America Online, Prodigy, and CompuServe, the guest's name and likeness could appear on the log-in screen where everyone will see it. This advance publicity may reach millions of people no matter how few actually attend the chat. That's why it's so important to provide the host with advance materials. But you can't rely on the venue to properly promote the chat, so in the next section, I'll show you how to help out.

Promoting Online Appearances

You can expect the host to do some promotion for the chat, but it may be limited. Big-name guests get the biggest promos, with announcements on the log-in screen, photos and bios installed weeks ahead of time, and regular announcements to the membership. Probably the ultimate in advance publicity came in August 1995, when pop singer Michael Jackson did a *simulchat*—simultaneous appearances on America Online, CompuServe, Prodigy, and MTV.

Jackson is no slouch when it comes to publicity. His advance team was out hyping the simulchat weeks ahead of time. Each of the commercial online services was pumping the event as hard as it could. Jackson made national news with this stunt, including a small write-up in *TV Guide* the day of the chat. It's fair to say that the little piece in *TV Guide* had more reach than all the online services combined.

Announcements

You might not be able to get a write-up in *TV Guide,* but there's a lot you can do to increase the turnout at your chat and expand the impact of the guest's appearance. A chat is a perfect excuse to post announcements to online discussion groups. If you were to invite people to visit your Web site, you might get flamed for bad netiquette. But announcing a chat appearance is usually perceived as a news item and as such is tolerated and even welcomed.

Figure 9.17 shows an announcement we used to promote a chat on Delphi, the ill-fated online service. The chat took place in Delphi's bookstore, and we received advance publicity in the bookstore a week ahead of time. We also got a log-in announcement on the day of the chat, telling everyone who connected to Delphi about the scheduled appearance.

The difficulty with this posting was that very few people had access to Delphi, and it would have resulted in a lot of flames if we hadn't offered to provide transcripts for those who couldn't attend. Between using a little humor and offering to pass questions to the moderator and provide transcripts, we didn't get any heat for this message; in fact, we received a lot of positive reactions.

Figure 9.17 A discussion group posting for a chat on Delphi.

SUBJECT LINE: Elvis Sighting on Delphi!

Is the King of Rock'n'Roll still alive? Find out Sunday night as
Delphi Internet Service presents a live forum with the authors of
ELVIS AARON PRESLEY: Revelations from the Memphis Mafia.

Here's your chance to find out:
* Whether the King is still alive?
* If Elvis had sexual relations with his mother?
* What Elvis' greatest fears were?

The forum will be held in the Online Bookstore at 7 p.m. Eastern
Time. I know not everyone has access to Delphi; if you e-mail your
questions to me, I will forward them to the moderator. If you
would like a transcript of the appearance, let me know and I'll
send it to you via e-mail as soon as it's available.

You can post announcements on appropriate Usenet newsgroups, Internet mailing lists, and on commercial online services. See the Announcements chapter for detailed instructions on how to do them. It's nice to be able to promote a whole "cybertour" in one posting, with a list of the places the guest will be appearing.

You have to be judicious when posting announcements for chats on competing services. For example, America Online hosts aren't thrilled about notices of chats on CompuServe. Even CompuServe hosts get unhappy if you promote a chat in another CompuServe forum. One way to avoid trouble is to promote a giveaway file in conjunction with the chat tour, and put the tour schedule inside the giveaway file. We do this a lot with authors doing book tours and we've never had a complaint. You can also just skip the advance publicity on a competing service and instead upload the transcript when the chat is over. Then you can post an announcement about the "interview" you made available.

News Releases

You would be surprised at how many media outlets have a calendar of chat events. The sole purpose of magazines such as *Net Guide* is to help people find interesting events online. Many electronic zines, such as *Netsurfer Digest*, give advance notice of major online appearances. My local newspaper, *The Seattle Times*, has a column called Chat Session once a week listing promising chats for the coming week. Radio talk show guests plug chats, and major events such as the Michael Jackson simulchat can make it on TV network news.

The more notice you give for your chat, the better your chance of getting offline publicity. Monthly print magazines have a three-month lead time, so you don't often see chat announcements on their pages. But most magazines also have a "news bits" column that's the last section they put to bed before going to press. If your announcement is sufficiently "newsy," it might get noted. For online publications, newspapers, radio, and TV, it's nice to give notice a month in advance, but you can sometimes get coverage with less than a week lead time.

Chapter 6, E-Mail News Releases, has all the information you need to create an attention-grabbing release and distribute it via e-mail. The Resources chapter (Chapter 12) lists Web sites where you can find the e-mail addresses of the media, and gives contact information for professional online publicists. You may want to create a few different versions of your news release to cater to different audiences. Local television stations, radio stations, and newspapers will write up your chat if the guest is a local resident—be sure to mention the hometown in your news release.

As you can see, the coverage you get offline for your chat may be much more important than the chat itself. The chat gives you an excuse to go to the media and to post messages where the vast online audience will see them. The name recognition and "buzz" that results from these announcements can have a dramatic impact on sales and lead to interviews and news stories offline.

Live and In Person

Everything is in place and the day of the big chat has arrived. If you're in an auditorium, you probably received a set of instructions from the host in advance of your appearance. The instructions might include a special I.D. name or number to use when logging in to the service.

If you've never been on that particular service before, you should try and check it out a few days in advance. For example, if your chat is on America Online and you've never been on that service, it's a good idea to install the software and visit a few days ahead of time. There can be many technical glitches trying to get a piece of software to work correctly the first time. In fact, I don't recommend putting people on chats unless they have a lot of experience online or they're using a "ghost typist," which is what America Online calls someone who keyboards your chat. You can do your chat over the phone or in the studio and just recite your answers and let someone else type them in. That's how Michael Jackson could appear on three online services at once. Most chat venues provide transcriptionists for major celebrities who don't want to deal with keyboarding their own answers. In the case of the simulchat, Jackson sat on a stage at MTV's studio; the questions came in from the different services and were read to him, and he responded verbally as typists recorded his answers.

Moderators

Moderators are a blessing and a curse. Most auditorium chat is moderated. The moderator controls the pace of the chat by passing through questions, asking follow-up questions, plugging the guest's new release, and other functions. Some people don't like moderators because they can channel the chat into less interesting avenues and stifle the spontaneity.

Most people do wish they had a moderator when there is a jerk in the house. Chats can be ruined by overzealous fans, competitors, customers who have a gripe, bored teens with nothing better to do, or anyone determined to make your chat an unpleasant experience. With a moderator, these folks can only bother other members of the audience not the guest, and moderators usually have the ability to disconnect someone and block their access to the chat area.

If you're in a forum chat without a moderator, and someone is pestering you, it's best to ask that person to continue the conversation via e-mail so that you can take other questions. If that doesn't work, you're just going to have to ignore the nuisance or call off the chat and try to reschedule.

Communicating in Chat

If there are a lot of people involved, chats can become confusing. If you think it's difficult handling multiple conversations, try doing it online where the only way to tell people apart is their screen names. You might have the moderator passing private messages to you, while audience questions are piling up. It's hard to keep your wits about you.

Probably the most distressing thing about being on a chat is the pressure to communicate quickly. Someone asks a question and the clock is ticking away while you type as fast as possible. There's no time to check spelling or verify a URL or even to make sure you don't sound like a complete moron. Fortunately, many services clean up the transcripts before making them available to the public.

There is also a limited amount of space in which to type an answer (about two lines). If you want to type more, you have to send the first part of your answer, then continue typing the next part, but communicating this way can be very frustrating. It's best to keep your answers short, and refer people to your Web site (or elsewhere) for more in-depth information.

Short is one thing, but some guests just clam up in chat, providing one-word answers and forcing the moderator to draw the responses out of them. Here are some snippets from an America Online chat with author Robert Jordan:

Question: Have you written any books previous to the WHEEL OF TIME set?
RJordan2: Yes.
Question: Where did you get the concept for Perrin?
RJordan2: Out of my head.
Question: Your plots are so detailed and intricate. Do you ever get confused about what should happen when?
RJordan2: No.

Compare this clipped style with the responses of Eric Tyson, author of *Personal Finance for Dummies,* also from a chat on America Online:

Question: What is the best credit card? How can I transfer to it?
Eric Tyson: If you carry a balance, there are a number of cards with rates less than 10 percent. Try Consumer's Best Bankcard or Wachovia. Phone numbers and a longer list are in the book.
Question: Something I did not see in your book was stock options or index options...could you briefly explain this?
Eric Tyson: Options are a gambling type vehicle that payoff or not based on short term price movements of a security. I recommended avoiding them in chapter 10.

It's handy to have some resources at your fingertips to refer people to. Keep a list of your favorite Web addresses nearby, and any other reference materials you think will help. Your host will appreciate it if you plug his or her forum as a good source of information. If you're a guest on HotWired, for example, find out whether they have relevant excerpts or interviews stored in their archives to point people to.

Just like radio and TV interviews, if you connect with the chat host, you tend to connect with the audience. It's hard to get any chemistry going online, though. Try to personalize the chat by using people's names. The host's name might appear as Moderator or BJenks213 on the screen, but you can call her Betty (or whatever her real name is) in your replies. Another tip is to use humor; it will help you relax and enjoy the chat.

After the Chat

The chat will pass incredibly quickly. It will seem like you just got started when the host thanks you for your time. After you have time to reflect on the chat, you probably will wish you had told people about some other resources. Consider following up on some of the questions by digging out information for people.

You can contact the host and ask him or her to install links to Web sites or other resources. You might want to upload a file on the service, perhaps putting an article or excerpt in its library for people intrigued by the chat. You can also ask to have material added to the transcripts.

Transcripts

Most services provide transcripts within a few days after the chat (see Figure 9.18). As we discussed earlier, these transcripts can reach many more people than the chat. Transcripts vary in quality tremendously. Most services clean-up the transcripts, removing extraneous comments, correcting spelling, and pasting replies together that were posted in little bits and pieces.

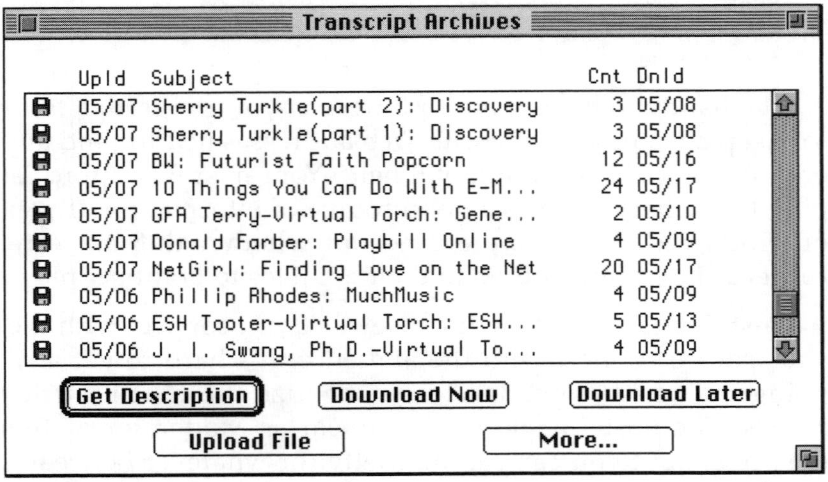

Figure 9.18 America Online's Transcript Archives, showing the title of the chat, the date it was uploaded, and how many downloads it received.

As soon as the transcripts are available, download them and check for mistakes. Here is a piece of a transcript from a chat I promoted on Delphi. Who would want to read such a horrible file?

```
/noxl xlon
XLON>  what is your favorite Elvis song/album?
BILLY_SMITH> It may sound like a cop out but all of them
how about you, Allanna?
QUEUE from XLON> 2 lines, 96 chars, subj: ?
BOOKSTORE> how about you, Allanna?
BILLY_SMITH> ALANNA-_ The early rockabilly stuff like "That's
BILLY_SMITH> Alright Mama".
BILLY_SMITH>
Thanks very much, to both Billy and ALANNA-.
BOOKSTORE> Thanks very much, to both Billy and ALANNA-.
If you are looking for the book Elvis Aaron Presley, and
BILLY_SMITH> ALANNA—It was fun.
```

Compare this to the following excerpt of a transcript of author Dean Koontz' appearance on Prodigy. Prodigy does an excellent job of cleaning the transcripts, correcting them, and putting them into an easy-to-read format with a short line length:

TSAbrams (PRODIGY Member)
I'd like to say that your books are great
and that ever since The Bad Place I have
been hooked. Where do you get your flare for
wording or do you sleep with a thesaurus?

Dean Koontz (Speaker)
Actually, I don't own a thesaurus. But I've
always loved the language and when you are
raised reading Ray Bradbury, Charles
Dickens, and Lovecraft, you become a walking
thesaurus.

bumblebeebz (PRODIGY Member)
Here's a loaded question... Are you
satisfied or slightly happy with the way
your work has been modified in the movies?

Dean Koontz (Speaker)
Thus far, filmmakers have behaved with me in

```
such a fashion that I feel comfortable
calling them jackbooted thugs. Lately, I've
been working with people of a higher talent
level than was often the case in the past,
but none of those projects is filming yet.
```

Moderator (Speaker)
```
Dean's literary successes have propelled
him into the world of Hollywood. He has
written the screenplays for the film
adaptations of his novels "Midnight,"
"Phantoms," and "Mr. Murder." In addition,
"Dark Rivers of the Heart" will soon be a
CBS TV movie, and last year, the film
version of Dean's "Hideaway" was released,
starring Jeff Goldblum.
```

I didn't attend the Koontz chat, so I don't know if the information about his movie projects was inserted into the chat transcript or if he was just blessed with an exceptionally knowledgeable moderator. I know the chances of two people spelling thesaurus correctly in a live chat are remote. If the transcripts for your chat aren't up to snuff, ask the service to fix them or do it yourself.

When evaluating your transcripts, here are some things to ask yourself:

- Is there a good introduction at the beginning of the file telling people who the guest is and when and where the chat was conducted?
- Is there information at the end of the file telling people how to get more information, order merchandise, visit a Web site, or whatever?
- Is there a proper copyright notice in the file?
- Have "noise messages" been culled out? These include log-on and log-off messages and any debris that disrupts the flow of the chat.
- Has the file been spell-checked?
- Is the file in ASCII text so that anyone can read it?

Transcripts are the property of the service that put on the chat, and this fact is reflected in the copyright notice. You need to request permission from the copyright holder to use the transcripts. This is true even if you are the guest! It's unlikely that your request will be denied, especially if you make it clear that the transcripts will include the copyright notice and a statement about where the chat was conducted. You might want to ask for permission to use the transcripts *before* you commit to a the chat.

Once the transcripts are cleaned up to your satisfaction, you can e-mail them to people who couldn't attend the chat. You can also put the transcripts on your own Web site and make them available by FTP. If there's something controversial that came out during the chat, you can issue a news release about it and make the transcripts available to reporters. You can also post another message on newsgroups and mailing lists notifying people that the transcripts are available at your Web site.

Fifty-Dollar World Tour

There's more than one way to skin a chat. One of the things I've done to help authors promote their books is get them set up on the Net and give them a road map of forums to visit. As I discuss in Chapter 11, Firefighting and Follow-Up, participating in online discussion groups is the most effective method of online marketing.

If the expert or celebrity or company representative you want to put online has a computer and a modem, it's a simple matter to get him or her going on America Online, CompuServe, or the Net itself. Offer to walk your guest through the process to remove the fear of being online. Through CIS or AOL, they will have access to Usenet newsgroups, Internet mailing lists, and the World Wide Web. If your guests use the services for more than a couple hours a week, however, it will be cheaper to go for a direct Internet connection.

My personal recommendation is that either AOL or CIS is a good place to get your feet wet in cyberspace. America Online has a younger audience, with good resources for parents, kids, and entrepreneurs. Because AOL allows you to have multiple screen names, it's a good service for the home computer. CompuServe, on the other hand, is more businesslike, with good resources for professional people and educators. It has terrific research tools and databases, and strong vendor support forums. Both AOL and CIS have good news, entertainment, and chat services.

The alternative is a direct Internet account. The advantages are that it is much faster working the Web from a direct account and a lot cheaper if you spend more than two hours a week online. The disadvantages are that it's much more difficult to set up a good suite of Internet software, and the help resources are often hard to find and hard to use. Being on the Net can be very frustrating to newcomers because most people don't realize that it requires mastery of a *family* of software programs, not just one.

Software and Hardware

Once you've determined which service to use, you need to access the software. All basic software is free. If you aren't receiving America Online and CompuServe disks on a daily basis in your mailbox, you can get them bundled with computer magazines at your favorite newsstand. You can also get the software free through a toll-free call. Here are the phone numbers:

CompuServe Information Service, 1-800-848-8990
America Online, 1-800-827-6364

For a direct Internet connection, you'll want to find an Internet Service Provider (ISP) within the guest's local dialing area. Nowadays, you can find these services listed in the phone book. Many phone companies are starting to offer cheap Internet access, so calling the phone company might be the easiest way to get started. You can also ask for referrals from businesses in the area; or look in the local newspaper's classified ads, or surf the Net comparing rates.

The ISP might provide you with free software and install it for a small fee. If the ISP doesn't provide the software, you might have to buy a kit such as *Internet in a Box* or *The Internet Starter Kit*. Your ISP might sell these. They include all the basic software you need in one package, and they usually come with books that are helpful for the beginner. You can buy these kits at bookstores, computer stores, even large warehouse-style retail outlets.

It doesn't take much hardware to participate online. All you need is a modem, a computer, and a phone line. You don't need a dedicated phone, and whatever computer you already have will probably work fine. However, the more up-to-date your equipment, the easier your online experience will be. In particular, it pays to buy the fastest modem currently on the market to reduce connection time and charges, and to lower your frustration level as you wait for graphics to appear on your screen.

The Road Map

One of the problems with the Internet is that it contains so much material it's hard to know where to start. Whether you've been on the Net for five minutes or five years, you can still use the help of other people who know the territory. I was doing some fact-checking the other day and it took me three hours to find something on the Net I could have gotten from a librarian in about 15 minutes. As a publicist, you can act as an advance scout for your clients, culling through the resources available and preparing a short list for your clients.

The Announcements chapter has a lot of detailed information on finding newsgroups, mailing lists, Web sites, and forums related to any given topic. Buying a recently released book is also a good source of leads. I was looking for quality business-oriented Web sites recently, and after spending a half-hour visiting poor quality sites online, I turned to Jill and Matthew Ellsworth's *Internet Business Book* where I found a nice, annotated list of exactly what I was after. Magazine articles that include lists of Web sites are also excellent tools for drawing a road map.

Figure 9.19 shows a road map a banker might use to find discussion groups related to online banking and business. It's not a comprehensive list, but it's better than digging up all these sites yourself. For AOL and CIS forums, the list begins with the Keyword or Go word for each forum, then the name of the forum. These services have many more excellent resources for business users, but we were looking for forums with discussion groups.

Figure 9.19 An Internet road map for someone wanting to find discussion groups dealing with online banking and commerce.

Internet Road Map
For Banking/Business Discussion Groups

Usenet Newsgroups:

    comp.internet.library

    alt.books.technical

    misc.books.technical

(continues)

Figure 9.19 (*Continued*)

misc.entrepreneurs.moderated

biz.misc

alt.business.misc

misc.business.credit

misc.business.records-mgmt

alt.security.pgp

comp.security.misc

comp.security.firewalls

talk.politics.crypto

America Online:

STRATEGIES - Business Strategies Forum

AD SIG - Advertising Forum

CRAINS - Crain's Small Business Forum

BWFORUM - Business Week Forum

AAII - American Assoc. of Individual Investors

INBIZ - Internet Business Forum

MONEY- Investors Network

HOC - Home Office Computing

WORTH - Worth Magazine

CompuServe:

INETCOM - Internet Commerce

SMALLBIZ - Small Business

PRSIG - PR & Marketing

FINFORUM - Financial Forums

AICPA - Accountants Forum

ITFORUM - International Trade Forum

FORTUNE - Fortune Magazine

Prodigy:

Money Talk Bulletin Board

Your Business Bulletin Board

Web Sites:

Galaxy Banking Product and Service Descriptions
<http://www.einet.net/galaxy/Business-and- Products and Services/
Finance/Banks.html>

Banking on the WWW - Guides
<http://www.gwdg.de/~ifbg/bank_1.htm>

Banks, Banking and Finance
<http://www.qualisteam.com/aconf.html>

Banking on the Web, Omega Performance
<http://www.omega.sf.ca.us/bankweb.html>

Internet Banking and Financial Index
<http://pages.prodigy.com/MI/ddsi/ddsi.html>

Nijenrode Business Resources Finance, Economics, and Banking
<http://www.nijenrode.nl/resources/bus/finance.html>

FINWeb - A Financial Economics WWW Server
<http://www.finweb.com/>

Sources: Business
<http://www.cc.emory.edu/WHSCL/sources.business.html>

NewsPage Sources
<http://www.newspage.com/NEWSPAGE/nptb-sources.html>

Bank.Net
<http://bank.net/home.rich.html>

UltraNet Communications
<http://www.ultranet.com>

FILL The Financial Information Link Library
<http://www.mbnet.mb.ca/~russell>

GNN Select: All Topics
<http://gnn-e2a.gnn.com/gnn/wic/wics/alltop.toc.html>

The Money Page Index
<http://www.moneypage.com/invest/>

Mortgage Market Information Services, Inc.
<http://www.interest.com/msource.html>

Mortgage Market Information Services, Inc.
<http://www.interest.com/mortgagemkt.html>

Dakota State University
<http://www.dsu.edu/departments/bis/finance/resources.html>

Virtual Library
<http://www.w3.org/hypertext/DataSources/bySubject/Finance/Overview.html>

Information Innovation's Professional Web Guide -
Banking, Finance & Investment
<http://www.euro.Net/innovation/ift/FinMap/FinTOC.htm>

Commercial Finance ONLINE!
<http://www.cfonline.com/cgi-win/cfonline.exe/getadd>

KiwiClubWeb (The Kiwi Club Server provideslinks to
financial information. Univ of Austin TX)
<http://www.ai.mit.edu/stocks/finance.html>

InfoSeek Finance Sites
<http://204.162.96.5/doc/netdir/finance.html>

Ivestments and Personal Finance
<http://www.umd.umich.edu/resources/finance.html>

Federal Yellow Pages
<http://www.info.gov/Info/html/fed_yellow_pgs.htm>

The Michigan Electronic Library
<http://141.211.190.218/business/BU-Banking.Finance.html>

"Banking and Finance" in Electronic Media
<http://www.wiso.gwdg.de/ifbg/medien.html> Requested link

The Banking Ready Reference
<http://ipl.sils.umich.edu:80/ref/RR/BUS/Banking-rr.html>

The Chartered Institute of Bankers (CIB) World Wide
<http://www.cib.org.uk/supersite.html>

InfoBank. - provided by Bank Rate Monitor
<http://www.wiso.gwdg.de/ifbg/bank_6.html>

JPB Corporation
<http://remus.rutgers.edu:80/~jburns/>

Investment Resources
<http://www.infomanage.com/investment/>

Custom Internet road maps can be extremely helpful to the clients you are putting online. You can even transfer the road maps as bookmark files that can be uploaded right into the person's Web browser. For example, I have prepared much of the information in the Resources chapter as an HTML file that can be uploaded in any Web browser. If you can't find it at my Web site or the Web site for this book, just drop me a line and I'll send it to you attached to e-mail. My address is IPS@olympus.net.

When you're putting someone else online, you might also want to provide them with resources they can use to answer people's questions. Using the information in the Document Transfers chapter, you can prepare text files to use in response to inquiries. You can also set up autoresponders or give your clients other materials they can use as they participate in the discussion groups.

Top Tips

- **Go the Distance:** Online chats have little or no impact unless you put in the effort to prepare advance materials and promote the chat. If you're going to do it, do it right.

- **Provide a Photo:** Your photo may be more popular than the transcripts of your chat. Provide the host with a publicity photo that has contact information embedded in it.

- **Promote Your Chat:** There are few occasions when you have good reason to post announcements and news releases; online appearances are just such an occasion. Don't miss this opportunity to get a little buzz going.

- **The Announcement Is More Important Than the Chat:** Very few people will be able to attend your chat, but millions might see the announcement, especially if it gets attention offline in the broadcast media or in print.

- **Make a Back-Up Plan:** What are you going to do if you can't connect for your chat? Make sure you have an emergency phone number if all else fails.

- **Connect with the Host:** If you can get some chemistry going with the host, you'll connect better with the audience. Use people's names and humor to personalize the chat.

- **Refer People to Resources:** You won't have enough time to get into deep discussions. Be prepared to refer people to your Web site or offer to send files with more detailed information.

- **Work the Transcripts:** The transcripts will probably reach more people than the chat. Make sure they look good and contain the proper contact information before you send them. Remember to get permission to use transcripts on your own Web site or distribute them through e-mail.

CHAPTER 10

Contests and Other Fancy Promotions

Let's put on a show!

By now you're tired of reading about boring subjects like announcements and news releases and appropriate postings. You're probably wondering what about the fancy stuff, the sneak previews, the fabulous contests, the spiffy interactive quizzes? None of these fancy promotions will work unless you understand the boring basics, but now that you're well-versed in netiquette and media list management, let's go for the limelight!

Fancy promotions are a part of any big marketing campaign—and they work particularly well on the Net. Instead of passively watching a show, people participate. We can join Web treasure hunts and scour the Net for clues. Instead of watching the show *Jeopardy*, we can play it at Sony Online. We can quiz celebrities on America Online, or register our disgust using Prodigy's polls. We can have our fortune told, win a T-shirt for filling out a survey, or watch a sold-out Cleveland Indians baseball game from a camera hooked up to the Web.

A big event always attracts a lot of attention. The Michael Jackson simulchat was a benchmark moment for the online entertainment industry. The sneak preview site for the movie *Toy Story* set the standard for movie promotions online. Everyone loves a parade, and the Web has become an endless stream of marching bands, floats, and hot air balloons.

Some of the balloons have burst, however, and that's part of the fun and the danger of online promotions. Imagine spending millions of dollars to broadcast your URL on television, radio, and in print ads, then not having the Web site ready. Sometimes, pulling off a big promotion seems like Mission Impossible.

This chapter will help your promotion soar. We'll take a look at some of the great successes and biggest blunders in Internet promotions. You'll learn some of the pitfalls to watch for and how to plan for success. And because creativity and novelty go a long way online, I'll toss in plenty of examples to spark your imagination. Now on with the show!

Topics covered include:

- **A Tale of Two Promotions:** Which would you rather have, $10,000 cash or a brand new Nissan Sentra automobile? People online voted with their mice.

- **Developing Good Promotions:** A good promotion comes out of the character of the product; it is creative, interactive, and irresistible to the target audience. I'll help you design a promotion that is memorable, functional, and on schedule.

- **Co-Branding:** Many large promotions involve partners, each contributing something special that makes the whole thing happen. With partners come problems, however. I'll help you prepare.

- **Contests:** Who can resist a clever contest? Not me. I've promoted some real winners and some real losers. I'll help you steer clear of the latter.

- **Quizzes:** No matter how smart you think you are, there's always somebody smarter on the Net. You have to design your quiz carefully if you don't want to be outsmarted.

- **Traffic Builders:** The Trojan Room Coffee Machine is the most famous in a long line of stupid Web tricks that reel in the browsers despite being incredibly lame.

- **Events:** You can come as you are to these gala events and leave anytime the chat gets boring. We'll discuss the benefits and drawbacks of putting on "a really big show."

- **Top Tips:** How to become the P. T. Barnum of the Net in 50 words or less.

A Tale of Two Promotions

It was the winter of 1994. The online community was all abuzz about a new "killer app" called Mosaic. *Business Week* had just run a cover story titled "The Internet: How it will change the way you do business." Then one company stepped forward to demonstrate that the old business models still work pretty well: If you want to get people's attention, give away something big. It gave away a car over the Internet.

The company was DealerNet, its virtual showroom was selling new and used automobiles (Figure 10.1). DealerNet represented a new way of doing business. Now you could shop for a car from the comfort of your home (more likely from work) without the pressure of a salesperson. You could visit dozens of dealerships without having to get out of your chair. You could easily prepare a list of the makes and models available and compare features and prices throughout the country. It was going to revolutionize the way cars were sold.

Figure 10.1 DealerNet ran one of the most successful promotions in the history of the Internet.

To promote its service, though, they relied on that tried-and-true marketing gimmick, the contest. They gave away a brand new Nissan Sentra. The Net went nuts. Usenet newsgroups hummed as people swapped the URL for the online entry form. The contest was written up, not only in the Internet trade journals, but in newspapers and magazines from coast to coast. The DealerNet home page was getting thousands of hits a day. It's still one of the most successful promotions ever run on the Net.

It was the winter of 1994. The online community was all abuzz about a new "killer app" called Netscape. Microsoft just announced that it would be building its own commercial online service. Then one company stepped forward to prove that greed was still the strongest marketing tool—or so it hoped. Carol Publishing announced it was giving away $10,000 cash. The Net yawned.

I was the publicist for the $10,000 giveaway. It was a promotion for the book, *Who Should Melissa Marry?* The book was an unfinished romance novel. The contest was to find the best concluding chapter, answering the title question. The promotion resulted in negligible media coverage and only a couple hundred requests for the rules. It was a disaster.

I take solace in the fact that the Melissa contest was not my idea. It had been running for several months offline. The media had not responded to Melissa's plea for help. Her prose was rotting on bookstore shelves, moving closer to the recycling bin as the contest deadline approached. The idea to put the contest online was a last-ditch effort to take advantage of the Net's ability to reach a large audience quickly. It didn't work.

I must admit I was a little surprised at Melissa's poor results. When DealerNet gave away a car, the Net exploded with activity as people burdened the bandwidth with entry forms, and the press ran interviews with the "geniuses" behind the promotion. Melissa was giving away $10,000 cash, which could be considered more valuable than the car and certainly was costing the sponsor more. So why was response so lackluster? Because it was not a good promotion, and I'll explain why not in this chapter.

Developing Good Promotions

A good promotion is like harnessed lightning. It rips through the heavy atmosphere of routine living, crackling with energy. It commands our attention with its sudden brightness. "Did you see that," people ask, spreading the word. The media hear the buzz and move in. A lightning strike is a good story. Then, just as quickly as the powerful bolt appears, it is gone.

DealerNet caught lightning in a bottle. Melissa caught nothing but heat. It's not easy catching lightning, but it's not completely up to chance. There are certain shared attributes of any great promotion. They include:

Integrity: A promotion grows out of the product being promoted.

Appeal: The promotion is irresistible to the target market.

Scope: The scale is perfectly suited to the product and the audience.

Timing: The right gimmick at just the right time.

Novelty: The concept has a unique twist to it.

Preparation: You must be ready to capture the lightning.

What Went Right

The DealerNet promotion was near-perfect. The giveaway—a car—was in total keeping with the client's product line. If the company had given away, say, an all-expenses-paid vacation to Ireland, the contest would not have resonated with the public. The contest was compelling for the target market: adults with ready access to the Internet. The point was to get people with automotive purchasing power to visit the site. It worked.

The scope of the contest was just right. A car giveaway is nothing new. In a magazine ad, it might draw only modest response. But it was an order of magnitude larger than anything previously given away on the Net. The timing was flawless, too, with the contest appearing just as people were buzzing about the Web. Today, you'd have to give away something more interesting than a car to get the media coverage DealerNet received.

That brings us to perhaps the most important ingredient for success: novelty. Giving away a car is nothing new; giving it away over the Internet, however, made it fresh again. It's not easy coming up with a perfect hook for a promotion. The best you can do is delve deeply into the product being promoted, research the target market, and look for some bolt linking the two.

If you find the lightning, you have to be ready. DealerNet had a professional team of publicists in place who knew how to use the lightning. Once they caught a journalist's attention, they were ready to roll out the tale of a new company revolutionizing the way cars were sold. They were prepared for the jokes: How can you test drive a car online? They were prepared for the questions: How many people have bought a car using your service? The contest was a bolt that punched a hole in the media's tough crust. DealerNet's publicity team used the opening to turn a news item about a contest into a feature story about a whole new way of selling cars.

What Went Wrong

Now let's look at poor Melissa. The product was a book, and the contest asked readers to become writers and provide the final chapter. That had some integrity. But the prize—cash—worked against it. A date with Fabio, the famous book cover hunk, probably would have resonated more with the target market: people who read romance novels.

The scope of the project was off. For a cash giveaway, it was too small. Thanks to lotteries, factory workers become millionaires on a nightly basis. In 1996, software maker Corel ran a million-dollar promotion. If you're giving away cash, anything less than a million bucks just isn't newsworthy on a national scale. As for timing, do you think a title like *Who Should Melissa Marry?* is in keeping with the times?

It's interesting to look at the origin of the Melissa contest. Bill Adler, the contest's creator, caught lightning in 1984 with a book called *Who Killed the Robins Family?* The publisher gave away $5,000 for that. The contest was a sensation, capturing the imagination of the general public. With more than 100,000 entries, the book with a built-in expiration date became a best-seller. But lightning wouldn't strike twice. Even the novelty of putting the contest on the Net and giving Melissa an e-mail address was not enough of a twist to command media coverage.

One of the only things Melissa had going for her was preparation. We set up an autoresponder and were ready to handle the thousands of requests for information that would pour in every day. Fewer than 200 people responded, and only three entries were submitted using the Net. Once the winner was announced, bookstores began returning the novel in droves. Just as the contest was recycled, so copies of Melissa's unsold story have probably been turned into newsprint.

Designing a Promotion

The difference between a successful promotion and a failure can often be attributed to the planning process. If you want to make a big splash online, the following are some questions you should try to answer before embarrassing yourself:

What Are the Characteristics of the Target Audience?

You have to immerse yourself in the target audience if you want to be successful reaching them. For many online promotions, the real audience is the media. You're hoping the promotion will catch fire and you'll make the evening news and the morning paper. The media is a tough crowd, though, and when you invite their attention, you may also be inviting disaster. If the promotion is a flop, the press can be merciless.

If the goal is to get media attention, then be prepared to handle the press. Offer some sort of press packet to flush them out. It's hard to schmooze a journalist if he or she is an anonymous lurker, so you have to entice them into making contact. Have the materials ready to turn a short news item into a feature story. Prepare artwork in advance and assign a spokesperson who can anticipate and answer media inquiries.

I've worked on many promotions where inquiries from the press were never followed up. Once I offered to give journalists press credentials for a trade show. It was only *after* many of them responded favorably that the show's management decided it needed to figure out what "press credentials" included. With major media outlets, you must follow up by telephone. It's a common mistake to try to do too much by e-mail.

If your target market is the general public, a completely different approach may be called for. If you're looking for nothing but numbers—reaching the most people possible—then your promotion must be accessible as well as compelling. You may want to partner with someone who has a server powerful enough to handle the traffic. To estimate traffic demands, try to get advertising information from popular Web sites; they will often tell you how many hits they get for popular events. You can find information like this at Rosalind Resnick's Interactive Publishing Alert site, http://www.netcreations.com/IPA/adindex/index.html (Figure 10.2).

To reach the masses, design your promotion so that you don't exclude people from America Online or Prodigy, people who have out-of-date Web browsers, people who use Macintosh computers, and so on. Of course, a text-based promotion has the widest possible audience, but it's unlikely to captivate much interest. You may want to offer several alternative versions of your promotion for people with different software and/or hardware configurations. Your clever creations will not reach the masses if enjoying them requires a T-1 line and a 21-inch monitor.

If your goal is to reach potential customers, you may want to design your promotion for utility instead of entertainment. Too many promotions are geared to generate traffic and nothing else. If you have 10,000 people a week coming to your site to play some silly game, you're probably making it more difficult for potential customers to get through. When customers arrive, does the site help them make a buying decision and provide them ready access to your customer support team?

Is the Target Audience Online?

Maybe you have a good idea of the people you're trying to reach. Are they on the Net? I've done a lot of work promoting items for kids on the Internet, and I have to keep reminding my clients that there aren't a lot of kids online. If you're promoting a product for children on the Net, you have to design the promotion for parents or teachers or the press.

Figure 10.2 Interactive Publishing Alert contains an index of Web sites, their advertising rates, and reported traffic counts.

In order to participate in an online promotion, people need two things: a computer and an account with an online service. Those criteria exclude 95 percent of the population. The characteristics of the remaining 5 percent look nothing like the demographics of the population as a whole. You can have a crystal-clear image of your target audience and design the perfect promotion to attract them, but if they aren't online, it won't work.

Chapter 2 has a lot of information about who's online and what they do while connected. The statistics are pretty weak, though, and you have to adjust them with common sense. One of the reasons my promotions are geared toward getting media coverage is that the press *is* online. Journalists, writers, researchers, and producers *are* a wired group of people. My promotions seldom result in online sales, though, because the broad consumer market is not online.

Many moons ago I worked in politics. The most painful lesson I learned was that people who don't vote, don't vote. You can't run a successful campaign for public office based on getting nonvoters to cast ballots. The only way to win an election is to compel the majority of the people who *do* vote to vote for your candidate. There may be millions of people with access to the Net, but it's a mistake to think you can tap that consumer buying power through an elaborate online promotion.

If This Promotion Is Successful, What Will the Results Be?

We all want to be successful, but would we know success even if we were basking in it? To design a good promotion, you need a more definitive goal than achieving a vague feeling of accomplishment. You should have a clear, detailed vision of the results you hope to achieve before launching an online promotion.

Site traffic is certainly one measure of success. The fact that a lot of people were drawn to the promotion is usually a good sign. But don't lie to yourself about what those numbers mean. For example, consider WebChat, a very cool online conferencing tool that could be part of a successful event. But in order to follow the discussion in WebChat, users have to reload the screen every few seconds; thus one browser could easily account for thousands of hits during a single event. Some sites get more hits because they are poorly designed and require a lot of searching to find information.

Sales is another measure of success that is hard to argue with. If your goal is to generate sales from your promotion, then the amount of traffic you get means little. There's some information in Chapter 2 about the ratio of sales online to sales offline, but it's still hard to quantify how many people buy based on something they saw on the Net.

Inquiries, prospects, or leads could be more important measures than sales, especially if you're marketing big-ticket items such as appliances, cars, or real estate. Inquiries are also important when you're selling services, not products. It's hard to buy a service over the Net without making some inquiry first.

A more sophisticated approach to measuring results involves the use of ratios. Compare the traffic you get with the inquiries or sales you generate. How does the ratio change over time? If you are consistently converting 1 percent of traffic into sales, what can you do to improve the sell-through. Either the hit count or the sales level alone can be misleading, but their ratio is a number you can work with. What percentage of inquiries do you convert to sales? When people buy, how much do they buy? How can you increase the sales per customer?

In my work promoting books online, I've found that the best results (other than media attention) come from one or two major customers. A single foreign distribution agreement could be worth tens of thousands of dollars. A bulk sale to a statewide library system could be worth thousands. A movie rights deal could be worth more than a million. You have to service an awful lot of retail customers to equal one big trade deal. But guess what? The foreign agent, the librarian, the Hollywood producer—they're all online. And the retail customer isn't. If success for you means the overall financial health of your enterprise, then I suggest you focus your promotions on business-to-business accounts and leave the entertainment to Sony and Starwave.

Another facet of online success is *presence*, that most mercurial of measures that includes such intangibles as brand recognition, goodwill, and cachet. It's hip to be online and it's embarrassing to be absent from the scene. It's true that having a Web site can improve your standing with stockholders and customers. If you have a substantial marketing budget, it makes sense to allocate an appropriate portion to online activities. Your presence online will help your traditional marketing activities work better.

Co-Branding

Many promotions succeed because they bring together two or more powerful partners. At Internet Publicity Services, our motto is to "go where the traffic is." Our experience has proven that it's a lot easier to place promotions on popular Web sites than it is to drag the audience over to a client's Web site. When you work with other sites on a promotion, the entire project becomes much easier. You reduce the amount of overhead required to carry out the promotion. You don't have to build a chat interface if you can use a successful one in place elsewhere. You don't have to worry about the technical problems as much—that's someone else's job. You don't have to buy a server that can handle the huge traffic good promotions draw; you use the server that someone else invested in.

A good promotion is called *content* online, and there are hundreds of well-known Web sites starved for good content. They need content to attract an audience and satisfy their sponsors, so if you've got a contest, a sneak preview of a movie, a celebrity, an author, an expert, a clever game—you name it, they want it, they *need* it. And you need the audience. So go where the traffic is; work with the big sites that need content, and leave the technical details to them

Finding the Top Sites

Where do you find these sites? Chapter 12, Resources, has a good section on SuperSites and webzines. You can also find suggestions in Chapter 5, The Linkage Campaign, for finding the premiere sites on any given subject. If you're looking for sheer volume of hits, however, the best place to go is Web21's weekly list of the top 100 Web sites, http://www.web21.com/services/hot100/index.html. Figure 10.3 shows a portion of the list. Yahoo, Point, Infoseek, and other catalogs have lists of popular Web sites. The editors of *PC Magazine* put together a pretty good list of the top 100 Web sites at http://www.pcmag.com/special/web100/top100f.htm.

The top Internet sites are dominated by Internet directories and adult content boards. Here, too, use common sense before partnering. Co-branding with a triple-X site might not be the best idea for most promotions. Co-branding with a directory service is an excellent idea,

Figure 10.3 The busiest sites on the Web, courtesy of Web21.

however, with one caveat. Directories are not destination sites; people don't linger in them long enough to participate in most promotions. They are probably more useful for building brand recognition than as a place to locate the promotion.

Destination sites are what I call webzines. These include HotWired, Playboy, ESPNet, Family Planet, iGuide, Pathfinder, Sony Online, and others. These megasites often include directories, chat rooms, news, features, and stores. They may draw millions of hits a day. Don't you think it would be a lot smarter to place a promotion on one of these sites rather than trying to get those millions of visitors over to your site?

Be aware that you can't always tell a good Web site by the traffic it's getting. For one thing, as of this writing, there is no reliable measure of site traffic. People will give you "hit counts," but they are often meaningless. "Views," "visitors," and "clicks" are other counts, but it's hard to know what they mean and whether you're being misled. Employees can run up hit counts, and caching by services like America Online can artificially deflate hit counts. You have to combine traffic statistics with common sense when choosing a site.

You can tell a quality site when you see one. Just ask yourself: Is the site workable? Does it have good content? Quality illustrations? Talented writers? Does it have name recognition? Is it a place you feel good being associated with? Do the people behind the site seem like good people to work with? Can you trust them to communicate with you; to get something in place on time; to tell you the truth about traffic, problems, delays?

Once you've worked with a few sites, you'll get a good feel for the process, particularly for a realistic time line for getting things done. It might turn out that you want to partner with one site on all your promotions. I place a lot of work at Book Stacks Unlimited, the giant bookstore at http://www.books.com. The traffic isn't as good as the big entertainment sites, but it's the right kind of audience for book promotions. The people there don't give me false statistics about traffic or sales, even though the numbers are sometimes so low they're hard to believe. They consistently do exactly what they say they're going to do, on time, so I can rely on them when setting a schedule. I've become spoiled by working with them.

You may find a similar partner site. If you're marketing to kids, look for the biggest kid sites on the Web. I'm sure they could use your financial support or the content and marketing your promotion will bring. When you find a good partner site, stick with it. Both of you will benefit from the ever-growing audience coming online.

A Co-Branding Success Story

In early 1996, Random House Juvenile Publishing launched an interactive Web promotion called The Lurker Files (Figure 10.4). The staff created a fictional online college complete with a chat room called The Ratskellar where the Lurker laid in wait. Behind the site was a professional writer (Scott Ciencin) who would spin out stories about the Lurker and other fictional characters attending the university. Visitors to the Web site would comment on the stories in the chat room, then see their comments turn up in the next episode as some plot twist. In other words, Random House's writers would work material from the chat room into the story.

This rather elaborate Web site was a big gamble. You never know if people are going to come, if they'll participate, if the chat room will work. But Random House had a couple things going for them. First, the graphics were amazingly good. Someone at that company understands that you can't take good offline graphics and just transfer them to the Web. You have to create graphics that work in this environment. They

Figure 10.4 The Lurker Files was a joint effort between Random House and Yahoo.

have to load quickly, yet look sharp. It's not an easy balance to achieve and few Web sites have done as good a job with their graphics as Random House.

Second, they co-branded the project with Yahoo, the giant Internet catalog and one of the top ten traffic sites on the Net. Yahoo had grown into a huge site and it was segmenting into a series of special-interest catalogs. The first one to roll out was Yahooligans, a catalog for kids. Yahooligans became a co-sponsor for The Lurker Files. Debuting almost simultaneously, The Lurker Files got a premium link spot off Yahooligans' entertainment page.

Random House also included a contest with the launch of The Lurker Files Web site. Kids were invited to write a fictional account of what it's like being online. The prize was not money, which isn't much of a motivator, but fame: the chance to be published online or in print by Random House. The contest was positioned for teachers to use as a writing assignment to get kids to talk about their online experiences. My firm promoted the contest on newsgroups, mailing lists, commercial online services—everywhere we thought we might find a teacher or a kid interested in the concept.

Figure 10.5 Yahooligans is a catalog of Internet resources for kids.

Even though The Lurker Files involved enticing the audience to a new Web site rather than working through a high-traffic site, it succeeded well beyond initial expectations. The site drew so much traffic that Random House decided to spin off a line of books, clothing, and other merchandise, and shop the concept to television producers. The gamble paid off because the site was well-constructed, and Random House did a good job of co-branding with Yahooligans and marketing the site to educators and not just kids.

A Co-Branding Horror Story

Whenever you are dependent on a co-branding partner, there is the potential for trouble. The biggest problem I've had with co-branding is the time lag. Everything has to be approved by two companies, and this process really slows down your ability to roll out a promotion and adjust it as necessary. Be sure to plan extra time into your schedule. Just ask Apple Computer.

Apple partnered with Paramount Pictures on a Web site for the movie *Mission Impossible*. (Apple's product line is prominently displayed in the film.) Their mission was to build a fancy Web site that demonstrated the value of their products. They should have turned down the assignment.

Apple launched the site with a series of television commercials and expensive print ads all built around the URL for the Web site: http://

mission.apple.com/ (Figure 10.6). But the site wasn't up in time. Millions of dollars in advertising, and only thing people connecting to the site saw was a "coming soon" graphic. I don't think many browsers planned to come back soon.

The site was six weeks late according to the buzz on a mailing list for computer journalists. But things went from bad to worse for Apple when the site finally appeared about a week after the TV spots started running. To enjoy the site, you had to have Netscape 2.0 and four plug-in software programs that most people didn't have. Those requirements eliminated a large portion of the potential audience, including everyone on America Online and Prodigy. Nothing like alienating seven million people.

But the story gets worse. Even if you had Netscape 2.0, and even if you found and installed all the plug-ins, the site didn't work. In fact, one wired journalist I know reported that the site crashed his system every time he tried to visit. First it was late, then it was broken. That's not the kind of PR Apple was hoping to achieve with its huge dollar investment.

Who knows whether the delays were caused by the co-branding relationship or by the difficulty of the programming or what. Certainly, whenever you are in a partnership, progress will slow. Time and again, I have been hired by companies to promote sites that are not ready. No

Figure 10.6 Connecting to Apple's partnership site with Paramount turned out to be a Mission Impossible.

matter what, don't invite millions of people to a site that is broken. Give yourself enough time to make absolutely certain the site works before you tell the world about it.

Steps in Successful Co-Branding

Successful co-branding requires a good match between partners. Hopefully, each partner has some strength that the other lacks. Most of the promotions I put on the Net offer content and publicity in exchange for my partner's audience and technical expertise. A familiarity with the Web and its search tools will make it easier to find such a partner. Patience will help you plan for the extra time a partnership arrangement requires.

At Internet Publicity Services, we partner with other sites to put book excerpts on the Net. Figure 10.7 shows a Web Excerpt Report prepared for Maximum Press, showing sites we contacted while placing an article based on two PowerPC-related books.

Figure 10.7 A report on attempts to find a partner site for a PowerPC promotion.

Web Excerpt Report

Client:	**Maximum Press**
Book:	**PowerPC Books**
Date:	**January 29, 1996**

Web Sites Visited & Results:

PowerPC News

http://power.globalnews.com/ppchome.htm

One of the most prominent sites dealing with PowerPC information. Run by Chris Rose. They have news and advertisements, so they will likely want a fee for hosting the article. They already have an article in the bookstore from a competing title called "The PowerPC Revolution." December 22, 1995: Pitched the article to Chris Rose for the News or the Bookstore. Also asked about selling Maxpress Books from their store.

Response on December 22, 1995, from Chris Rose:

>Thanks very much for your mail, I've seen the books - very nice. We
>don't tend to take placed articles on the editorial side, but I've passed your

(continues)

Figure 10.7 (*Continued*)

>message on to the publisher, Julian Marszalek, who is better placed to
>work out how best your books could be sold via the site.

Motorola PowerPC Home Page

http://www.mot.com/SPS/PowerPC/index.html
They have a strong site including a library and a page of links. December 19,
1995: Pitched article to webmaster.

Response on December 22, 1995, from George Paap, Motorola PowerPC Webmaster. Files transferred to him.

>I'll take a look at it. We already have a link to you in our Bibliography
>section of the library. We really don't have the infrastructure yet to
>sell products from our site.

Sat, 6 Jan 1996: George declined to take the page, but did correct the URLs for
two links to Maximum Press that were not working.

IBM RISC System/6000 Products & Services

http://www.austin.ibm.com/indext.html
Have some articles on their site, though mostly of a technical nature. December 19, 1995: Pitched article to Ed Costello - Technical manager & webmaster
<epc@www.ibm.com>

Fri, 29 Dec 1995: Ed Costello passed my note to Alex Wright.

16 Jan 96: Alex Wright bounced me to two other folks who have never replied.

The IBM PowerPC Microprocessor Web Site

http://www.chips.ibm.com/products/ppc/index.html
Similar to the RS/6000 site above, but focused on the PowerPC Microproces-
sor. December 19, 1995: Pitched article to David Gardner - World Wide Web
Program Manager <medialab@vnet.ibm.com>

January 29, 1996 : See IBM RISC/6000, above. My requests were consolidated
in a message to Alex Wright. No response to date.

PC Week Online

http://www.zdnet.com/~pcweek/
Mostly archives content from the magazine. They have a "Special Reports"
section where the PowerPC article might work. December 19, 1995: Pitched article to Jeffrey Frentzen - Technical Director <jfrentzen@pcweek.ziff.com>

January 29, 1996: Never responded.

X Computer Company

http://www.bossnt.com/xhome.html
> Manufactures a computer based on the PowerPC chip. Site is very thin. December 19, 1995: Pitched article to webmaster, <mbusam@boss1.bossnt.com>

> Response on December 28, 1995, from Matthew Busam. Files were FTPed to his site.

>>I'd very much like to see the article and include it at my site. Please
>>send it along with the button. You can ftp to my ftp server: ftp.bossnt.com.
>>Login is anonymous, with email as your password. Place the documents in
>>the incoming directory. It is easier than if you email (at least for me.)

> January 19, 1996: Article installed at: http://www.bossnt.com/PCPower.html

FirePower Systems, Inc.

http://www.firepower.com/
> Manufacturer of PowerPC-based computers. Site has no editorial content. "Points of Interest" has links. December 19, 1995: Pitched article to Philip Schiller, head of marketing.

> January 29, 1996: Never responded.

Chris Bennett's PowerPC Page

http://www.mcs.com/~bennettc/WWW/PowerPC.html
> Chris is involved with GEnie's PowerPC roundtable. His (her?) site has links and some original content. December 19, 1995: Pitched article to Chris Bennett <bennettc@mcs.com>

> Response on December 19, 1995, from Christopher E. Bennett. Files sent.:

>>I'll forward this information on to my friend Sheppy, the head sysop of the
>>PowerPC Programmer's RT on GEnie. He'll certainly want post your articles
>>on the system. There is also a "PowerPC Hotspots on the Internet" area
>>where we can add a link to your page. So do send the information... I may
>>not be enthusiastic any more, but I know some people who are. ;)

Microprocessor Architechture Survey

http://www.eng.uci.edu/comp.arch/processors/index.html
> Collection of articles and links dealing with PowerPC processors, among others. December 19, 1995: Pitched article to Mark Pontius <mpontius@ece.uci.edu>

> Response on December 27, 1995, from Mark Pontius. Files sent:

(continues)

Figure 10.7 (*Continued*)

>I would like to see this article, and would be happy to put it onto
>my site (assuming it's not too much over 1MB). You could send me the HTML,
>either straight or uuencoded.
>
>Again, thanks for the offer, and I'll look forward to hearing from you.
>—Mark Pontius

Mon, 22 Jan 1996: Article installed at
http://www.eng.uci.edu/comp.arch/processors/default.html

We started our search for a partner by using the standard Internet
directories and search tools to look for PowerPC SuperSites. (Chapter 5,
The Linkage Campaign, has more information about finding SuperSites
devoted to specific topics.) We then visited the sites and, when we
found a good match, looked for a person to approach about a partnership. Figure 10.7 shows some of the information we tried to glean at
every site.

Some of the information we collect in our Web Excerpt Report is
easy to take for granted, but not so easy to find. Basic things to note are
the name of the site, the URL or Web address, the name of a contact person and his or her e-mail address, the page on the site where you believe your promotion will work. We found through painful experience
that just bookmarking sites does not provide enough information to
work with. Bookmarks often don't capture the true name of the site; it's
very frustrating to go searching for sites one day, only to come back the
next and see a bunch of links to *index.html*.

You can prepare a report like the one in Figure 10.7 by creating *annotated bookmarks*. Chapter 12 is based on these kinds of bookmark files.
When you visit a site in Netscape 2.0, you can bookmark it, then edit
the bookmark to clarify the name of the site and add notes about why
you put it on your hotlist. Figure 10.8 shows the Edit Bookmark window in Netscape 2.0.

It is most important when trying to partner with a site to get the
name of the person who can make decisions for the site. Many sites
don't have credits or provide the names of people responsible for site
content. You may have to send e-mail to a generic address, such as Webmaster, explaining your interest in working together and asking for the
name of a contact. But don't forget the phone! I've worked with a lot of

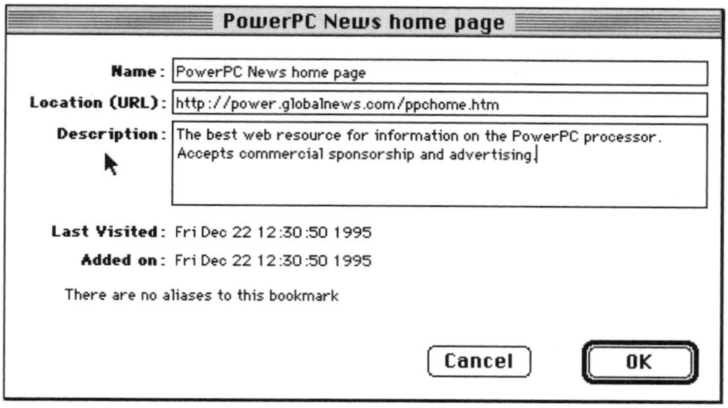

Figure 10.8 You can edit bookmarks in Netscape 2.0 and add descriptions that will help you at a later date.

popular webzines, and I rarely get a placement without telephone contact with the editor. These people get many more e-mail messages than phone calls, and it's easier to get their attention over the phone.

Once you've found a partner site and its interested in the promotion, you need to work out a timetable and decide who will provide what materials. You will speed the process by offering as much support as possible. With any promotion, there is usually text and artwork that must be prepared. Web sites often have a very definite look they're trying to cultivate, so they might not want you to provide the HTML code for the Web pages. However, they will probably be pleased to accept text and artwork files electronically, saving time in keyboarding and scanning.

When I'm co-branding with a site, I try to have all the resources my partners might want, ready to go. I don't want to lose momentum while people are keyboarding text or scanning graphics or waiting for permission or legal review. I've lost a couple of good placements as initial enthusiasm cooled due to long delays. Now I'll provide the graphics, the Web pages, and the programming if necessary. If they want to promote the placement, that's fine, but I'll have my own plan for promoting the installation.

One of the most important items you can get from your partners is a detailed report on the traffic the site is generating—a so-called hit list. Ask exactly how they measure traffic, and if they can provide a good approximation of the number of people visiting the site, not just the number of hits. Without a good measure of traffic, it's difficult to know how successful the partnership arrangement is and how to modify it for improved results.

Contests

Contests are very popular promotions offline, and they have successfully made the transition to the digital world. In fact, they are perfectly suited to the Net because they take advantage of the interactive character of online communications. Contestants can enter online at no cost to the sponsor. The contest links at Yahoo are among the catalog's most-used resources (Figure 10.9).

One reason that contests are so popular with publicists is that they entice people into providing the demographic information that companies crave. Marketing people want to know everything they can about

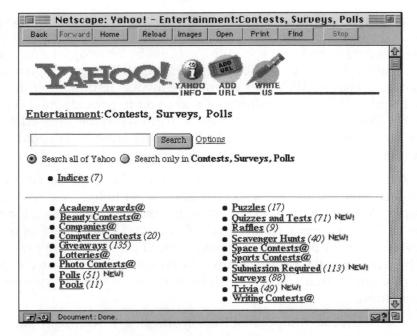

Figure 10.9 The Contests page at Yahoo—it was one of the first categories set up at the site.

who is visiting the company Web site. Your server software can tell you the domain name for all visitors, possibly even individual e-mail addresses, but it can't tell you how old visitors are or what their favorite flavor is. So Webmasters resort to bribes.

Contests are used to channel traffic in desirable directions especially Web treasure hunts, which have a cultlike following online. Clues are scattered at participating Web sites, and those who provide a list of URLs for all the pages where clues are found win a prize. One of the most popular contest sites is The Riddler (Figure 10.10) at http://www.riddler.com, where browsers can participate in several advertiser-supported trivia games and treasure hunts.

Some Webmasters have incorporated treasure hunts into their own sites. To get people to explore more of your Web site, consider hiding something and giving a prize to those who find it. Or enter them in a drawing for a monthly prize. You can also prompt people to fill out a survey by offering to enter them in a contest. Figure 10.11 shows a contest offered by Hamilton Beach/Proctor-Silex.

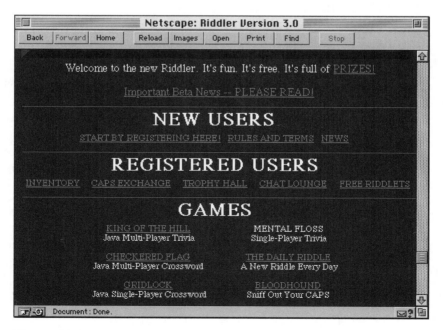

Figure 10.10 The Riddler is a favorite Web site for contests.

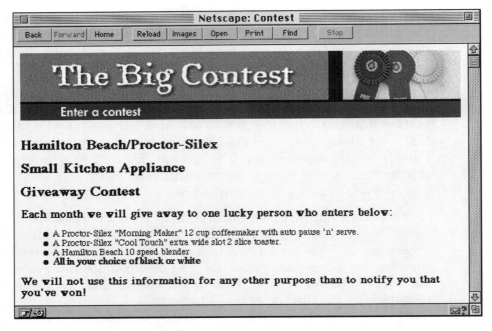

Figure 10.11 Visitors at this Web site can win appliances just by providing their contact information.

Choosing a Good Prize

One of the biggest mistakes made by people sponsoring contests is giving away the wrong prize. I did a promotion for a publishing client that included a contest for a free copy of the book. Who is going to buy the book if they think they might win it? Let's say you're visiting the site because you're interested in this book. You are the target market—a potential buyer. You have the choice of buying the book, or entering a contest to win it. Many people choose to enter the contest.

What happens next? The potential customer moves to some other Web site and probably forgets about the book. Are you going to notify all the losers: "Hi! You didn't win the contest for the book, but would you like to buy it?" That's not a very effective marketing strategy. But if you don't notify them, they might pass up the book in stores, thinking they still have a chance to win it. Your product loses either way.

In short, don't pick a prize that's going to cost you sales. If anything, give something away that reinforces your marketing: logo items such as T-shirts, mouse pads, caps, coffee mugs, screen savers, and so on, are good giveaways because they are also ads for your company's products. Money usually fails as a giveaway because it seldom reinforces marketing efforts. As I said earlier, a good promotion is both original and grows out of the product being promoted. You can spend very little money on a giveaway but provoke an incredible response, especially from the media, if there's something unusual about it.

Legal Considerations

Nothing slows down the planning of a promotion as much as lawyers. It seems like they're paid to think up novel reasons why you shouldn't do a contest, rather than helping you launch it quickly and legally. Still, you could be in a world of hurt if you don't get legal counsel before putting your contest online.

Figure 10.12 shows the boilerplate from the Hamilton Beach/Proctor-Silex contest described earlier in the chapter. Most boilerplates focus on three things: no purchase necessary to win, employees are ineligible, and the people putting on the contest aren't responsible for lost entries. I'm sure you can find an attorney who will lengthen that list for you. I've seen some boilerplates that are so long and complicated that they requires their own Web sites.

There are probably all sorts of federal and state laws governing contests that you should consult. Since the Internet is truly international, you never know who is going to claim jurisdiction over your contest. Is

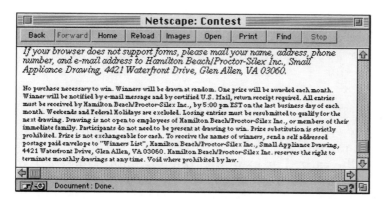

Figure 10.12 Contest boilerplate, courtesy of the legal department.

it the state where the Web server is located, or perhaps the state where the company headquarters is located? These are the sorts of questions attorneys get paid $300 an hour to ponder on your behalf.

My point is, if you need legal advice, *factor it into the timetable*. I have never worked on a contest that involved attorneys and made the target launch date. You may actually want to consult them *before* any other planning to determine whether you can get a list of demands in advance, then build the contest around the boilerplate. It doesn't sound very inspiring, but neither is a subpoena.

Quizzes

Quizzes are a special type of contest that work very well online. They require entrants to provide answers, thereby taking advantage of the interactive character of the Net. Quizzes work best when their nature is in tune with the product being promoted.

We prepared a quiz to promote the book *The Seinfeld Aptitude Test* (Figure 10.13). A quiz was a perfect promotion because it attracted fans interested in trivia about the popular television series, and gave them a taste of what was in the book. We didn't even have to think-up the questions; we took them straight from the book. Still, there were problems crafting the test.

When we developed the quiz, it was a one-page promotion. We partnered with Book Stacks Unlimited, the aforementioned popular Web bookstore, in hopes of increasing sales by being linked with a fulfillment service. The staff there agreed to install the quiz at no charge. In fact, they were so taken with the quiz that they offered to have their programmers power it up at no charge. This is exactly the sort of benefit you hope for in a co-branding relationship.

The original version of the quiz had the answers at the bottom of the page, and people graded themselves. Book Stacks wrote a program that enabled entrants to click on a button and score the quiz. The problem with many quizzes, though, is that some entrant is smarter than the writers of the quiz. For example, one question we asked was, "What color was the defective condom George used?" We thought the answer was blue, but an astute student of *Seinfeld* informed us that the condom was not, in fact, defective—George only *thought* it was.

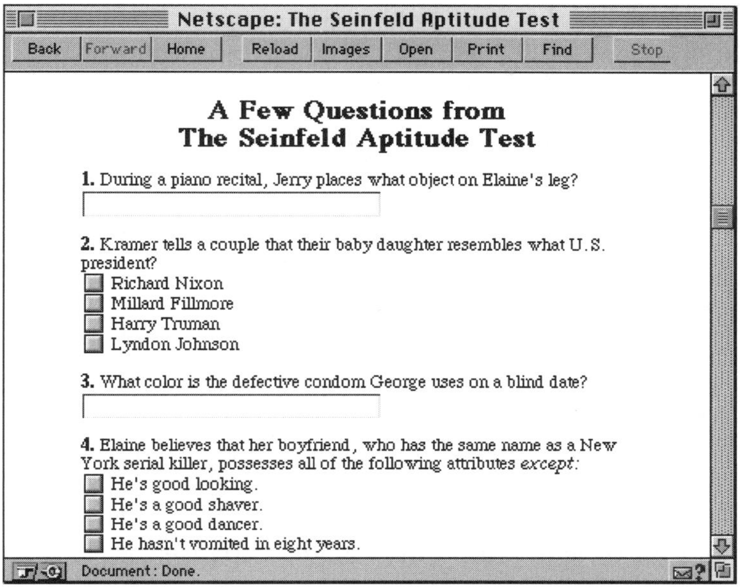

```
╔═══════════════════════════════════════════════════════════╗
║ ▦ ▦       Netscape: The Seinfeld Aptitude Test      ▦ ▦ ║
╠═══════════════════════════════════════════════════════════╣
║ │Back│ │Forward│ │Home│ │Reload│ │Images│ │Open│ │Print│ │Find│ │Stop│ ║
╚═══════════════════════════════════════════════════════════╝
```

A Few Questions from
The Seinfeld Aptitude Test

1. During a piano recital, Jerry places what object on Elaine's leg?

[   ]

2. Kramer tells a couple that their baby daughter resembles what U.S. president?

☐ Richard Nixon
☐ Millard Fillmore
☐ Harry Truman
☐ Lyndon Johnson

3. What color is the defective condom George uses on a blind date?

[   ]

4. Elaine believes that her boyfriend, who has the same name as a New York serial killer, possesses all of the following attributes *except:*

☐ He's good looking.
☐ He's a good shaver.
☐ He's a good dancer.
☐ He hasn't vomited in eight years.

Document : Done.

Figure 10.13 We created a quiz to promote *The Seinfeld Aptitude Test*, a trivia book by Beth B. Golub.

We also had a fill-in-the-blank question that asked what model computer Jerry originally used on the show. The correct answer was a Macintosh Duo. But what happens if someone types in "Mac Duo?" The program counts anything less than a perfect match as a wrong answer. Even switching to all multiple choice questions didn't fix that problem.

Fortunately, our quiz didn't involve any prizes, or even a tote board with the names of the top scorers. We had no way to prevent people from taking the test twice using different Internet accounts, learning the answers the first time and propelling themselves to the top spot the second time. If we had been giving away prizes, the problems with that quiz would have been substantial. Just scoring the quiz may have cost us some customers who would have given themselves a better grade if they self-scored. However, the interactive scoring feature made the quiz more exciting to play.

Now that I've described the pitfalls of quizzes, what about the results? Did the Seinfeld Aptitude Test sell books? No! Thousands of people played the quiz, yet fewer than 10 people bought the book at Book

Stacks. We were crushed by the low numbers. One reason was the shipping cost: the book only cost $7.95, but shipping was $3.00.

This points up one of the many pitfalls of online contests. Just because people like playing your contest doesn't mean they will buy your products. In our case, it seemed like most of the hits were coming from college students. That's great if college students are your target market. But if they're not your market, and they're not buying, do you want to spend thousands of dollars on programmers and hardware to entertain noncustomers?

The Seinfeld Aptitude Test actually worked well by our standards. It's true nobody bought the book online, but the quiz caught the eye of a *People Magazine* reporter, and the book got a nice write-up. The coverage in *People* and the other recognition the quiz received would make any publisher happy, knowing that sales will likely follow. Without that *People* article, though, the quiz would have been little more than some amusement for college kids at my client's expense.

Traffic Builders

As just noted, a quiz might not sell products, but it can sure bring a lot of traffic to your site. And if you're selling ads or sponsorships, traffic might be all you want. Judging from the list of top Web sites, putting pictures of naked people on your site is the most surefire way of pumping up the hit count. You might want to use a more creative traffic booster, though, like the famous Internet coffee pot (Figure 10.14).

Figure 10.14 The Trojan Room Coffee Machine, tucked away in a computer lab at Cambridge University.

The story of the Internet coffee pot is now a well-worn legend. Some programmers got tired of going to the break room only to find the coffee pot empty. They decided to hook up a camera to their network, then wrote software to deliver updated images of the coffee pot to their computer screens every 20 seconds. Now they could check the coffee level before embarking on a journey to the break room.

As rumors of the coffee server percolated through the online community, the camera was eventually hooked up to the Web. Hundreds of thousands of people have visited the site. You can see this wonder of the webbed world at http://www.cl.cam.ac.uk/coffee/coffee.html.

The Internet coffee pot generates a lot of traffic, but at whose expense? The traffic from a popular promotion can overload a server and overwhelm a Web site. Of course, if you are a coffee roaster or appliance maker, wouldn't you want to sponsor the Internet coffee pot and get all that brand recognition? You bet!

All kinds of silly traffic builders have gone on to fame and fortune on the information superhighway. Glen Davis started his Cool Site of the Day on InfiNet, and it grew into one of the most popular spots on the Web, with hundreds of sites linking to it. Word of the Day inspired one of my clients to develop Dirty Word of the Day as a protest against Internet censorship. It featured a new euphemism every day that people could use in place of a common cuss word.

These traffic builders are terrific if all you're looking for are hits. But beware. People get upset if they can't connect to your site because you don't provide enough hardware muscle to handle the load. They also get upset if the site doesn't work as promised or is not updated regularly. Making people mad is not a good sales tactic, and it can result in mischief at your expense.

If you use a traffic builder, tap into your creative talents to think of something that resonates with the product being promoted. Recently, the *Los Angeles Times* joined with United Airlines for a co-branded Web promotion (Figure 10.15). People using the *L.A. Times* custom news filter, called Hunter, were entered in a contest for frequent flyer miles from United Airlines. What do airplane travel and news retrieval have in common? The logo for the *Times'* Hunter service is a Golden Retriever. A joint promotion with Alpo or the ASPCA might have been a better match. As all marketers know, people can't resist a cute dog. If

Figure 10.15 United Airlines joined with *The L.A.Times* in a frequent flyer promotion.

the Hunter search service had an airplane as a logo or used a flight metaphor, I might understand the partnership with United Airlines better.

If your traffic builder really works, consider franchising it to other sites. You can ask for a graphical hotlink to your site directly from the gimmick. That way, you get brand recognition, but you only get visitors to your site who are interested in your products, not the gimmick. A good traffic builder is commodity worth quite a bit online. Webmasters at sites that rely on advertising or sponsorships will pay dearly for anything that boosts their numbers. Sony Online offers many people free Web sites in exchange for putting content on their server. Infoseek lets browsers connect to daily comics, such as *Dilbert* (Figure 10.16).

One of my favorite traffic builders was the Magic 8-Ball. Some college kids put the famed oracle on their site. Visitors asked a question,

Figure 10.16 Comics are great traffic builders, which means they're a franchise worth marketing.

clicked a button, and the 8-Ball returned one of its pat answers, such as "It is Decidedly So!" I think the makers of the Magic Talking 8-Ball must have cracked down on these sites for trademark infringement, because it's very difficult to find Magic 8-Ball sites anymore.

I was able to find Kurt Cobain's Magic Talking 8-Ball, though, where you can ask the late rock star a question and he responds from beyond (Figure 10.17). If you're building a device to bring the online hoards clicking to your site, be sure you aren't infringing a registered trademark, or you might find that most of the traffic originates from legal domains.

Events

One of the most under appreciated promotions is the Web event. Too many companies focus on building regular traffic at their sites, and end up using silly tricks in order to get enough hits to please the boss. Consequently, the company's computing and creative powers are put in the service of entertaining people on the Net instead of serving the needs of customers, suppliers, employees, and others who would benefit from a well-designed Web site.

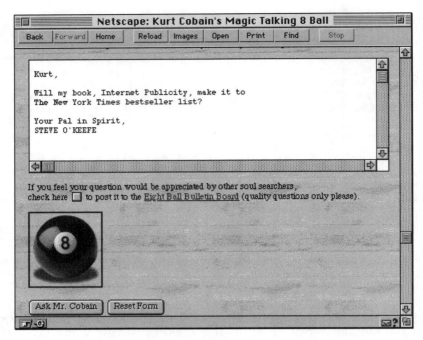

Figure 10.17 Let Kurt Cobain answer your questions from the comfort of his eternal resting place.

If you are an auto parts manufacturer, your Web site may be a huge success if you attract only one person: the buyer for a chain of auto parts stores. If the buyer likes your site—finds it a convenient way to learn about your products, ask questions, and place orders—you might pay for the whole operation by landing this one account.

Instead of trying to generate repeat traffic to your site, you can go for a big, annual blowout to introduce the site to your target market. Plan an open house or a trade show or some similar major exhibit that lasts for a week or a month. Instead of changing your home page every day to make the site fresh, save your money and hold an annual event for which you make over your Web site with a new theme every year.

A good example of Web events are the exhibitions at the University of California Irvine's bookstore, http://www.book.uci.edu/Exhibitions.html (Figure 10.18). The bookstore's Webmaster has teamed up with content providers to create lavish exhibits that educate as well as

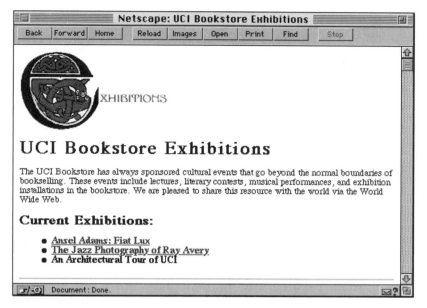

Figure 10.18 The UCI bookstore offers well-crafted exhibitions that work in conjunction with the store's inventory.

entertain. Their first project was called The Big Island of Hawaii, sponsored by Moon travel handbooks. As a jazz fan, I loved their exhibit on the jazz photography of Ray Avery, which included biographies and discographies of jazz musicians, all linked to buying opportunities from the bookstore's collection of CDs and jazz books.

When you do an annual promotion like this, you have time to plan. You can iron out the legal details of contests or quizzes. You have time to look for partners, sponsors, advertisers. You can develop artwork, audio files, video clips, and databases that mesh well for a premium browsing experience. You have time to test the event to make sure it works before you put it online. Best of all, you have plenty of time to promote the event.

Instead of chasing after the media every week or month, you're asking them to visit just once a year, and you're hopefully providing an event with enough pizzazz to warrant the coverage. You can promote the show with printed invitations to customers, suppliers, investors, and the press. You can buy print ads or get the event written up in magazines and journals that have long lead times.

Once the show is over, you can leave the exhibits on your Web site. The point of the "grand opening" is to debut the new site with the goal of enticing your target audience to stop by. If they find your site useful, they will be back later. And if they missed the gala event, there's no great loss. UCI keeps its exhibits up for years, with a big bash for each new show.

Possibly the biggest advantage of holding an annual event is to preserve the sanity of your Webmaster and staff. I've seen many a programmer burn out trying to create the latest, hippest, coolest thing on the Net. With an annual event, there's a schedule, a plan. Of course, as the deadline approaches, people will be stressed trying to get everything in place, but afterwards, they can relax, take some time off, and start thinking about next year's show.

The one drawback of the annual event is that you are pulling in a lot of traffic in a short period of time. Therefore, you need a server that's powerful enough to handle the load. The rest of the year, traffic might be a lot lighter. However, for most events this won't be a problem. If you're promoting a business, you don't want the masses to visit your Web site; you want the trade to visit: customers, employees, sales reps, distributors, wholesalers, investors, partners, the media. Any decent-sized server should have no trouble with that kind of load. If your event is geared for the general public—for the masses—consider partnering with one of the larger entertainment sites on the Net.

Top Tips

- **Look for Lightning:** A good promotion is like a bolt of lightning ripping through cyberspace. It harmonizes with the nature of the product being promoted and resonates with the target audience.

- **Look for Partners:** The Internet has grown so large that it takes an event of significant proportions to get the attention of the public and the press. Look for partners who have strengths where you need help.

- **Be Creative:** If you want to captivate the online audience, cleverness goes further than money. A photo of an empty coffee pot can be more compelling than a Web extravaganza packed with multimedia installations that are disappointing even if they *do* work.

- **Define the Target Audience:** Who are you trying to reach? What do they look like, *smell like*, think like? If you can visualize the destination, it's a lot easier to forge the path.

- **Take Your Time:** Major promotions are never ready on time. Budget extra time in your schedule if you have partners or need to consult attorneys. Give yourself time to test.

CHAPTER 11

Firefighting and Follow-Up

What happens when you put 30 million people together and give them the ability to communicate at no charge? *People will talk!* The Internet may have more or less than 30 million participants, and there might be small charges for message delivery, but you get the drift. Sometimes the Net feels like a giant talk radio program, and conversation can get pretty hot.

Imagine you're the CEO of a giant computer company and someone just posted a message that your new model has a major flaw. How long will it take for you to find out about the message? How long will it take your competitors to find out? How quickly can you respond and what should you say? What will you do if the message spreads, your stock price plummets, sales drop off, people organize boycotts of your products, and hackers attack your electronic communications?

Welcome to the wild and wooly world of the Internet where, thanks to fiber optics, stories—true and false—really do spread at the speed of light. If the preceding scenario sounds a little frightening, wait until you read about some of the companies that have been there, done that. Damage control is part of any public relations plan, and this chapter is all about what can happen to you online and how you should respond.

Obviously, you can't respond to a problem online until you know about it. This chapter shows you how to get up-to-the-nanosecond information about your company's image online. You also learn about the sexy field of *competitive intelligence*, and the amazingly powerful tools for stalking your competitors online.

I tell you how to deal with bad publicity, beginning with dousing minor flames and progressing to Internet blacklists. I also tell you how to avoid these unpleasantries altogether while successfully promoting your company on the Net. Here are some of the vital subjects covered in this chapter:

- **Internet Firefighters:** Some companies try to manage their image online; others wish they had.

- **People Are Talking:** How to find out what folks are saying about you. How to search the Net for hot gossip.

- **Competitive Intelligence:** How to find out what your competitors are doing, and why you often have more to gain by working together than apart.

- **Success through Participation:** Sometimes the best sales promotion is just being there when people need you. How to use your time online more efficiently.

- **Responding to Flames:** How to put out flames before they escalate beyond control. How to work with moderators, forum hosts, and other Internet authorities.

- **Advanced Medialist Management:** Keeping track of people on your list, updating procedures; what to do when someone complains or asks to be taken off.

- **Canceled Messages and Blacklists:** How to deal with canceled messages. How to find out if you're on a blacklist, and what you can do about it.

- **Top Tips:** Best suggestions for getting close to the action without getting pulled into a fight.

Internet Firefighters

The Internet has had its share of defining moments in its short history, when the technology was challenged by some crisis and rose to the occasion. The Canter & Siegel affair was one such moment. A couple of inconsiderate attorneys gleefully plastered the Net with ads for their legal services. The Net returned the favor by showing its ugly side: death threats, sabotage, and general meanness. The Net discovered its strength: the ability to spread information at lightning pace and to organize people instantly.

The Net's power was shown in a more flattering light on a couple of other occasions. After the January 1994 earthquake in Los Angeles, people used the Net to check on missing relatives or friends. During the revolt against Boris Yeltsin in Russia, the Net was used to transmit information that was blocked from normal channels.

Another defining moment for the Internet was the Pentium Chip Scandal of 1994. Intel had been getting nothing but praise for its new Pentium chips. Then Thomas Nicely, a professor of mathematics at Lynchburg College in Virginia, posted a message about a bug on the Usenet newsgroup comp.sys.intel. Intel responded by acknowledging that it knew about the bug and had corrected the problem. The company said it was highly unlikely the average user would be effected and offered to replace the chip upon request. But this response wasn't satisfactory to many members of the online community. They demanded that Intel recall the defective chips or at least notify owners about the problem.

Intel eventually made further concessions, but not before the company was thoroughly scorched online. For weeks, all the newsgroups crackled with jokes about the Pentium chip. Electronic zines spread the controversy even further. Then the controversy itself became a news item, reported on TV and in print. The technical details of the flaw were buried beneath the impression that something was wrong with Pentium processors. The "Intel Inside" sticker came to be a warning signal to potential buyers. Intel recovered from this catastrophe, but who knows how much the fiasco cost them in terms of sales, momentum, and reputation?

In the glow of the Pentium scandal, people online felt like they had taken on a giant and won. The Net was now a force to be reckoned with, and companies ignored it at their own peril. The next major recipients of the Net's wrath were CompuServe and Unisys, following an announcement on December 29, 1994, that CompuServe would start collecting licensing fees for software used to make GIFs. GIF, as I've mentioned, is a format for storing images and it dominates graphics storage on the Web. There had never been a charge to use the GIF format before, and CompuServe had, in fact, encouraged its use. Users panicked, believing they would have to pay CompuServe a royalty on every GIF in use.

Immediately, the online community organized to protest the GIF fee. Unisys and CompuServe were excoriated. People called for retaliation, including a boycott on H & R Block, CompuServe's parent company. As programmers scrambled to find a substitute format that would circumvent the underlying patent, Web developers were encouraged to switch to the freely available JPEG format. When the controversy made it into the hallowed pages of *The Wall Street Journal*, CompuServe and Unisys were faced with a public relations nightmare.

CompuServe hurt its own case by releasing poorly worded announcements that fed the online frenzy. The fact that they released the announcement over the Christmas holiday, giving developers one month to register for a license or risk legal action, didn't help their cause. As the online community turned up the heat, CompuServe and Unisys came out with "clarifications" to stem the controversy: the licensing fee applied only to software for making GIFs—not the GIFs themselves—and would not be required for software released before January 1, 1995. Web developers breathed a collective sigh of relief, and companies learned once again the potentially devastating power of the Net.

The Net had won again. By generating so much bad publicity so quickly, the Net had shown it was a force to be reckoned with. Companies could no longer take the Net for granted. If they wanted to be successful with the family of computer users, then they had to court the Net's goodwill—or at least learn to tame its wrath when necessary. People who relied on the Net for the success of their businesses learned an important lesson: they would have to get in the trenches, listen to the buzz online, and try to influence it.

And so a whole new profession was born: Internet *Firefighters*. Today, many companies have assigned employees the task of monitoring their image online. You'll see many of these people working discussion groups and chat rooms, correcting misinformation and offering to take care of problems.

Microsoft Bashing

Probably no company needs a firefighter more than software maker Microsoft. There are entire newsgroups devoted to Microsoft bashing.

There's an anti-Windows Web site and numerous other home pages that wallow in their hatred for the software giant. Just take a look at this news item reported in the webzine *Netsurfer Digest* on November 26, 1995:

```
Once glance at Joan Grove's home page will tell you that she
doesn't exactly rank as Microsoft's greatest fan. Joan, a
former Microsoft employee, displays proof of what she
considers to be crucial Microsoft math bugs, a report on how
"Microsoft Destroyed My Family", and accusations of sexual
harassment and thuggery. This WWW site won't make Bill Gates'
day. She claims Microsoft's legal department warns all
potential employers of her, as well any who try either to work
with or help her. For good measure, she accuses her ex-husband
of molesting her children and includes a photo of him naked.
There's lots of other stuff, too, but is it fact or fiction?
Either option's truly scary.
<URL:http://www.halcyon.com/redrose/joan.html>
```

Microsoft has a lot to lose from a poor image online. There's no way of knowing if this bad image contributed to the failure of the Microsoft Network, the company's ill-fated commercial online service which is now being converted to a Web site. Certainly the bad press didn't help. Microsoft is betting that the Internet will become the dominant channel for delivering software to its customers. If Bill Gates hopes to be successful on the Net, he had better deploy some professionals to clean up the company's online image.

Polishing the Apple

Apple Computer has learned how important the Internet is to its survival. According to recent statistics compiled by MIDS (see the Who's Online chapter), Apple's share of Internet-connected machines is growing while Windows' share is actually falling. This is surprising considering how much Internet software is available for Windows as opposed to Macintosh users.

Recognizing the Internet as the world's biggest rumor mill, Apple Computer actively seeks out discussions concerning its products. When people need information, the company provides it. When false rumors are being spread, Apple tries to correct bad information before it gets out of control. Here's one of Apple's firefighters at work in the Usenet newsgroup biz.marketplace.computers.discussion:

```
From: Macintosh Technical Support Team
Newsgroups: biz.marketplace.computers.discussion
Subject: Apple Computer is doing just fine...
Date: Mon, 22 Jan 1996 12:23:12 -0500

Since everyone lately thinks that Apple is on it's way out —
think again.  The company is actually doing quite well in
comparison to other "big business" companies out there.

Due to a number of requests to have this information reprinted
and disseminated more widely, here is another posting
regarding Apple's quite healthy financial and market
situation.  News providers are encouraged to write articles
utilizing this data.  Sources are listed as appropriate along
with a list of Web-based resources used in this profile.

   [SNIP]
```

What followed was a rather lengthy dissertation on Apple's financials, arguing that the company is in better shape than some misanthropes would have you think. The point is, by consistently being there to defend its image online, Apple is able to confront rumors before they cause serious trouble. I wouldn't be surprised if bad PR on the Net leads to lower stock prices. Most large investors rely on computers to gather and analyze information and to make trades. Stock traders are some of the most wired people on the planet. They can't help but be influenced by gossip they hear online.

While Apple's use of firefighters is apparent, America Online's is less so. AOL was suffering from a bad reputation on the Internet. Long considered a service for novices, when AOL unleashed its membership on the Net, long-time netizens howled. They complained that people from AOL were poorly educated about netiquette and were clogging newsgroups and mailboxes with spam and stupid questions.

I noticed, however, that wherever I heard AOL being bashed, I soon after heard someone defending them. This happened often enough that I came to suspect that America Online uses firefighters to protect the company's image online.

Benefits of Firefighting

A lot of good can come from protecting a company's image online. In halting the spread of false rumors, a company circumvents damage to its brands and its stock price. Bad PR online can cause ill will among employees and government regulators and can lead to expensive lawsuits. Firefighting not only curbs negative PR, it also reveals opportunities to promote a company's brands and products.

When a company puts feelers out on the Net, it's going to get back a lot of information. Not all of it will be bad. Hearing about the problems caused by its members, America Online took efforts to improve its image. The company bought the electronic rights to books on using the Internet and netiquette, and installed these as help files at its Internet Connection center. America Online went from no support to the best support available online.

America Online also established procedures for disciplining members who abuse its terms of service by spamming the Net. The service posts announcements on the Net telling people how to turn in AOL members who violate netiquette. It also makes regular postings to the Internet abuse newsgroups, documenting disciplinary actions taken against its own members.

People can say what they like about America Online, but they have to credit the company with listening. It hears the negative criticism and has gone well beyond defending itself to actually doing something about it. How many other companies can say the same?

People Are Talking

So, how exactly do you find out what people are saying about you online? This is precisely the sort of activity computers are designed for: sorting through enormous amounts of digital information looking for the most relevant bits. Programmers have developed several useful tools for doing custom searches of information available online. Some of the best of these tools are listed in Chapter 12. The best place to start an information-gathering campaign is at the University of Maryland's Information Filtering site, http://www.ee.umd.edu/medlab/filter/.

From this site, you can find links to free and fee-based Internet filters. But be aware, some filtering programs are poorly designed, some are brilliant, still others are frightening. By setting up filtering services, you can monitor such Internet activities as Usenet newsgroup discussions, Web pages, news resources, and more. You can use these services to paint a complete picture of your company's presence online. You can also find out exactly what the competition is up to.

After looking at the filters currently available, you might want to head over to Infoseek and set up a personal news service. Infoseek is at http://www.infoseek.com/. Figure 11.1 shows a personal news page I set up for my dog, Joe Rude. By indicating my preferences on a series of set-up screens, Infoseek created a custom Web page giving Joey the latest information on subjects of great concern to him.

Whenever my Joey checks his Infoseek page, he will be shown such things as the weather here in Port Townsend, news stories of dog rescues and animal control activities, the latest stock quotes for the Ralston-Purina corporation, any sports stories about the Iditarod race in Alaska, and any appearance of his name in Usenet newsgroups. Joe can

Figure 11.1 A personal news page put together by Infoseek for my dog Joey.

also select the names of 10 individuals or businesses and Infoseek will track them in Usenet.

Infoseek's personal news page was still in beta testing when I set one up for my dog. It was free, but the results were disappointing. The top news stories were the same as you would find on any news page and had nothing to do with dogs. The Usenet searches are not performed automatically; if you want to find out who's talking about you in Usenet, you have to submit the search and wait for the results. If Infoseek can power up this service, it could be very useful. Until then, try some of the other filters mentioned in Capter 12 and in the following sections.

Searching Newsgroups and Mailing Lists

Most public dialogue on the Internet happens in newsgroups and mailing lists. There are several good resources for searching Usenet newsgroups. The Stanford News Filter service (http://woodstock.stanford.edu:2000/) allows you to set up a search profile and have any matching results e-mailed to you on a regular basis. Figure 11.2 shows the form used to set up the filter.

The Stanford filter will search all its newsgroups and send you an e-mail report of matching entries. Each match contains the header of the newsgroup message and a few lines of text. This filter is, however,

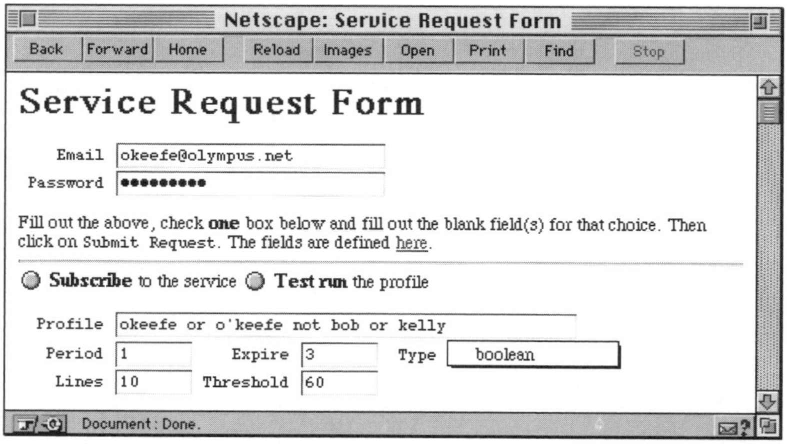

Figure 11.2 Stanford's news filter e-mails matching items to your mailbox.

somewhat cumbersome to work with. If you set your search criteria too broadly, you'll get a lot of posts you couldn't care less about. Set it too narrow, however, and you may miss something important. You can't set up one profile to search for multiple items the way you can at Infoseek. Rather, you must set up a separate profile for each company or person you're tracking. Finally, the reports the Stanford filter generates have too much superfluous information in them compared to DejaNews.

DejaNews (http://www.dejanews.com/) lets you search Usenet for any word or phrase (a company name, an e-mail address, etc.). It returns a nice listing of matches with one line for each match. Figure 11.3 shows the results of a DejaNews search for the word "microsoft." This service is very fast, and the results are compact and easy to use.

There are many other Usenet news filters available. Try them to find those you like. One of the easiest to use is your own Usenet news reader program. I use a program called NewsWatcher. It enables me to set up a list of the groups I want to follow. I can highlight any number of newsgroups and search them using various criteria (keyword, To, From, etc.). My firm tracks the results of our Usenet postings this way. The process is described in the Announcements chapter.

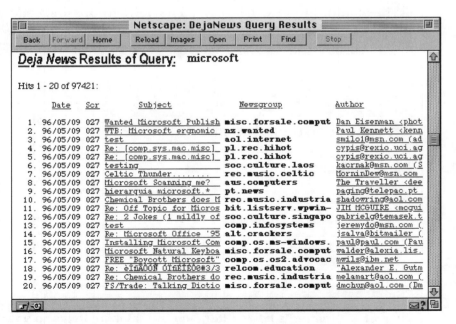

Figure 11.3 Results of a DejaNews search for "microsoft."

Mailing lists are a little harder to search. If the list is available as a bit.listserv newsgroup, you can use a Usenet filter to search it. If it's archived on the Web, a Web search may catch any mentions of the items you're tracking. If you subscribe to the mailing list, you can search it in your e-mail program or port it to your word processor and search it there.

Searching Other Services

For business users, NewsPage may be the best filtering service on the Net (http://www.newspage.com/). You can search for news items using keywords (for example, "General Motors") or browse categories (such as "automobiles"). Figure 11.4 shows the NewsPage home page, including a list of the categories available.

NewsPage returns a list of links to news stories with one- or two-line summaries of the content. Some of the articles are available free;

Figure 11.4 NewsPage lets you search a database of news articles.

you click on the link to read them. Other articles you must pay to see, either by subscribing to the news service or on a pay-per-view basis. You can get more information about the costs at the Web site.

You can search the Web for items of interest using all the Web search engines described throughout this book (Yahoo, Alta Vista, Infoseek, etc.). Look in Chapter 12 for addresses and brief descriptions of the major services.

One of the more interesting Web searches you can perform is a link search. Go to Alta Vista (http://www.altavista.digital.com/) and in the search window, type in the following: "link:URL," where the URL is any part of the address of a Web page. Alta Vista will return a list of pages that contain a link to the URL you typed in. This is a very handy way of checking who has linked to your page—and who's linked to your competitors. Figure 11.5 shows the results of a link search for the URL, www.okeefe.com (my brother's Web site). There were 106 matches, and the first two are shown in detail.

Don't be surprised if you don't see all the links on the Alta Vista results page. It doesn't catch links kept in databases. For example, if you registered with WebCrawler, your link is in a database and not on a

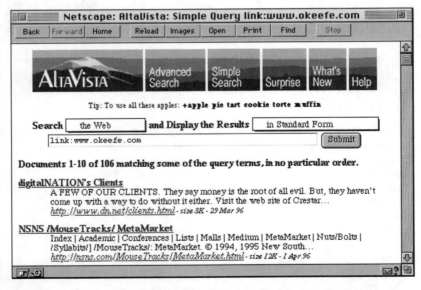

Figure 11.5 An Alta Vista link search for www.okeefe.com.

Web page. I wouldn't rely on Alta Vista to deliver a comprehensive set of links; however, you might find some that surprise you.

Some Ominous Implications

Many companies were concerned that the freewheeling ways of the Internet would result in unchecked piracy and copyright infringement. In fact, the truth online is weirder than the predictions. The Internet has come to be used not so much as an instrument of theft as a tool of surveillance. Using the described resources, companies are finding out about copyright infringements and trademark violations that would have otherwise gone unnoticed.

It's a fairly simple matter to have Alta Vista or DejaNews search for your trademarks. This kind of investigation happens all the time on the Net. Companies then send out their minions to defend their trademarks and enforce their patents and copyrights. If companies used to be afraid their stuff would be stolen on the Net, they now fear a letter from an attorney informing them of an actionable infringement on their Web site. You gotta love the Net!

The Internet has flipped conventional logic on a number of fronts. Companies formerly fretted about employees spending time entertaining themselves on the Web. After all, what's to stop someone from hanging out at the Playboy site all day long? WebSense, that's what. WebSense is a program developed by Net Partners that blocks access to certain Internet sites. There are many programs like this on the market now. They run on the server and block connection to a specified list of sites. Some Webmasters are using these Net censors to reduce the potential liability from access to sites containing images or information that might be illegal to view or possess. But there's another, more sinister side to this software.

WebSense doesn't just restrict access to Net destinations. It also logs every attempt to connect to a site and every minute of time spent online. Instead of employees surfing entertainment sites on company time, we now have employers monitoring every moment of an employee's online life. The Internet is making possible the kind of total surveillance only hinted at in books such as George Orwell's *1984*.

This leads us to an examination of our next subject, *competitive intelligence*—using the Internet to gather information on your rivals.

Competitive Intelligence

If you can use the Internet to find out what people are saying about your business, you can also use it to gauge the gossip on your competitors. You can use the same tools just described to keep track of companies or people whose online activities interest you. For example, you can use Infoseek's personal news page to track any Usenet postings mentioning your main competitors. You can also use Infoseek to track stock quotes and gather other intelligence.

Using Alta Vista, you can get a list of any Web sites with links to your competition. Many of these sites would probably be happy to add a link to your home page. Chapter 5, The Linkage Campaign, describes a campaign to get other Web sites to link to your Web site. By following the instructions in that chapter, you will develop a pretty good sense of the state of your industry online. As you search the Web for information on your competitors, try to bookmark the following types of resources:

- **SuperSites:** For every industry, profession or hobby, there is probably a SuperSite out there that catalogs Internet resources related to that subject. These sites will be of continuing importance to your online success.

- **Webzines:** Webzines are World Wide Web sites that function like magazines. Examples include *HotWired* and *The Wall Street Journal* Web site. You'll want to get on a first-name basis with the editors of webzines covering your industry.

- **E-zines and Mailing Lists:** E-zines are similar to webzines, except they are distributed to subscribers via e-mail, just like Internet mailing lists. They tend to be text-only documents, more focused on news than entertainment. There are sure to be a few devoted to your type of business.

- **Discussion Forums:** Don't forget about commercial online services such as CompuServe and America Online. Most of the action on these services happens in the forums. When you find a healthy forum discussing issues related to your business, add it to your hotlist and check it regularly. Get the names of the hosts or sysops of the forums.

By tracking the online periodicals and sites related to your business, you'll be alert to any activities by your competitors. You can use search tools to quickly wade through a stockpile of e-zines for names or phrases. Articles of interest can be cut and pasted into a personal newsletter, which can then be archived for later reference. There is a growing cadre of "information brokers" and clipping services online that can prepare custom reports like these for a fee. Look for listings at Yahoo.

Another excellent method for tracking your competition is to subscribe to the electronic newsletters they offer. Chapter 8, Document Transfers, has information on setting up a list server or mailing list, and commands for subscribing to the major brands of list servers. Many of my customers have company newsletters, and I follow them to find out what they're doing online. You might also want to subscribe to newsletters put out by suppliers, major investors, government regulatory agencies, and anyone else with a direct impact on your business. Don't forget to subscribe to *your own* company's newsletter—many managers don't know what their own online people are doing.

You'll hear a lot of gossip in chat rooms and at online appearances. There's no law that says you can't ask questions about your competitors. Frequently people ask, "What do you think about this company," or "Has anyone ever dealt with XYZ Corp," or "What are the best businesses in this field," or "Where can I find help on the Web?" You too can ask people what they think about your Web site or a competitor's Web site.

If you know that a representative from a competing company is going to be a guest speaker at an online chat, why not stop by and ask a question or two? You'd be surprised what people will reveal in these chats. A common question for guests is, "What are your plans for the future?" Wouldn't you like to know your competitors' plans for the future? If you can't attend the chat, you can usually download transcripts, and these often contain tasty tidbits of competitive intelligence.

Although you might want the information, you might not want the competition to know that you're checking up on them. Sometimes it's difficult to disguise your identity, but often it's very easy. I've had accounts on America Online, CompuServe, Prodigy, GEnie, Delphi, the WELL and several other services, although I only use my main Internet address in my printed materials and online communications. My Prodigy address is TUPZ36A. None of my competitors would recognize that account as belonging to me.

When you subscribe to electronic publications and want to remain anonymous, use only your e-mail address, not your name. If you must provide a name, you can certainly make one up—there's no law against it. America Online and Prodigy allow you to have multiple *screen names*; it's pretty simple to use one as your main account and a less recognizable one for competitive intelligence. But because Web-masters can tell who's visiting their sites, you might want to surf from a CompuServe account (or any secondary account) when scoping the competition.

All this cloak-and-dagger business is seldom necessary, though. In most cases, you'll find that you have more to gain by working *with* your competitors. No two companies produce exactly the same product; there's always some difference, if not in the physical product, then in the way it's marketed. Engaging in competitive intelligence will give you a good picture of the marketplace. You can use that information to improve your results by shifting your company's focus or working with others.

Case in point: People I formerly considered competitors are now my suppliers. Why? I simply can't handle all the inquiries I get. When folks want to build a Web site, I send them to a competitor. If I'm too swamped to take their publicity business, I refer them to a "rival." I also buy services from my competitors when I'm too busy to do the work myself. Likewise, my competitors refer their book publishing clients to me—it's my specialty. We often team up to serve a client's online marketing needs. Business today means cooperation more than competition, and online marketing is more about participation than advertising.

Success through Participation

Certainly, the most effective strategy for online marketing success is to participate in discussion groups. The country club of my parents' generation has been replaced by the virtual club: the forums, mailing lists, and chat rooms that make up the online community. All you have to do is maintain a helpful presence and then satisfy the customers that come your way. This strategy is so successful, in fact, that I've had to *stop* participating in my favorite discussion groups.

I'm a big fan of Glenn Fleishman's Internet Marketing mailing list. I used to enjoy talking about online publicity, pointing people to help resources, providing advice about doing online chats, and the like. But Glenn's list got so popular I was overwhelmed with e-mail asking for help or requesting information. I found I was spending 25 percent of my workday helping people learn about the Internet—people who were not likely to benefit from my publicity services and who would not make good clients. In order to get my work done, I had to curb the urge to contribute to these groups.

Of course, having too many prospects is a problem most businesses would welcome. To use your time online efficiently, though, it helps to have resources prepared in advance to give to people. The chapter on Document Transfers has detailed instructions for preparing files for electronic delivery. Here are some items you may want to have handy:

- Basic information about your company.
- The address of a Web site, FTP site, and/or Gopher site where people can find more information.
- Giveaway files, prepared as text, ready to paste into outgoing e-mail.
- An info file for every major product or service you sell.
- A list of clients or references.
- A hotlist of helpful resources you've found online.
- Answers to commonly asked questions.
- A referral list of other people who might be able to help.

These items will help you cut down on the amount of time you spend assisting people with basic Internet navigation. You can use autoresponders and list servers to deliver many of these documents (refer to the Document Transfers chapter). You can use your signature to tell people how to get these help files.

As I've explained, a signature is a small bit of text automatically appended to all your outgoing messages—like an electronic letterhead. Jill Ellsworth, author of *Marketing on the Internet* and many other excellent books, says a good "sig" is the most useful online marketing tool. The following is a signature from Susan Klopfer at Vanatech Press. She offers Internet help and provides two contact points: a Web site and e-mail.

```
**** VANATECH PRESS ****========================================
You're invited to visit the Internet's ONLY two-book bookstore
at http://www.branson.com/branson/vanatech/ and discover how to
FIRE YOUR BOSS in '96! ALSO... get some FREE and easy Internet
help from "Fred" (a really nice guy) OR... Send today for a
FREE online Vanatech Press Catalog from sklopfer@vanatech.com
========================================****VANATECH PRESS****
```

You don't have to participate in many discussion groups, as long as you're involved with the *right* ones. It's not the quantity that counts—it's the quality. If you're a game developer, the Game Developers Forum on GEnie might be the most important place for you. If you're in marketing, CompuServe's PR and Marketing SIG is one of the hottest forums online. Writers who haven't seen America Online's Writers' Club are really missing out; the joint is jumpin' with agents, publishers, authors, fans, and lots of folks who can help you out. A reminder: Chapter 12 lists Web sites that will help you find the happening discussion groups online.

If you can't find the perfect discussion group, you can start one of your own. This is a tried-and-true method for developing customers, but it comes at a substantial price. In order to be successful, you will have to do a lot of work monitoring the group, providing good content, and dealing with technical details. If you have a large company and you have a lot of content you can bring to the discussion group, it may be worth hiring someone to run the group for you.

An alternative to starting your own forum is to co-host an existing group. America Online, CompuServe, and the Microsoft Network pay their forum hosts. A successful forum can be very lucrative by itself, not to mention all the customers it can generate. Wherever you find a busy forum or mailing list, you'll find a host who could use some help. Your offer to co-host will probably be gratefully received by the host and the membership.

Responding to Flames

If you're following good netiquette and contributing something of value in your online postings, you'll have very few problems with flames. But there's always someone out there who will object to *any* message. Someone once torched me for using the word Triscuits in one of my posts. He argued that the plural of Triscuit should, in fact, be Triscuit, and that adding the s was a sign of my ignorance. You gotta love the Net.

Throughout this book, I promised that I would give you detailed instructions on handling flames. Now's the time. As I sketched out earlier, the general procedure is to remain calm, check the facts, defend your posting if it was appropriate, remove your posting and apologize if you were wrong. Let's look at these steps more closely—you'll appreciate the detail next time you're in a flame war.

Power Considerations

If you get flamed, *stay calm*. Don't go firing off a Molatov e-mail until you assess your position. You probably don't know the person who flamed you or what he or she is capable of. Malicious people can wreak havoc with your electronic communications and, in some cases, can destroy your computer system. Don't make a bad situation worse by inspiring a malcontent to visit evil upon you.

Even if you are 100 percent legally, morally, and netiquettely in the right, that won't necessarily stop the person at the other end of the torch from making your life miserable. Here are some of the things Internet vigilantes can do to you:

- Cancel messages you put on the Net.
- Get you listed on an Internet blacklist.
- Spread lies about you and inspire others to attack you.
- Keep you under online surveillance.
- Subscribe you to thousands of mailing lists.
- E-mail bomb you with thousands of identical messages a day.
- Try to trick you into downloading a computer virus.
- Redirect your incoming e-mail.
- Respond to anyone trying to send you e-mail with a bogus message.
- Completely shut down your e-mail account.
- Forge messages so they look like they came from you.

In short, these people can make your life online a living hell. And we haven't even talked about your life *off* the Net. Physical stalking, death threats, calls to your employer, anonymous tips to the IRS, property damage . . . am I getting through yet? The Internet puts you in contact with millions of people around the globe. A certain percentage of them are wound up and ready to cut down the first good target they see. Don't inadvertently volunteer to be that target. Now you see why I say, *stay calm*.

That's one aspect of online power. Another is the legal authority of the person flaming you. If you posted to a moderated group, then the moderators have the authority to remove your postings for whatever reasons they choose. Similarly, all commercial online services are private and thus have the authority to remove your posting and / or revoke your membership. Almost all Internet service providers also have terms of service you agreed to when you signed up, and they can cancel your account for violating those terms.

In unmoderated discussion groups, no one can tell you what to post, although they may try. They can *suggest* that you follow certain guidelines, such as the charter for a newsgroup or the recommendations in a FAQ file, but they have no right to dictate behavior. Still, some people act like they own discussion groups and chastise anyone for posting something they don't like. These pyromaniacs have driven many good people out of unmoderated groups and into more temperate discussion areas. You, too, might find it smarter to leave a group rather than try to reason with such a person.

Assess the Facts

Once you've determined the status of the flamer, double-check the circumstances surrounding the posting. Does your message fit with the current tone of discussion in the group? Are there many similar messages in the group? If so, then you have reason to believe your message was appropriate, and you have one line of defense.

As an Internet publicist, most complaints I receive are about commercial content in my messages. I've learned to avoid anything smacking of commercial content. I don't put prices or order numbers in my postings. I never offer to sell anything to anyone; I either offer a free file containing some hopefully valuable information, or I point them to a

Web site containing free information. I recommend you limit any sales talk in your messages and emphasize free information resources. Check other messages in the group to see how much commercial content they contain. Although I don't use a signature file in most of my postings, most people do, and their signatures often contain what could be seen as commercial content. People have flamed me for commercial content, only to sell products or services in *their* sigs. This is your second line of defense: He or she who is without sin cast the first stone.

Check your posting against the charter or FAQ for the group. The Resources and Announcements chapters have lots of suggestions for finding these documents. Several times I've been flamed for posting new book announcements in newsgroups, only to find that the charter reads "book announcements are especially welcomed." Many charters and FAQs say that commercial information is allowed in response to a question, or when it isn't an overt advertisement. Charters and FAQs are a third line of defense.

Dousing the Flames

Once you understand the power relationship between you and the flamer, and you are armed with all the facts, you can act in the most judicious manner. If your posting was in error, attempt to make the situation right by removing your post if possible and apologizing to the flamer. Most discussion groups have a way to cancel your own posts. If you can't figure it out, ask the host to remove it for you.

If you believe you are in the right, you might choose not to respond at all. If the flame arrived by e-mail and was not posted to the group, it might be wise to just forget it. But archive the flame, just in case funny things start happening to your computer—you might have to contact the authorities and the flame could be evidence. I don't mean to alarm you with all this talk of vigilantes, but I've seen their handiwork elsewhere and I don't want to see it happen to you. I've posted thousands and thousands of messages online and I've never had a serious altercation with anyone.

If the flamer contacted your Internet service provider or a forum host or some legitimate authority, this is the time to defend your posting privately to stay in the good graces of those who can revoke your account. My service provider, Ned, gets notes about my activities from time to time and forwards them to me for comment. He knows I run a clean operation and he has never asked me to change the way I run my business.

If you're scorched in public unjustifiably and it's necessary to defend your reputation, try to keep your response from getting personal. Simply state the facts: why you believe your message was appropriate.

I receive about one flame a month, on average, and I've gotten a written apology from every single flamer except two. Most of the flames were form letters sent by people who monitor their favorite discussion groups and routinely blast anyone who posts commercial announcements. Needless to say, these types don't examine my messages closely enough to see that I'm not selling anything. Upon reflection, they at least understand why I thought the posting was appropriate. Case closed. No hard feelings.

The two flames to which I didn't receive apologies were interesting. One was a posting to a moderated discussion group. In this case, the woman who flamed me should have taken it up with the moderator, who thought the message was appropriate. The other was from someone who didn't like my offer of a free Q&A file in the newsgroup alt.invest.stocks. He told me the posting would have been acceptable if I were a regular contributor, but because I wasn't, it was "too commercial." I had to laugh when I double-checked the newsgroup: it gets about 1,000 messages a day, almost all of them blatant sales pitches. My message was one of the only noncommercial postings in the group. You gotta love the Net.

As noted some protectors of the Net use form letter flames. I use a form letter response which you can modify to suit your needs:

```
Perhaps you don't care for my posting to _____, but it is
neither commercial nor off-topic. I am not selling anything,
nor asking people to buy anything. I'm simply informing them
of the availability of an excellent help file. I would have
uploaded the entire file, but such long posts are considered
bad netiquette.

I posted this message because I believe the file will be of
keen interest to many people in the group. After going back
and looking at other postings in the group, I feel my posting
was more on-topic than most of what appears there.
```

```
You may not agree, but this is an open discussion group. I
could understand your objection if I was posting a
"make.money.fast" pitch, but the information I provided was
clearly within the bounds of the charter.
```

When you are dealing with moderated discussion groups or forum hosts, the approach is slightly different. Since they can remove your message if it doesn't meet their approval, always ask how you can change the message to satisfy them. They will usually tell you to tone down the commercial content if you include information such as prices and toll-free numbers in the posting. They also don't like you referring people to URLs or sending them to other forums. You can usually adjust the message to satisfy them.

If you feel your message is on target, try to work with the host. Once you have established a working relationship, you will have little trouble with that host in the future. These forum hosts want to run attractive discussion groups, free of commercial clutter and full of valuable content for their members. If you are participating in the discussions and offering genuinely useful advice, tips, and resources, your contributions will be welcomed.

The Controlled Burn

Here's an old trick from the promoter's black bag: there's nothing like a little controversy to attract a crowd. Sometimes the best thing you can do for a flame war is stand back and watch it burn. That's what I did after I posted a message comparing notorious spam artists Canter and Siegel to persecuted author Salman Rushdie. Here's a portion of the posting:

```
What do Salman Rushdie and Canter & Siegel have in common?
They received death threats and had their books banned. You'll
find them together with Andrei Codrescu, Senator Exon, Sandra
Coliver and others at the "Book Banning, Burning and
Censorship" exhibit at Book Stacks Unlimited
<http://www.banned.books.com>
```

No sooner did this message go up than someone fired back, "How dare you compare Canter and Siegel with Salman Rushdie?" The next message read, "He has a point. Go look at the documents. They were both victims of book banning." Then the fire took off. Over the next two days, there were 14 messages in the thread, and the topic spilled over into other forums. It was the perfect discussion for people to have during Banned Books Week.

The banned books controversy wasn't planned—it just happened. In Usenet, when a thread is getting a lot of activity, it feeds on itself. People see double-digit replies and they want to know what all the fuss is about. I've seen threads where I suspect all the controversy is a scam: two people flaming each other just to get some heat going. You might be able to pull that off once or twice, but in general deceiving people is not a good marketing strategy.

If I'm genuinely being flamed in a discussion forum, I might decide to reply just to raise the temperature a little. When my messages have been removed by forum hosts on commercial online services and I can't reason with them, I sometimes take my case to the membership. I'll start a thread called Forum Censorship or something similar. The forum host can either respond or shut down the thread, in which case they just add fuel to the fire. I've gotten some interesting discussions going about commercial speech and censorship online.

Advanced Medialist Management

Once I cost a forum host his job. He was a co-host, actually, and he threatened me with a lawsuit after I sent him a news release offering a free review copy of a book. His threatening e-mail was a form flame, and although I recognized that it wasn't personal, hey, I don't like being threatened. I looked him up in my records and found that just a week earlier his boss had sent me e-mail asking to have their names added to my mailing list. At the time I told them if they ever wanted off the list, just let me know. Then came the flame.

I responded to the flame saying, "I hope this was a form letter and not a personal attack. Last week, I got e-mail asking to add your name to the list. If you don't want to be on my list, just say so—there's no need for threats. I don't want to send mail to anyone who doesn't want it. If you only want certain kinds of announcements, let me know and I'll document my files." I sent a copy to his boss, since he was the one who requested the names be added to my list. The next thing I know, all hell broke loose. The flamer apologized. His boss apologized. Then I received e-mail from the boss saying he fired the guy for being unprofessional. Then I got another apology from the flamer. Then I tried to patch everything up, and I think the guy got his job back. You really have to use your head online or something will come back and bite you.

I bring all this up to illustrate the importance of good mailing list management. That's how you get the information to deal with issues like the preceding flame. In the chapter on News Releases, I covered all the basics about maintaining an e-mail medialist. Now we're going to quickly look at some of the advanced skills for those of you who plan on repeatedly using your own medialist.

The first rule of advanced mailing list management is to remember that you're dealing with *people*, not companies or e-mail addresses. Your list should be focused on the people who report on your industry. Your goal is to become a personal, reliable source of information for your contacts. In order to give them what they want, you have to collect as much relevant information on them as possible. The following is a sample record from my database of media contacts, showing the kind of detail I like to have:

Name: David Hipschman
E-Mail: <dochip@netrix.net>
Address: 5445 Hwy 83 North, Whitefish, MT 59937
Notes: * Requested WWW Marketing. Formerly the international news editor at the San Francisco Chronicle. Doing reviews on GNN. I think this is the guy who puts out Kinesis. Author of Cyberland, the Internet newspaper column. Contributing Editor, Web Review.

David is on my freelance list. If he were employed by a media outlet, I would have his title, the name of the publication or station, and perhaps the name of the publishing company. As you build your own medialist, you might want to note how someone got on your list. It can come in handy if you get flamed. People often want to know how they got on my list even though they seldom ask to be taken off.

I like to put an asterisk at the beginning of the Notes field indicating every time we receive a positive response from a journalist. Several times when people have asked to be removed from my list, I go back and see they've requested review copies of books from me in the past. In such cases, I'll send them a letter asking, "Are you sure you want off the list? Last month you requested such-and-such, and I've got similar promotions coming up. Would you prefer it if I noted in your file that you only want certain types of announcements?" Without exception, people choose to remain on my list. This sort of attentiveness will earn you bonus points with press people. They simply don't have time for stuff that is not in their niche. So you have to prompt them to tell you what their niche is. If you pulled their name from a magazine or TV broadcast, note the kinds of stories they work on so you know what to send them.

Always be looking to update your medialist when people respond to your news releases. I often send e-mail to an organization's address and get a response from an individual. Bingo! A new e-mail address for the list. And check the replies against your database to confirm that you have the person's name spelled right, their correct title, the names of the publications they write for, and so on.

Journalists are a fleet-of-foot bunch. They move around from job to job, but they almost always stay in the fourth estate. When you focus on the person—not the publication—you'll find that your medialist stays flexible and up to date.

Canceled Messages and Blacklists

In the preceding section on Power Considerations, I listed some of the nasty things that Internet vigilantes can visit upon their enemies. Most of these activities are illegal, but they are difficult to defend against or prosecute. In an effort to bring some civilized law to the Internet, many of the key organizations and people online are working together to find legal and peaceful ways of disciplining bad netizens. We'll look at two such attempts here: canceled postings and Internet blacklists.

Canceled Postings

If you post to newsgroups and mailing lists, and your messages don't appear in the customary time frame, they might have been canceled. Canceling is usually accomplished by someone issuing forged cancelation notices; that is, the request to remove the message appears to have come from you. It is illegal to forge messages this way, but if the messages are sent through an anonymous remailer outside of the country, it becomes impossible to track them to their source.

If you suspect your messages have been canceled, try posting again. If you're concerned about triggering an automatic canceling program, follow these tips:

1. Limit the number of groups you're posting to. I've heard that posting to more than 15 groups will activate some cancelers.

2. Vary the subject line of your messages. Changing capitalization won't make a difference—slightly alter your phrasing.

3. Don't cross-post to more than five groups at a time. If you're posting to 12 newsgroups, break them down into several smaller groups, cross-posting where the readership of the groups is likely to overlap.

4. Divide your postings between multiple accounts. You might do half your postings from your Internet account, the other half through America Online or CompuServe.

5. Start your subject line with the abbreviation Re as though you're responding to a previous message. This will help you escape the notice of people who check all new postings to a group.

If your postings are canceled, you will sometimes get an e-mail message from the Cancel Moose or whoever did it. If you get one of these messages, or if you suspect your postings were canceled, visit the newsgroup news.admin.net-abuse. The people who canceled your messages will often place notices here to cut down on redundant cancelations. An appearance on NANA, as it's called, is really a form of blacklisting.

Blacklists

The infamous Green Card Lawyers, Canter and Siegel, threw a monkey wrench into the Net with their unapologetic, repeated spamming of thousands of newsgroups. One of the upshots of that crisis was the newsgroup alt.current-events.net-abuse (a.c-e.n-a), where people discuss how to deal with folks like Canter and Siegel.

As canceling became a common way of handling spam, a.c-e.n-a became a place to coordinate cancelation. By posting to a.c-e.n-a, other vigilantes would know that the spam had been taken care of, thus reducing duplicate efforts. Postings to a.c-e.n-a would also broadcast the evil spammers' names to the vigilante community so they could follow up with other punishments, such as hate-mail, e-mail to Internet service providers asking that accounts be revoked, and other acts of terrorism described earlier in this chapter.

Like everything else online, a.c-e.n-a has evolved. It has been pretty much replaced by NANA (although you should check both newsgroups if you suspect cancelation). If you are written up in NANA, it could seriously impact your online activities. Among other things, it could result in your postings being automatically filtered off before they reach any newsgroups. If you find your name in NANA, the first thing to do is determine whether you have been the victim of a prank.

A few malicious souls have found that one way to make life miserable for their enemies is to post their names in NANA. Some will go so far as to forge spam in your name, then cancel it and post your name in NANA. Many innocent people have had their reputations destroyed by being written up on these blacklists. If you are the victim of such a prank, plead your case in a hurry.

I once had a close brush with this problem. Someone redistributed an announcement I posted to a bunch of mailing lists. They weren't trying to do any harm; they were just trying to spread the word. Unfortunately, they spread the word a lot further than good netiquette allows, and I ended up getting flamed for their enthusiasm. I didn't end up on any blacklists, but I had to do a lot of explaining to keep the tarnish off my reputation.

If you feel you can make a good case for your actions, try and defend yourself in NANA and other groups where you are being flamed. An apology goes a long way with a lot of people. A public act of contrition and a promise not to spam again may cool the blowtorches and spare you from electronic hell. An explanation of why you thought your postings were appropriate also may help, although some people will not listen to reason.

For further information about NANA and what you should do if you find your name on a blacklist, consult the FAQ for net.admin.net-abuse. You can find FAQ resources and the locations of other blacklists in Chapter 12. The best defense, of course, is to follow netiquette and only post messages where you believe they will be welcomed.

Top Tips

- **Respect the Power of the Net:** There are roughly 20 million people online and gossip spreads fast. Controversies like the Pentium chip fiasco can cost corporations millions. It's wise to keep track of your company's image online and defend it when necessary.

- **Keep Track of the Competition:** By monitoring your competitors, you'll get a sharper picture of your industry and see opportunities as they arise. Don't be surprised if your competitors end up becoming your partners.

- **Participate:** Maintaining a consistent, helpful presence is the most powerful online marketing tool.

- **Get Organized:** Make the best use of your time online by preparing help files in advance and making them readily available through e-mail, autoresponders, FTP, and your Web site.

- **Stay Calm:** It's a jungle out there. If you're attacked online, act out of self-preservation, not anger. Often the best response is no response at all.

- **Assemble the Facts:** When challenged online, assemble the information you need to defend yourself. Consult any written guidelines (terms of service, acceptable use policies, bulletin board guidelines, charters, FAQs, etc.) and note the current standards for acceptable behavior.

CHAPTER 12

Internet Publicity Resources

In order to keep this book more readable and useful, I have tried to cut down on the number of URLs in the text and gather them together in this chapter, where I can make sure they're as fresh as possible. Of course, the Internet is a Protean beast, constantly shape-shifting, and this chapter is but a snapshot, albeit with a very good camera. Some of these addresses will go out of date, but fear not—I groom this list of resources continuously on my own computer.

If you would like the latest revision, please send me e-mail at IPS@olympus.net with the subject line: Send Hotlist. I will send you back the latest version of this list. You might also check the John Wiley & Sons Web site; they usually provide updates and help files to support the fine books they sell. The site is located at http://www.wiley.com/compbooks.

If you have any corrections or suggestions for this list, I invite you to share them with the rest of the online marketing community. Please send them to me via e-mail. For additions to the list, be sure to include the name of the site, the URL, and a brief description of why it merits a position on the list. I don't promise to include every recommendation, but I'll do my best to continue to provide a list of the most valuable Internet publicity resources available online.

This chapter is divided into 14 sections. Some resources overlap; for example, Infoseek is included in the Searching Resources and also in the Firefighting Resources, though for different reasons. For each re-source, we have provided the "street name" for the site (not necessarily the official name), a URL, and a short, biased description of what you'll find there. Here's a brief rundown on each of the 14 sections:

Self-Promotion Resources

For the do-it-yourself publicist, links to sites where you will find not only general information about online marketing and publicity, but also online tools for promoting yourself, your business, and your Web site.

Paid Promotion Resources

The hired guns of the information frontier. I am proud to include myself in this list of professional online publicists. Also includes sites that track online advertising opportunities and rates.

Registration Resources

Use these links to get your Web site listed in dozens of directories, in-dexes, catalogs, search engines, and online malls. Includes both free and fee-based services.

Chat Resources

A nice set of links to chat software, conferencing software, and popular chat clubs on the World Wide Web to help you plan your world tour.

Searching Resources

A round-up of the usual suspects: Yahoo, Alta Vista, Infoseek, and the rest of the gang that make it their business to help you find your way online.

Media Contacts and People Finders

Links to the e-mail addresses of the media, as well as Internet white pages where you can find the e-mail address of just about anyone.

SuperSite Finder Resources

SuperSites are often the key sites for any particular subject or industry. The links in this section include lists of the top 100 Web sites, best of the Web lists, and other resources to help you find the SuperSites.

Webzine and E-Zine Finder Resources

Webzines are entertainment sites on the World Wide Web; e-zines are delivered by e-mail. There are webzines and e-zines to suit every imag-inable taste. These resources will help you find the best and the rest.

Mailing List Resources
Amazing resources for finding the appropriate mailing lists on which to post messages. Also included are mailing list software sites, and other sites that help you understand and use these powerful tools.

Newsgroup Resources
You'll cut down on the number of flames you get if you use these resources to find the best Usenet newsgroups for your announcements.

Firefighting Resources
A collection of links to information filters so that you can track exactly what people are saying about you or your competitors. Also includes links to Internet blacklists and other Net abuse discussions.

Software Resources
Giant repositories of software for any computer platform. You'll find an incredible amount of freeware and shareware to help you create and deploy better promotions.

Web Page Design Resources
You may not be able to paint like Picasso, but you can learn to sling HTML like a HotWired intern with these sites devoted to the design of great Web pages.

Demographics Resources
Lies and statistics: we've got them both here in the demographics section. Get the latest guesses on how many people are using the Net and what they like to do online.

Self-Promotion Resources

Public Relations Online Resources
http://www.webcom.com/impulse/resource.html

An excellent set of links from Impulse Research Corporation covering PR services, associations, self-promotion sites, people finders, and various online publications. Links are annotated and kept up to date.

Marketing SuperSite
http://www.ntu.ac.sg/ntu/lib/advrtise.htm

This resource list from the National Technology University in Singapore is almost too big. Contains links to a massive number of articles and

Web sites concerned with promotion, marketing, and commerce on the Internet.

CyberPulse
http://www.cyberpulse.com/

Bob and Varda Novick know their stuff when it comes to online marketing. Excellent resource area covering mailing lists, newsgroups, advertising, promotion, and more. Don't let the plain graphics fool you.

Promote-It!
http://www.iTools.com/promote-it/promote-it.html

Nice self-promotion site that includes the popular Submit-It! registration service. You'll also find links to "cool site of the day" sites and a few other promotion resources.

The Delphi Group
http://www.cam.org/~delphig/index.html

A nice set of links to marketing, advertising, and publicity resources on the Internet. Delphi also provides Web site development and online marketing services.

A1 WWW Promotion Sites
http://www.vir.com/~wyatt/index.html

Excellent resource for locating hundreds of directories, indexes, and catalogs that will list your site for free. Also has a handy tool for locating large Webzine sites. Provides paid marketing services.

Paid Promotion Resources

Internet Publicity Services
http://www.olympus.net/okeefe/PI

Steve O'Keefe's excellent service for promoting books and authors on the Internet. Contains a large collection of articles for the do-it-yourself publicist.

NetPOST
http://www.netpost.com/

Eric Ward is possibly the best in the "Web site awareness" business, as recognized with a 1995 Tenagra Award for Internet Marketing Excellence. NetPOST does mostly registration, news releases, and announcements.

NetCreations/PostMaster/IPA
http://www.netcreations.com/

Rosalind Resnick's amazing site of Internet Marketing Resources. Includes PostMaster, the popular announcement service (see Registration Resources). Also includes IPA, which tracks online advertising opportunities and rates.

Multimedia Marketing Group/WebStep
http://www.mmgco.com/

John Audette's Internet marketing service. Includes registration, press releases, marketing consulting, and more. See also WebStep in the Free Registration listings. John's rates are quite reasonable.

WebTrack
http://www.webtrack.com/

This site tracks online advertising, showing you who is spending money to advertise, who's getting that money, and how much is changing hands. Very interesting site to follow.

Registration Resources

Submit It!
http://www.submit-it.com/

FREE service to register your site with the top 20 (plus or minus) directories and catalogs. A real time-saver!

WebStep 100
http://www.mmgco.com/top100.html

John Audette of Multimedia Marketing Group put together this list of the top 100 directories, indexes, and catalogs. The links are all annotated, and you can reach each site's registration page from the link on WebStep.

PostMaster
http://www.netcreations.com/postmaster/

Rosalind Resnick's resource for registering your Web page with hundreds of sites. Provides other marketing services as well.

Announce-It
http://www.netcom.com/~karyntag/web.html

Registration service. In summer of 1996, rates were $49, $89, and $179 for submission to 50, 100, and 200 directories, respectively.

WebPost96
http://www.webpost96.com/

A clever do-it-yourself registration service that helps you register in the top 60 directories for about $50. You can save your registration form and use it to check your listings later.

Chat Resources

WBS
http://wbs.net/

The WebChat Broadcasting System, with over 50 million hits a month, is a major interface to multimedia chats via the World Wide Web.

WebChat Communications
http://wbs.net/wcc.html

Makers of WebChat software and operators of the WebChat Broadcasting Service (WBS). Check out their services for putting on chats or selling you the capabilities to put them on yourself.

Club Wired
http://www.hotwired.com/Piazza/Club/

HotWired's chat service. There are many channels to choose from, some of which have guest speakers. This is a text-only chat. HotWired will soon have a more functional Java-based chat interface.

NetSpace
http://www.swnetworks.com/

This is Sony Online's chat service, run by SW Networks, Sony's syndicated radio programming division. This is one of the most active chat services on the Web.

Internet Chat Guide
http://www.quarterdeck.com/chat/schedule.html

Sponsored by Quarterdeck and Global Chat. Lists sites that use Global Chat servers, including Pathfinder, Sony, ZDNet, and many other top-level chat sites.

Talk City
http://www.talkcity.com/eventscalendar/

A good place to get easy instructions for using chat software. Talk City hosts over 100 live chat events every week, dealing with everything from computers to relationships.

Searching Resources

Point
http://www.pointcom.com/

Affiliated with Lycos. Excellent catalog of Web sites that includes reviews. Point gives out the popular Top 5% of the Web awards.

Alta Vista
http://www.altavista.digital.com/

The reigning King of Spiders, Alta Vista is the best Internet search engine currently on the market. Use it to search the Web, Usenet, or to look for links to your site.

Yahoo
http://www.yahoo.com

The grandpappy of Internet catalogs. Yahoo maintains annotated links to thousands of Internet resources, but since most links are user-contributed, the lists are spotty and sometimes deceptive.

Infoseek
http://www.infoseek.com/

A combination catalog and search engine, Infoseek does an excellent job of cross-referencing resources. This is a good site for finding topic-specific SuperSite lists.

Lycos
http://lycos.cs.cmu.edu/

Another excellent search spider. Lycos was the original search engine for the Internet, and it's still one of the best. Similar to Alta Vista.

Galaxy
http://galaxy.einet.net/

Comprehensive catalog of Internet resources. Galaxy is much more "scholarly" than Yahoo; resources are classified in a hierarchical structure that would make Linnaeus proud.

c l net's search.com
http://www.search.com/

Links to more than 250 search engines on the Internet. Allows you to search by subject classification. Pretty amazing!

excite Netsearch
http://www.excite.com/

An excellent search engine that also allows you to customize a personal Web search page. Includes searches of the Web, Usenet, and a database of site reviews.

Media Contacts and People Finders

MIT Usenet E-Mail Addresses
http://usenet-addresses.mit.edu/

Amazing resource for finding people's e-mail addresses by searching Usenet postings. Try searching for nbc.com and take a look at the media contacts you get!

Four11
http://www.Four11.com/

The phone book of the Internet. Four11 is used to find the e-mail addresses of people online. It doesn't have everyone, but there are millions of people in its database.

Internet Address Finder
http://www.iaf.net/

A large Internet white pages. You must provide a last name, or you can do a "reverse search" if you know the exact e-mail address. Provides 10 matches per screen. Based mostly on names lifted from Usenet postings.

Peter Gugerell's Medialist
http://www.ping.at/gugerell/media/

From Vienna, Austria, comes this magnificent list of the e-mail addresses of the media. Includes hundreds of U.S. addresses. Compiled by hobbyist Peter Gugerell.

Adam M. Gaffin's Media List
http://www.webcom.com/~leavitt/medialist.html

The e-mail addresses of the media. WARNING: This list was last revised 1/26/95. Unless it has been updated, it's pretty useless. I include it here in case there are some addresses you want to test.

SuperSite Finder Resources

Hot100 Websites—Updated Weekly
http://www.web21.com/services/hot100/index.html

In my opinion, the best and most up-to-date list of the most active Web sites. Lists most active sites in more than a dozen different categories, including business, sports, adult, chat, tech, and more.

Bestweb List
http://www.rt66.com/~korteng/besturl.htm

Catalog of the "Most Valuable and Useful Internet Sites" from The Bestweb List. Short, annotated lists covering a wide range of subjects.

WebCrawler Top 25
http://webcrawler.com/WebCrawler/Top25.html

The top 25 hits from WebCrawler's catalog. Most of these are search engines, and obviously excludes adult-content sites.

GNN Select Top 50
http://gnn.com/wic/wics/top.new.html

The most popular 50 links from GNN's catalog of 2,500 top Web sites. This used to be the Whole Internet Catalog Top 25 until GNN took it over.

GNN Best of the Net
http://gnn.com/gnn/wic/botn/index.html

Quality sites in many different categories. GNN picks an "amateur" and "professional" site, so there are a lot of personal favorites that don't necessarily get a lot of traffic.

SuperSites
http://www.basenet.net/~tci/sites.html

Maczynski's Info Page with a terrific list of over 100 Internet Super-Sites.

Lycos/Point Top 10
http://www.pointcom.com/gifs/topsites/

Not based on traffic, but on qualitative reviews in three areas: content, presentation and overall experience. You can find some worthy sites here.

***PC Magazine* Top 100 Web Sites**
http://www.pcmag.com/special/web100/top100f.htm

Selected by the staff of *PC Magazine*—not based on traffic. Divided into 10 categories. Annotations and links for each site.

Yahoo! Best of the Web
http://www.yahoo.com/Computers_and_Internet/Internet/World_Wide_Web/Best_of_the_Web/

Yahoo's category of sites that compile Best of the Web lists. Most of the links are pretty useless, but you never know.

Magellan
http://www.mckinley.com/

Rates and reviews Web sites in dozens of different categories. Good way to find partner sites or co-branding opportunities.

Webzine and E-Zine Finder Resources

Ecola's Newsstand
http://www.ecola.com/news/

Ecola maintains an amazing collection of links to newspapers and magazines that have an Internet presence. Divided into such categories as daily papers, weekly papers, computer magazines, and many others—all hotlinked. Nice!

NewsPath
http://www.niu.edu/newspath/news.html

Links to all the top news resources on the Internet as well as entertainment sites and electronic publications. No annotations. Also has a list of other e-zine SuperSites. From Northern Illinois University.

John Labovitz's E-Zine List
http://www.ora.com:8080/johnl/e-zine-list/index.html

A comprehensive list of electronic publications, including e-mail zines, webzines and others. So comprehensive it can be difficult to work with. A lot of microcirculation zines.

CREAM of ZINES
http://www.rubyslippers.com/creamzines/index.html

List of national magazines that have Web sites. Not all these are webzines—just the online homes of their parent publications. Includes Time, People, Mother Jones, Sportline, Money, Internet, USA, NY Times.

Webreference
http://www.webreference.com/magazines.html

Annotated list of webzines that cover the Internet. Good list for finding educational resources about the Internet and online marketing that you can use in training staff.

Mailing List Resources

Liszt
http://www.liszt.com/

Stunningly good resource for finding mailing lists. Searches bring up a list of matching mailing lists with one-line descriptions and hotlinks for more information or to subscribe. Superb!

E-Mail Discussion Groups Megasite
http://www.webcom.com/impulse/list.html

Bob and Varda Novick operate this fantastic site with everything you want to know about every kind of mailing list and links to all the resources you could want. Excellent!

Inter-Links
http://www.nova.edu/Inter-Links/cgi-bin/lists

Another searchable catalog of mailing list descriptions. The advantage of using this one is that all results are output on one long page, including descriptions of the lists and how to subscribe.

CataList
http://www.lsoft.com/lists/listref.html

Listserv only. Another resource for finding mailing lists run on Listserv software; 9,000 groups; several ways to search. One nice feature: it tells you how many subscribers each list has!

Vivian Neou's List of Lists
http://catalog.com/vivian/interest-group-search.html

Nice, searchable list of mailing lists (originally compiled by Rich Zellich). Vivian is the author of Internet Mailing Lists Navigator from Prentice-Hall.

Mailing Lists by Subject
http://www.neosoft.com/internet/paml/bysubj.html

Stephanie da Silva's Publicly Accessible Mailing Lists Web site has mailing list descriptions cross-referenced by name and subject. Updated once a month.

Majordomo (FAQ)
http://www.math.psu.edu/barr/majordomo-faq.html#what

Information about the majordomo list server program, updated monthly by Brent Chapman.

Newsgroup Resources

Indiana University's Usenet Resources
http://scwww.ucs.indiana.edu/NetRsc/usenet.html

Links to everything you ever wanted to know about USENET, including FAQs, charters, netiquette, how to start a newsgroup, and so on. An excellent starting point.

Sunsite Search for Groups
http://sunsite.unc.edu/usenet-i/search.html

The absolute best way to search for appropriate newsgroups. If your browser is forms-compatible, don't waste your time anywhere else—try this first! Brought to you by the University of North Carolina.

Ohio State's Newsgroups and Mailing Lists
http://www.cis.ohio-state.edu/hypertext/faq/bngusenet/news/lists/top.html

Excellent resource for finding one-line descriptions of newsgroups, along with descriptions of publicly accessible mailing lists. Updated monthly.

Oxford's FAQs
http://www.lib.ox.ac.uk/internet/news/

An easy-to-use interface for finding newsgroup FAQs. The best FAQ finder of the resources listed here.

Ohio State's FAQs
http://www.cis.ohio-state.edu:80/hypertext/faq/usenet/

Alphabetical list of Usenet FAQs. These can help you determine which postings are welcome in a newsgroup, although Oxford's FAQs may be a better place to look.

Yahoo—News:Usenet
http://www.yahoo.com/News/Usenet/

Yahoo's directory of information about Usenet. This should help you locate other Usenet resources.

Usenet Charters
ftp://ftp.uu.net/usenet/news.announce.newgroups/

FTP directory maintained by UUNET. By drilling down, you can find the charters of Usenet newsgroups. Not a very easy way to learn about newsgroups.

DejaNews
http://www.dejanews.com/

This is a good resource for scanning newsgroups to find out what people are saying about you (or your competition).

Zippo
http://www.zippo.com/

Commercial news service. For a small fee, you can read newsgroups and post to them. For a larger fee, you get faster access to more groups. More than 17,000 newsgroups!

Firefighting Resources

Information Filtering Resources
http://www.ee.umd.edu/medlab/filter/

University of Maryland's collection of links to information filters. A good place to find and try various Internet filters and news-gathering services.

Infoseek Personal
http://personal.infoseek.com/

Infoseek allows you to search the Web, Usenet, and certain news summaries. You can also search for e-mail addresses. Its personal news service lets you store search criteria in order to have a custom home page whenever you visit Infoseek.

NewsPage
http://www.newspage.com/

Excellent resource for business news. Search by category or keyword. Has both a free service and a paid, personalized service.

Stanford News Filter
http://woodstock.stanford.edu:2000/

Fantastic free services that allows you to set-up a search of Usenet newsgroups and have matching items e-mailed to you. Search daily, weekly, and so on, using Boolean or standard language.

DejaNews
http://www.dejanews.com/

Free, fast search of Usenet newsgroups. Results in a very clean report showing date, subject line, newsgroup, and author. Nice!

Alta Vista
http://www.altavista.digital.com/

Use Alta Vista's link query to find out who has linked to your Web site. The format for the search is link:URL where URL can be all or part of the address for the Web page.

Net Abuse FAQs
http://www-sc.ucssc.indiana.edu/~scotty/acena.html

Scott Southwick's humorous and useful archive of information about what constitutes net abuse and what people can and have done about it. Includes spam recipes and remedies.

Blacklist of Internet Advertisers
http://www.ip.net/BL/blacklist.html

Alex Boldt's list of bad netizens. You don't want to get your name on a list like this one.

Software Resources

Info-Mac HyperArchive
http://hyperarchive.lcs.mit.edu/HyperArchive/HyperArchive.html

One of the largest and most well-known repositories for various types of Macintosh-related software and shareware. Sponsored by the Massachusetts Institute of Technology Laboratory for Computer Science.

WIT Software Archive
http://www.wit.com/newwit/home/software/

A fairly large archive of DOS, Mac, Windows, Win 95, NT, OS/2, Unix, and Amiga software. Sponsored by World Internet Technologies.

Complete Idiot's Archive
http://www.mcp.com/softlib/IDIOTS-INTERNET/#Web_browsers

Archive of software mentioned in the popular *Complete Idiot's* computer guidebooks. Links to just about anything you could need for getting set up on the Internet.

Cross-Platform Helper Applications
http://home.netscape.com/assist/helper_apps/variety.html

Helper applications run in conjunction with your Web browser and other Internet software. This is Netscape's links page for finding all the helper apps the average surfer could use.

The Internet Goodies
http://www.ensta.fr/internet/

From our friends in France comes this site with beaucoup Internet software covering 23 different operating systems.

The Shareware Link
http://www.sdinter.net/~rbeck/

A shareware archive with links to other archives and home pages for various shareware programs (lots of games, too).

Web Page Design Resources

Laura's Web Zone
http://www.lne.com/web/

A great site for a beginner or an expert looking for information on creating perfect Web pages. Hosted by Laura Lemay, author of Teach Yourself Web Publishing with HTML.

WebReference.Com
http://www.webreference.com/

Amazing resource for Web designers. Includes links to book reviews, articles, legal considerations, trade shows, statistics, tutorials, software, graphics, image map helpers, and more.

Michael Shea's Internet Page
http://justice.loyola.edu/~mshea/html/internetpage.html

A more conceptual approach to Web design, with information on planning, designing, maintaining, and testing Web pages.

The Web Designer
http://web.canlink.com/webdesign/nl.htm

Lots of links, tips, and information on building Web pages. Includes forms, validation, counters, scripts, VRML, and Java. With links for registering your site when you're finished.

Web Masters
http://miso.wwa.com/~boba/masters1.html

Bob Allison's amazing page of information and resources for Web designers, journalists, surfers, or anyone interested in a behind-the-screens look at the Internet.

Lilly's Web Toolbox
http://members.tripod.com/~lirani/webbie.htm

A great resource for learning the basics of writing Web pages and then spiffing them up to the point of winning awards.

Webspinner's Workshop
http://dcn.davis.ca.us/~lacarrol/webspin.html

A page for getting ideas and information for creating outstanding Web pages. Includes validation, hit counters, and really cool bullets.

Demographics Resources

MIDS (Matrix Information and Directory Services)
http://www.mids.org/index.html

John S. Quarterman's company that conducts Internet surveys and publishes the results in regular reports. The best statistical work done so far on determining the number of people online.

GVU Web Survey
http://www.cc.gatech.edu/gvu/user_surveys/
User_Survey_Home.html

A voluntary survey of World Wide Web users conducted every six months by Georgia Tech's Graphics, Visualization, & Usability program (GVU). Prodigy participates in this survey. Good information about what people do online.

The Hermes Project
http://www-personal.umich.edu/~sgupta/hermes/

A research project into the commercial uses of the World Wide Web located at the University of Michigan. Works in conjunction with Georgia Tech's GVU survey.

O'Reilly Internet Survey '95
http://www.ora.com/www/info/research/users/index.html

Publishers and Internet pioneers, O'Reilly teamed up with Trish Information Services to conduct a statistically sound survey of online users.

InternetInfo
http://www.webcom.com/~walsh/stats.html

Statistics from InterNIC about the growth and geographical spread of Internet domains.

Nielsen Internet Survey
http://www.nielsenmedia.com/demo.htm

The famous TV ratings folks are working their magic online. This survey was done in 1995 in conjunction with CommerceNet, a consortium of large companies interested in Net demographics.

What's on the Web Site

The Web site that accompanies this book is located at http://www. wiley. com/compbooks. There you'll find:

Web Site Registration Hotlist: This is the same page used at Internet Publicity Services to register web sites with the top 20+ catalogs, directories, and search engines. For each directory, you will find a link to search it, to submit your site information, or to ask for help if your listing hasn't appeared. There is no charge to use this service.

Internet Publicity Resources: An incredible, easy-to-use hotlist of resources for anyone engaged in publicity work on the Internet. It contains annotated links to the critical resources in 14 different categories. Each link is accompanied by a description of what you will find there and why it's valuable. Here are the categories covered:

- *Self-Promotion Resources* For the do-it-yourself publicist, links to sites where you will find not only general information about online marketing and publicity, but also online tools for promoting yourself, your business, and your Web site.

- *Paid Promotion Resources* The hired guns of the information frontier. I am proud to include myself in this list of professional online publicists. Also includes sites that track online advertising opportunities and rates.

- *Registration Resources*   Use these links to get your Web site listed in dozens of directories, indexes, catalogs, search engines, and on-line malls. Includes both free and fee-based services.

- *Chat Resources*   A nice set of links to chat software, conferencing software, and popular chat clubs on the World Wide Web to help you plan your world tour.

- *Searching Resources*   A round-up of the usual suspects: Yahoo, Alta Vista, Infoseek, and the rest of the gang that make it their business to help you find your way online.

- *Media Contacts and People Finders*   Links to the e-mail addresses of the media, as well as Internet white pages where you can find the e-mail address of just about anyone.

- *SuperSite Finder Resources*   SuperSites are often the key sites for any particular subject or industry. The links in this section include lists of the top 100 Web sites, best of the Web lists, and other resources to help you find the SuperSites.

- *Webzine and E-Zine Finder Resources*   Webzines are entertainment sites on the World Wide Web; e-zines are delivered by e-mail. There are webzines and e-zines to suit every imaginable taste. These resources will help you find the best and the rest.

- *Mailing List Resources*   Amazing resources for finding the appropriate mailing lists on which to post messages. Also included are mailing list software sites, and other sites that help you understand and use these powerful tools.

- *Newsgroup Resources*   You'll cut down on the number of flames you get if you use these resources to find the best Usenet newsgroups for your announcements.

- *Firefighting Resources*   A collection of links to information filters so that you can track exactly what people are saying about you or your competitors. Also includes links to Internet blacklists and other Net abuse discussions.

- *Software Resources*   Giant repositories of software for any computer platform. You'll find an incredible amount of freeware and shareware to help you create and deploy better promotions.

- *Web Page Design Resources*   You may not be able to paint like Picasso, but you can learn to sling HTML like a HotWired intern with these sites devoted to the design of great Web pages.

- *Demographics Resources*   Lies and statistics: we've got them both here in the demographics section. Get the latest guesses on how many people are using the net and what they like to do online.

Index

What's on the Web Site

The Web site that accompanies this book is located at http://www.wiley.com/compbooks. There you'll find:

Web Site Registration Hotlist: This is the same page used at Internet Publicity Services to register web sites with the top 20+ catalogs, directories and search engines. For each directory, you will find a link to search it, to submit your site information, or to ask for help if your listing hasn't appeared. There is no charge to use this service.

Internet Publicity Resources: An incredible, easy-to-use hotlist of resources for anyone engaged in publicity work on the Internet. It contains annotated links to the critical resources in 14 different categories. Each link is accompanied by a description of what you will find there and why it's valuable. Here are the categories covered:

- *Self-Promotion Resources*
- *Paid Promotion Resources*
- *Registration Resources*
- *Chat Resources*
- *Searching Resource*
- *Media Contacts and People Finders*
- *SuperSite Finder Resources*

- *Webzine and E-Zine Finder Resources*
- *Mailing List Resources*
- *Newsgroup Resources*
- *Firefighting Resources*
- *Software Resources*
- *Web Page Design Resources*
- *Demographics Resources*